Were Mama's Tears in Vain?

By

Richard A. Byron-Cox

This is the second edition of this collection of stories, first published 2007. Both editions are self-published.

For the Mothers of the Caribbean

Who were, are, and will always be crucial to

The formation of our noble society

And

In Memory of past generations

Who sacrificed all to ensure our and future generations will suffer less

Voices from Around the World: Readers of Richard Byron-Cox's Stories

The following are commentaries from around the world on the stories you are about to read

The dead man living with us

The story captures you from the very beginning with its title and plot. In the end you realize that you have read a very subtle tale about superstition and the way modern society has forgotten to appreciate the world of the unknown and the mysterious. Very interesting read indeed.

Anja Thust

Bonn, **Germany**

It is very gripping. I like the suspense without the horror. A very good read indeed. Yes, I really liked it.

Jehann I.J. Jack

Eastern Caribbean Central Bank

Basseterre, **ST Kitts**

An interesting and wonderful story, simply but beautifully told from beginning to end. I really enjoyed it from the word go, the mystery held me to it.

Veronique Zidi-Aporeigah

Toulouse, **France**

A truly very good West Indian story, suitable for a moonlight evening; when the entire family should get together to remember traditions, superstitions, history and our culture. I liked it very much indeed.

Hazel Brookes

Newton Ground, **St. Kitts**

This suspense-filled story had an incredible hold on my attention. The reader is taken along to relive with the King family the inexplicable events in their house. It is a story where one is left unsure as to the boundaries between reality and fiction.

Esmeralda Hernandez Garcia

Chihuahua, **Mexico**

How Japheth met Lucifer

This is a hell of a story.

Joshua Byron-Cox 11 years old

New York, **USA**

Having read the first three pages I couldn't stop! I simply had to finish. Honestly it's a well-written story and holds the reader. I like the way Japheth is allowed to seek survival, declare independence, and ascend to the powerful position of Bad John. This story is excellent.

Cenio E. Lewis

High Commissioner of SVG

London, **England**

I enjoyed it from start to finish: Japheth is a kid only a mother could love! It takes me back to a nostalgic place and time with references to mud-houses, shaker temples, etc. I think every West Indian of a certain age would be able to relate to these memories. And the younger W.I. readers would be entertained by how the old folks lived. The writing style reflects the necessary balance of patois and proper English in a wonderful manner. The characterization is full-bodied and well developed and each person immediately becomes an individual in the reader's mind. The setting is typical West Indian and the scenery vivid and entertaining. The juxtaposition of superstition and religion is a fine thing to witness. A great story with a flowing, easy, engaging style.

Heather Byron-Cox

Columbia University

New York, **USA**

I read it all last night and really liked it. It is entertaining, flowing and keeps one's curiosity alive throughout. What I like most about it is that it gives you an insight to a culture, its people and values in a very accessible, plain manner. It allows outsiders like me to be able to learn as well as enjoy daily life events taking place in another part of the world. I felt a bit the same when I read that book of Naipaul I liked so much. This story made me laugh and worry. I really enjoyed it.

Veronique Zidi-Aporeigah

Toulouse, **France**

Sattou's pain and Mr. Penniston's burden

I read it all in one go. It's a story that took me back to Byrea Hill. Very interesting indeed.

Ken Boyea

Ratho Mill, **St. Vincent**

I see this well-written beautiful story turning into an equally beautiful and touching movie. Dr. Richard Byron-Cox is simply brilliant.

Adnan Al-Zoubi

Irbid, **Jordan**

I loved it. I got lost in Charlie and Sattou. It was as if I was there. I could relate to them. Here the true country farm life was real. The real meat of the matter was exposed. Racism, country life, life's truths, pride and not being able to say I'm sorry. It released emotions in me. I was mad, I laughed, I was upset, I started thinking. I must confess too, that because of the suspense, I cheated and read the last paragraph when I was halfway through the book. I got emotional. Yes, it is great. I enjoyed it.

Ann Marie Henny

Gordon Town, **Jamaica**

On first reading, the story is engaging and will be enjoyed by young people, and I hope it will be. Like all people in such situations, Sattou was searching for himself, determined to find the truth. It is lovely. In retrospect the issues it deals with - recognition, acknowledgement, and reparation - to some extent are evident all very apropos in 2007, during the bicentenary of the Abolition of the Slave Trade.

Hazel Brookes

Newton Ground **St. Kitts**

I became totally drawn to the world the story brought to me. It's about a place and time I've never known, yet, I feel like I was there, experiencing it myself. I was one of the children dying to hear the adventure of their uncle. I grew up with them to find out what the real world had to offer. It's an excellent story that gives you nostalgia and discoveries at the same time.

Yukie Hori

Kyoto, **Japan.**

The story is fascinating and keeps the reader captivated until the very end. After the first page, the reader absolutely wants to know what comes next. What I really liked in the story above all, is the surprise ending and the fact that the story reveals that despite the timeframe and contacts with other civilisations, people in the Diaspora maintain fundamental elements of their culture, which continue to manifest themselves in their daily lifestyle, their reactions and emotions. For me, as an African, this story could have taken place in any former African colony. The story is accessible to the public of any age as it is easy to read.

Nima Barry

Labe, **The Republic of Guinea**

An excellent story line where all the characters are well played out. Sattou at such an early age proved to be quite adventurous yet determined in his quest in finding the truth. This is truly a suspenseful story that makes you want to keep the pages turning.

Carlysle Hibbert

Red Hills, **Jamaica.**

Lord Orator in the Calypso Tent

This is funny yet very serious. It speaks to the writer's gift of being able to tackle serious subjects in such a way that keeps you turning the pages. You can see and feel the

Calypso Tent, singing, dancing, laughing and shouting "Blow man, blow!" with the Pit crowd. Then the Mighty Preacher and Lord Orator appear and you realise that the Tent is more than a big party, it is sometimes a university and sometimes a shooting range. This is story telling par excellence.

Sandrine Rastetter

Alsace, **France**

I enjoyed it most thoroughly. It's an insightful and inspired example of writing, extremely entertaining, written from the heart. Dr. Richard Byron-Cox captures the folk soul of the Caribbean and eloquently expresses the spirit of our culture.

Hugh Phillips

210 Elllesmere Rd

Toronto, **Canada**

I read this story twice. It is a good story and a good theme too.

Maxwell Haywood

New York, **USA**

This is such a joyful way of getting a glimpse of the Caribbean culture and history. The vivid description of the Calypso Tent makes you feel like you must go there against all odds!

Yukie Hori

Kyoto, **Japan**

Were Mama's tears in Vain?

I was engrossed by this story from start to finish. The style of writing is easy to read and will appeal to readers. Through well-drawn characters and skilful story telling Dr. Byron-Cox paints a vivid picture of life and society in the West Indies in colonial times, transporting the reader from the abject poverty of the tin shack to the luxury of plantation house to highlight the difference in the worlds inhabited by the main characters. He subtly delves into the prevailing divisions in society on the basis of race and class. The importance of education as a gateway to escape life on the estate from cradle to the grave will resonate with readers, many of whose forefathers have shared this common experience. Part of the story's appeal is that it could be set in any village in any part of the world with a history rooted in the plantation culture. I enjoyed the story immensely and look forward to reading more of Dr. Byron-Cox's offerings.

Claudia Clarke-Oderson

Oxnards St. James, **Barbados**

It will touch you, you will see. I know, for believe me, it moved me. This work is brilliance in simplicity at its best. Read it you will not be disappointed. This story penetrates the heart to touch the very soul, and like Sam Browne you are left crying tears of joy.

Sandrine Rastetter

Alsace, **France**

A story full of the tenderness, which surrounds you with and stirs in you the noblest feelings of a human being, it leaves you with hope through the demonstration of unending perseverance.

Esmeralda Hernandez Garcia

Chihuahua, **Mexico**

We read this work with great pleasure and confess that we were deeply touched by it. It tells of an important part of the crude, real, cruel and objective history of the Negro and his vicissitudes in this hemisphere. This brilliant work must be translated so that the Spanish-speaking peoples come to know it and we are prepared to help in this. Dr. Richard Byron-Cox is an exceptional talent.

Maria Antonia Fernandes

Oscar Oramas Olivia

(Former Deputy Foreign Minister of Cuba)

Havana, **Cuba**

A heartwarming and moving testimony to the endurance of the human spirit, that accurately captures the socio-political economic context from which we have emerged. This story stands as a glowing tribute to the sacred institution of motherhood and reminds us of the inspiration and determination necessary, if we are to realise our full potential even in the face of insurmountable odds.

Hugh Phillips

210 Elllesmere Rd

Toronto, **Canada**

Foreword

This text of five short stories, with a title story which is twice the length of the shortest story, was first published in 2007. I first read Were Mama's Tears In Vain ? in 2020. Within this thirteen year period, these stories have resonated within the Vincentian societies which have given birth to them. These stories are crafted out of St. Vincent and the Grenadines' historical and socio-cultural realities, and are presented with the throbbing energy of oral story-telling. Indeed, the 'orality' of the presentations carries a 'Vincy cadence' which lends authenticity to the stories' rhythms. Artfully multi-layered, the stories are accessible and lend themselves to enjoyable critical and literary analysis.

Through the writing of this Foreword, I am honoured to have been invited to join the literary discourse surrounding this text. My belated reading of Were Mama's Tears in Vain ? made me feel as though I had excluded myself from a vibrant intellectual movement which had energised not only Vincy story-telling, but the ingredients which contribute to the formation of perspectives in a post-colonial Caribbean. The making of a Vincy identity, in the mid-twentieth century, shapes this text. The villages, 'bay-sides', Baptist churches, grave-yards, 'rum-shops', calypso tents, estate huts and plantation houses serve as landmarks in the topography of an evolving socio-political and cultural landscape. The characters who inhabit these stories tend to be those larger-than-life persons who are yet very familiar to us. Even ghosts are familiar because they live among us.

Our history is presented as living and walking in the spaces with which we are familiar.

'Boysie', with the archetypal name for the impoverished black 'West Indian boy', is the protagonist in the title story. He is the only Boysie in this collection of short stories, and his painful path towards manhood, following the death of his mother, is rife with the symbolism of an emerging Vincy / Caribbean psyche. He seeks to embrace the nebulous promise of 'education' which was his 'Mama's' dream for him. Boysie's efforts allow us to assess the acculturating process of schooling / education, and we say to ourselves, like another 'Mama' did in Earl Lovelace's Wine of Astonishment (1982), "we push these children to this education…we stuff them with it…and we don't know what this education doing to the heart inside of them. But what else to do?"

Richard Byron-Cox deftly weaves these seminal consternations into the fabric of these stories, which challenge our 'education' and entertain us in the process. Enjoy the experience of his passionate story-telling!

Andrea Bowman

Ambassador of Saint Vincent and the Grenadines to the R.O.C.(Taiwan)

17th June, 2025.

Introduction

The English-speaking Caribbean, between 1900 and 1960, was a place where colonialism, superstition, poverty and mass illiteracy held sway. It was a place where colour prejudice, estate labour, ignorance and disenfranchisement kept the majority black population chained to a life of constant want, dependence and serious exploitation by those who possessed economic and political power on the islands. From the beginning, this was a Caribbean, not fully sure whether human value was the possession of black and white, coloniser and colonised in equal measure. And later, not certain whether it wanted to be in a federation, remain under British dominion, or if it had what it took to be independent.

But the Caribbean of this period was also a Caribbean of a hard-working, intelligent and determined people. It was a Caribbean of beautiful ring games played on moonlit nights, when families sat around in their outdoor kitchen listening to grandma and/or grandpa telling ghost stories of their childhood. It was a Caribbean that was seeking to find its way in this world and so gave birth to the steel band, Gary Sobers, The Mighty Sparrow, Eric Williams, C. L. R. James, Sir Arthur Lewis, George McIntosh, Ebenezer Joshua and many others, who were to chart a course for Caribbean development that would lead to universal adult suffrage and ultimately, independence.

This book covers this era of Caribbean development by showing the reality of the period through the lives of its characters. In it, the reader sees the poverty, nakedness, ignorance and deprivation of the Caribbean at that time, all portrayed through the lives of the characters and their cries of pain and sorrow. The reader sees that despite these hardships, the Caribbean people of that time still possessed a special ability to be happy and contented with even the smallest of treasures, and the simplest of pleasures. The reader is made to see that, even in their darkest hour, the Caribbean people never lost hope. And more than that, they still found time to sing, dance, laugh at themselves, and share with one another what little they had.

This book, using the lives, thoughts, hopes and dreams of the characters of its five stories, undresses the Caribbean person of that time, leaving him naked for the reader to see how the prevailing conditions tried desperately to make him a hopeless victim; yet he prevailed. It is therefore a book full of stories about a lot of laughter and tears, superstition and ignorance, poverty and need. But it is also full of courage and hope, determination and will, and trust and honesty, the substance that has produced the great Caribbean heroes the world recognises today.

The discerning eye can easily see that through this book, the reader is taken on a fantastic excursion of Caribbean history, culture, folk philosophy, politics, and the list goes on. But this is all done in a literary form that makes the reader sometimes laugh, cry, sing and/or dance, for it is all told as part of the lives of the living characters in the book. And, the reader naturally joins in, sharing it all with the characters. From the terrible troublemaker Japheth to the suffering Boysie, and from the unending search of Sattou for that which he never knew, never had, to the frightening idea of a dead man living among the living and the gaiety of the Calypso Tent, every reader, regardless of his or her interest, origin or taste, would find something not just interesting, but compelling in this book.

In short, the five stories told here are only fictitious in the sense that the writer manufactured the characters. But everything else is real, transporting the reader to the Caribbean of 1900 to 1960. I hope it brings you as much joy reading it, as it gave me pleasure writing it. It is now yours.

Richard A. Byron-Cox

April 2025

Konigswinter

Germany

The Dead Man

Living With Us

As the laughing began to die down, Tyrone or Balgo, as we called him, and my siblings realised that my mother had not joined in the fun. In fact, she just sat there and seemed to be in very deep and serious thought as she stared into space. Her quietness was unusual and disturbed us. We expected her to see the funniness of it all. This not being the case, we all stopped laughing and she, as if returning from some far away place, partially came back to us.

"He is right," she said, in a detached yet knowing and profound sort of a way. "Tony is right. There is an unseen guest living with us in this house. He has always lived here. I was told he lived here long before your father built this house, and I now realise, not only that he never left, but that he does not intend to leave."

My mother spoke slowly and deliberately, as if carefully weighing each word. I felt that she was not just speaking, but expressing a correct conclusion and an unquestionable truth. Although we always paid close attention to what my mother said, for she was a no-nonsense, strict disciplinarian at the most leisurely of times, in situations like this, she immediately had our ear. We, as if by instinct, knew that what followed on such occasions, was meant to be taken very seriously indeed.

"Who are you talking about, mom?" questioned my youngest sister Joan.

"Are you saying that Tony was speaking the truth? That there was somebody in this house?" asked Balgo.

"Yes Tyrone," my mother said quietly. "there is somebody in this house."

This certain declaration startled Balgo. Something didn't add up. "But how could that be?" he questioned, seemingly baffled. "I searched the whole house that evening, including the cellar, and I saw no one. Not even the ghost of anyone."

"Not only that there was somebody here, but there is always somebody here," continued my mother. "It is precisely because he is a ghost why you didn't see him, for not everyone can see spirits. In fact, I have a feeling that he is here right now watching and listening to us. He is probably having just as much fun hearing you mock Tony while having his own laugh at you, knowing full well that Tony was speaking the truth, and you all thought him a coward. You see, we are never alone in this house. There is an invisible man always watching us."

By this time, everybody was listening to my mother intently. But she seemed quite deep in thought, as if wanting to proceed but only with the greatest of caution. Joan, the youngest of the group, realising the seriousness of my mother's countenance, began showing signs of worry.

"You mean to say that we live in a zombie house?" she questioned.

"No, it is not a zombie house, but we do have someone living here, and it is time that you all know this."

My eldest sister Debra, became quite uneasy as well, and wanted our mother to explain it all there and then.

3

"Mom, so who is this person? And why did you not mention this before? Are you really saying that someone has lived in this house and you never told us all these years?"

"Well, as I said to Tyrone," my mother never calls him Balgo, "it is not wholly correct to say that it is a person, for a spirit is not really a human being. And as regards not telling you, I had very good reasons for that. Had you known in childhood of this reality, I don't think we would still be living here today."

I saw Joan edge closer to Balgo, and the expressions on all the faces had now changed. The laughter was now completely forgotten, replaced by concerned looks all around. An evening that started with family memories of the good times, and was supposed to culminate in Tyrone's fantastic story about my cowardice, had suddenly changed to one of uncertainty about the house in which we lived. This place we had called home from before I was born, some twenty years earlier.

I wasn't sure whether I should feel relieved that someone had finally vindicated me after two years of my being ashamed every time Balgo mentioned that story. Or to be worried that there was indeed a phantom living in our house, and might well do me harm sometime in the future.

My mother seemed more preoccupied with trying to find a mental answer to the case, than worried that this reality exists in her house. It was as if she had come to a sudden realisation, put in the final piece of a puzzle she had been working on for a very long time, and was now admiring it to make sure it was fitted up perfectly.

"Mom, who is this spirit? Is it someone we know? Is it someone from the village? Is it a dead member of our family?" The questions came in torrents from a very worried Debra.

"Oh no. This is someone none of us knew and who knew none of us. In fact, I think he was English or French. But he is definitely a white man from somewhere in Europe. He might have been a soldier or something of the sort. But I am not sure. I am trying to remember what Dina told me he said he was."

Now all ears were fully tuned to, and eyes fully trained on, my mother.

"Dina," said Joan. "Who is this Dina?"

"Dina is the daughter of Rhoda, the woman from whom we bought this land and the wooden house which stood on it."

"So did this Dina speak to this man? Did she know him?" asked Tyrone.

"Well no, her mother had a dream in which he appeared and gave her the money."

"The money? What money? And where does a ghost get money to give away?" asked Cameron, the eldest of my siblings. "This doesn't make any sense."

"Well, this is really a long story and for you to get the whole picture, I would have to begin from the start and this could take the whole night. So let's leave it for tomorrow," said my mother, now fully back in our presence.

"Why tomorrow? Nobody has to go to work tomorrow, so we can all sleep late if we so wish. Tell us now," demanded Cameron. "If I am sleeping in the same house with the spirit of a dead man, then I want to know everything there is to know. Suppose he, he…"

"Yes, mom," urged Debra not allowing Cameron to finish. "I think you should tell us tonight for who knows what…."

"If you are thinking that he is dangerous," said my mother interrupting her, "then you have nothing to worry about. We have lived here all these years and he has done none of us anything. Why would he start now? And again, if I thought for a moment that he was dangerous to our family, we would be long gone from here. We have lived in this house for thirty years and he has not hurt any of you."

"Well, he did attack Tony, didn't he?" said Cameron.

"Tony did not say that he attacked him. Did you now Tony?" she asked turning her eyes on me and clearly going on the defensive.

"No," I said, "I can't say that he attacked me."

As the discussion went on, my mother realised that my siblings were not about to relent; she had disturbed an ant nest. She was a fantastic storyteller, who made you relive the tales she told, and this was one of the reasons why we always insisted that she told us all the stories she knew. But in this case, it had nothing to do with her storytelling abilities. It had all to do with a rising apprehension we were all feeling about our home. My mother sensed that to restore our peace of mind so that we might trust her word and therefore be able to sleep that night, she had to tell the story. She knew there was no way that she could leave us all thinking that we were living under the constant surveillance of someone from the world of the dead, and expect us to sleep quietly. She did the reasonable thing and surrendered.

"When your father decided to build a new house," she began, "as our family was getting bigger and the small house we had bought just before our marriage was not going to be big enough, we went around looking at land to buy. Then we heard of this piece of land with a big wooden house standing on it. It was being sold cheaply, as the owners, Rhoda and her daughter, were leaving for Trinidad. So we came to see it.

"When we arrived and I saw the amount of land the house was standing on, I immediately fell in love with it. It was flat, was of the right size, was removed from the main road, and most importantly, had all these fruit trees. We walked around a bit, and I was so pleased with what I saw, that I impressed upon your father that he needed to seriously consider the offer. He agreed but said he needed some time to think about it. By the time we got back home, I was convinced that your father should buy this land. I could already imagine this house on it, and you children running around having a good time and enjoying all the fruits that are here. I wasn't wrong. We have certainly had a very good life here."

"So it's you that made daddy buy this house?" questioned Joan.

"Be quiet, Joan," came an impatient rebuke from Debra.

"But I was only asking a question," came the innocent response.

"Joan, please be quiet," said Balgo.

"Yes Joan, I made your father buy the land that this house stands on. But this house was built by us."

"So you found out about the ghost after you bought the place?" inquired Balgo.

"It would be more correct to say that I became convinced of its existence long after we had built this house. Indeed, it was Tony who, many years later, caused me to see real proof that this spirit definitely exists and lives here with us."

When my mother made this declaration, I saw the change in the composure of my sisters. The fear on their faces was real. I could see that Tyrone had finally accepted that what I had said I had experienced on that Kiddies' Carnival Saturday evening, might just have some truth in, and sense to it. Now, he more than anyone else was most determined to hear what my mother had to say about this spirit in our house.

Though going through a mire of muddled thoughts, I still found my voice and asked, "Mom, how did I cause you to see the proof of this ghost?"

"Like this spirit likes Tony?" said Joan before my mother could answer.

"Yes," my mother agreed, "he seems to be watching over Tony."

This made me even more uncomfortable, and I wanted to know what role I had played and seemed to be still playing in this very strange story of which I was completely ignorant. I was truly baffled by my mother's sayings, for they made no sense to me whatsoever.

"Mom, what do you mean by he is watching over me? I never asked him to watch over me. I don't want him to watch over me. Is it that he is following me around?"

"Son, you should be happy that he is doing that, for it means that he would do you no harm. More importantly, he will never let harm come to you."

"Could you all stop the cross talk and allow Mom to continue please? You all just interrupting after every word," said Clementine.

"Yes, Mom, let's get on with it," encouraged Debra.

"Well, the following weekend, we went back to visit, for your father had decided to make the owners, Rhoda and her daughter Dina, an offer. In those days, we only had Cameron and Debra, who were six and four respectively, and we took them with us. The wooden house standing on the land was built on stilts and, while your father and I were talking with Rhoda and Dina, Cameron, always Mr. Inquisitive, wandered under the house and found something which was like a manmade pond filled with water. There were ducks swimming in it. He came running to me. 'Mummy, Mummy! Can I have one of the ducks? Can I have one of the ducks?' When I enquired of what ducks he was speaking, he said there was a big pond under the house filled with water with white ducks swimming in it.

"Cammie, do you remember this?" my mother asked, her gaze lingering on him for a while.

A slightly smiling Cameron inclined his head to one side and wrinkled his forehead, giving the impression that he needed a few

9

moments of reflection. But he didn't respond in the few seconds pause that my mother had made. She continued.

"Well, anyway, Rhoda assured Cammie that he could have a duck, and I went around the house with her and Cammie to see them. And there it was, this big hole full of crystal clear water with these milk-white ducks swimming around. I found it strange that they would have a pond under the house, and asked Rhoda about it.

"Why did you put the pond under the house?" I asked.

"Oh, we didn't really put it there," she replied.

"You met it here when you came?" I asked.

"No, no. The hole was dug by us of course," she responded.

"Where does this water come from? Is there a natural spring here?"

"Well, sort of," she replied.

"By this time, your dad and Dina had joined us. And, looking under the house, he asked, 'And this, is it natural or did you dig it?'"

"Dina and Rhoda looked at each other for a second or two and then Rhoda finally said. 'Mr. King, we dug the hole, but that was some time ago.'"

"So you have been keeping these ducks a long time now?" I asked.

"'No,' she replied, 'the hole was not dug for the ducks at all, but for a purpose you would not believe if I were to tell you. As a matter of fact, I think you would laugh at me and Dina, for you might see it as superstitious nonsense. Anyways, it is a long story which needs time to tell.'

"When she mentioned superstition, this awoke my curiosity, for Rhoda seemed just a bit younger than granny Dey. I naturally thought this might be another one of those fantastic stories of their time, which I could later tell you children; for as you know, the stories from my mother's childhood are unique. I therefore pressed Rhoda to tell me the story, but she insisted that there was not enough time."

My mother was indeed a lover of stories, especially the tales that grandmother Dey, her mother, told. And although we had heard these tales time and again from early childhood, we were always ready to listen to them again and again from my mother. She had what Mrs. Charles, my literature teacher, described as the gift of storytelling. She was indeed one of the many Dickens that the Caribbean has produced and which the world would never hear about. The simple reason being, the many limitations and sheer poverty of these tiny islands at that time, did not allow many avenues for the expression of such talent. No wonder then that, when she had the chance, my mother relocated her family to the United States.

"I then told her that I was willing to come back another day, but yet she seemed reluctant," continued my mother. "so I openly asked her if it had anything to do with the land.

"'Oh no, Mrs. King,' she said, 'this is good solid land. You can't go wrong when you buy land here. You just ask anybody.'"

My mother was actually reliving the event as she told it to us, and I could see she was being transported back to the time when it all took place. This was her way when recalling the past, and it naturally spilled over into her storytelling. I couldn't appreciate it then, but now I have come to realise that this was a real gift my mother had. A special ability to tell stories in such a way that she was completely removed from it all. Consequently, it is not anymore a tale, but a living reality, which the listener could not only hear, but see and feel as well.

She continued, "Dina then came to her mother's aid. 'Mrs. King,' she said, 'it's just that when we told people this story in the past, the majority usually didn't believe us. Many others accused us of having done evil, causing it to befall us. But if you are really interested, you could come back this Sunday evening after we return from church, say around 3 o'clock and I will tell you the whole thing. But you must promise to keep an open mind and not to change your plans about buying the property.'

"So that Sunday evening, I sent Cammie and Debbie to Sunday school with your father and I headed up here to see Rhoda and Dina. After offering me a glass of lime juice, Dina sat me down under the orange tree in the backyard where they had a bench, and told me this story:

Mrs. King, my father inherited this land from his father who had inherited it from his father, that is, my great grandfather, who had always said that this was a rich land with a lot of money hidden somewhere. He also said that this money would only be given to a female member of the family. However, my great grandparents had only one son, as their daughter died at age one. That son, my grandfather, also had only one son, my father. Consequently, the money remained hidden from them, for there was no girl to claim it.

Mrs. King, according to my grandfather, it all began one day when his father, great grandfather Thomas, was working the land under the hot midday sun. It was so hot that at one point he felt he was going to faint, and so decided to go under the avocado tree and rest in the shade a while. Yes, I think it is that same avocado tree you see over there, down next to the stream. Within a short while, he must have dozed off, and that is when he had this dream. In fact, my grandfather said that great grandfather Thomas was not sure whether it was a dream, or if he actually saw it all. However, there was the sudden appearance of this man.

He was a tall and slim man, dressed in a maroon-red coat lined with golden buttons in the front and blue epaulets on the shoulders. This coat of hip length, covered a white shirt of which great grandfather Thomas could only see the collar. The coat fell over navy-blue trousers, which in turn reached down to just below the knees, where they entered tall black leather boots. He wore a navy-blue military-styled cap, the very colour of his trousers, and had a sword in a long leather case hanging down from his left hip. This sword was strapped to his body by a black leather belt.

My great grandfather was so surprised that although he wanted to speak, he couldn't utter a word. All he could do was stare in absolute amazement at his visitor who it seemed appeared from nowhere.

'Thomas,' the man said. 'I came to give you something, but it's not for you, it is for the girl. It is here on this land and I will return to show you where it is when the girl is here. This is a secret for you and your family to keep. I would reveal all in due course, but the girl must be here first.'

Before my great grandfather could respond, the man had taken his leave in the same way he came. As my great grandfather said, he seemed to vanish into thin air.

The impact of this dream or appearance, whichever one chooses to believe, never left my great grandfather for the next year and nine months. He would see this figure in the red coat continuously, time and time again in his sleep. Interestingly enough, it was exactly nine months after he first saw the man, that my great aunt Rena, his only daughter was born. When she died of diphtheria at age one, the man stopped appearing in his dreams.

Great grandfather Thomas kept this his secret for many years, saying nothing to anyone. And he would have forgotten the whole affair, had not his grandson, my father, seen the said man many years later in a small plot of cocoa trees they had on the farm at that time.

My father related that when he was about nine years old, he had gone to the cocoa plot to pick the ripened fruits as ordered by his mother. As he was getting down from one of the cocoa trees, he saw this white man dressed in a maroon-red coat, navy-blue trousers, black boots and navy-blue military-styled cap walking over to him.

He was transfixed by the sudden appearance of this man. Having never seen a white man before, he wanted to scream, for he had heard many stories of zombies dressed like normal people, who came and took little children away. But, although he opened his mouth, no sound came out, and he could only stare at the man.

The man came right up under the tree, looked up at my father and started speaking.

'Don't worry Alfonso; I am just tired of watching this money and want to give it up. If I could give it to you, I would; but the girl must be here. The girl must be here.' He then took the small stick with the sharpened point he was carrying in his right hand and stuck it into the ground, saying, 'It is here, right here; but the girl

must be here. The girl must be here.' The man said this, looking at Alfonso as if he could see right through him. My father wanted to shout, scream, jump from the tree; just do something to escape. But he was completely paralysed by the mere presence of the man.

Then he heard a sound, which at first he didn't recognise, for it seemed to be coming from far, far away. But it was enough to break the paralysis that had seized him. After a few seconds, he realised it was his mother's voice calling him. As if suddenly awakened from a trance, he fell out of the tree, hurting his left hand in the process. He got up and the man just stood there staring at him in silence. Moments later, my father found his legs and set off towards his mother, screaming at the top of his voice, which he found had returned after the fall.

When he got to the house, his mother came running out of the kitchen to see what had happened. He rushed up to her saying, 'A man, Mama, a man.' 'What man?' she asked? 'What man?'

'A man, down in the cocoa. A man down in the cocoa.'

She took him inside and tried to get him to calm down, but he was so frightened that this proved to be very difficult to do. Then she noticed he was holding his left hand and realised that he was in pain. She went and called my great grandfather and my grandfather. They checked his hand and realised it was only a sprain. My great grandfather massaged it and then bandaged it with some freshly picked and heated aloes. My father screamed so much during the massage that he was later hoarse for a few days.

After the massage, my grandfather demanded to know what had happened, and my father told him the whole story. When he was finished, his grandfather, that is to say my great grandfather Thomas, who was by this time in his 80s, asked him to describe again, how the man was dressed. As he did so, great grandfather added his own bits and pieces here and there to the description, all of which my father confirmed. Great grandfather Thomas was so precise on the details that his grandson, my father, was sure he had seen the man, and suddenly exclaimed to his mother, 'You see, Mama, grandpa saw him too!'

'Yes and no,' replied great grandfather Thomas. 'I did not see him today, but I saw him sometime before.' And, as if speaking to himself, added, 'So I wasn't dreaming after all, it is real. We have money on this land.'

His son, my grandfather, on hearing this latter statement, wanted to know what he was talking about. Great grandfather Thomas told him the whole story of what he thought he had dreamt many years earlier, and which he was now convinced was not a dream, but a real incident that took place. He wanted to go and see the spot in the cocoa plot where Alfonso claimed it all took place. But it was already dark, and so they had to postpone the visit until the following morning.

The next morning, they went all three straight to the cocoa plot. When they arrived there, they looked around, hoping to find the stick that my father had described, but it was not to be seen. Great grandfather Thomas insisted however, that there must be some sign of Mr. Redcoat having been there, and convinced the others that they should look more closely. And sure enough, on closer inspection of the tree from which Alfonso, my father, had fallen the afternoon before, they saw a hole in the ground at about the same spot that he had described. And it was clear, that it could only have been made by a stick stuck into the ground, in the manner he had described. My great grandfather grabbed his grandson and declared, 'You are rich, my boy! Real, real rich!'

After ascertaining from Alfonso that the man had said that the place where the stick fell was indeed where the money was buried, my great grandfather and grandfather decided to dig for it. This they decided to do two days later, and went back to the spot one afternoon and began digging. After four feet, they found nothing; but decided to continue for another two feet. But still there was nothing. They had no choice but to give it up and refill the hole they had made.

Later that night at about 12:30 a.m. when everyone else was asleep, great grandfather Thomas was on the porch smoking his pipe in his rocking chair. This was something he quite often did until one or two in the morning. He would pass the time just looking at the stars; reading the clouds for rain, so important to his crops; remembering his youthful days and my late great grandmother, whom he considered the perfect wife. Or just listening to the crickets, the frogs, the night owls and the insects joined together to sing that beautiful song in honour and praise of the wonder he knew and understood to be God's masterful creation.

On this particular night, his quiet reflections were interrupted by the arrival of a soft strange wind. It rustled the trees in a rather unusual way, drowning out nature's choir. Yet it wasn't really of any active strength. And suddenly there he was, standing at attention in his maroon-red coat and navy-blue cap and trousers, and black boots.

Great grandfather Thomas was startled and couldn't speak. His visitor stood and stared at him for what seemed to be a very long time and then he simply said, 'The girl is not here, the girl is not here. You must wait for the girl; you must wait, Thomas; do as I told you and wait for the girl.'

With that, he was gone, and the wind slowly died down. Great grandfather Thomas said he wanted to ask the man who was the girl he was talking about?

Why is it that she needed to be there? And what was really this money? But in the presence of this man, in his strange dress and with his particular accent and military conduct, great grandfather Thomas just couldn't find his speech. It was as if his vocal chords were under siege or had abandoned him. It was as if he was commanded to listen and do absolutely nothing else.

The next morning, he told his son, my grandpa Saga, the entire story. He warned him that he should not consider looking for the money until the girl came. He said he did not know who the girl was, but that he was sure when she finally came, grandpa Saga would know. Great grandfather Thomas died a few years later at the age of exactly one hundred, and in those years no girl appeared. With time, grandpa Saga just forgot all this talk, and stories about this money and life continued as usual.

Time passed, and Alfonso, my father, grew up and met my mother, who was from the other side of the island. They got married and she came to live with his family. They, that is, his parents, wanted it that way as my father was their only child, and they did not want him getting married and moving away, leaving them all alone. Apart from that, there was the farm to attend to and they were getting old, and therefore needed his assistance more and more. My mother, being from a rural background herself, fitted nicely into the existing framework, so life went on unchanged.

Everything went along as normal, with my father and mother helping my grandparents with the farm. They were not rich but weren't doing badly as the farm produced crops in some abundance. My mother and father recalled this time as one of peace, prosperity and great hope. Then there was the great storm.

When the hurricane season began that year, the newspaper, which was printed once a month, warned that this might be a very dangerous season. And so it proved to be. By early September, three major storms had hit the island and there was a forecast for a fourth which was anticipated to be much stronger than the previous ones.

As the expected destruction approached, the colonial authorities appealed to people to seek shelter in the nearest public school or church. There were many reasons for this stipulation. The most important however, was that in most villages on the island, these were the only concrete buildings. They were therefore expected to withstand the storm better than the wattle and daub that the majority poor lived in. Or the wooden structures which the few slightly better off were able to build.

Grandpa Saga was not the kind of man who would allow a hurricane to force him to leave his house and go to seek refuge somewhere else, regardless of how strong that storm might be. But he had no choice, for the colonial authorities sent an order to the sergeant at the local police station, compelling him to round up all the villagers and put them in the church for their own safety.

So grandpa Saga, grandma Isolyn, my father and my mother Rhoda, were huddled along with all the other villagers into the old Anglican parish church. Yes, the same one that you see up the road. There is where they sheltered from that storm. This was one time in our lives when the dictatorial style of governance practised by the colonial authorities, was absolutely necessary and did have a positive effect.

The next morning, when my father and grandpa went to check on their home, what they saw broke their hearts. There were just two of the wooden walls of the house standing and the roof was nowhere to be seen. The contents of the house were spread over different parts of the farm. The whole property looked as if the storm had a bitter personal quarrel with the family and was very determined to get even. If so, it really did. The destruction was such that grandpa Saga sat on a stump, the remains of one of the many trees destroyed by the storm, with his face in his hands for quite some time. When he finally stood up, his son realised for the first time that his father was able to feel pain that causes tears, and was so moved by it that he also broke down in tears.

Even surrounded by such great loss, my grandpa and my father knew they had to get up and get. They started with the rebuilding of their home. They were indeed typical of the Caribbean people of that time and before, for whom triumph over adversity was a way of life. It was a daily chore which had created in them an indomitable spirit. They were the grandchildren of a people who were, by and large, landless and penniless, illiterate and powerless, even though they had spent their entire lives working as hard as oxen. But they were simply never paid for their labour. After all, they were slaves, just part of the estate stock with a duty to work until death, deprived of even the right to hope for better. But they had prevailed, and here again they shall prevail.

After such destruction, Grandpa Saga promised himself not to build the new house on a spot exposed to the hurricanes. After careful study and consultation with my father, he decided to build it on the cocoa plot. This was an area of the farm that stood behind the mountain and therefore was shielded from the winds. And so it was that the cocoa plot was chopped down, and grandpa and my father, along with regular Saturday and Sunday help from the men in the neighbourhood, built their new house on the spot where my father was told the money was buried. This is the very house that you see here today.

But from the first day they moved into this house, my grandmother started seeing shadows. She never saw the man in the red coat or any other person for that matter. But she would sometimes see the shadow of someone disappearing into one of the bedrooms. However, on entering behind the shadow, she would find no one. Or she would see the rocking chair, rocking on its own with no one sitting in it.

Sometimes she would see the swing that my dad, Alfonso, had tied up on the big mango tree swinging all by itself. She would also hear noises in the kitchen and when she checked, there would be no one there. Most strange of all were the times when Frisco, the dog, would bark his head off like mad, aggressively daring someone or something to come closer; but when she looked out to see who it was, there was nothing and no one. Yet Frisco's menace and stare were definitely focused, threatening to rip whomever or whatever it was apart.

My father and grandfather also saw some of these things. These strange happenings caused my grandfather to come up with the idea that these things were the actions of the man in the red coat, as the new house was placed on the spot where he belonged, and where he buried his money. So, in his daily movement, they would see him, for even if he wanted to avoid them, he couldn't always do so.

So you see, Mrs. King, this man whom great grandfather Thomas referred to as Mr. Redcoat has been living in this house from the first day it was built. And as far as I know he has never left it. But there is nothing for you and your family to fear, for we have lived here all our lives in peace and quiet. I can assure you that you will too.

My mother stopped there, and we all thought that that was the end of the story. Joan beat us all to it, "So what happened next?" she asked anxiously.

"What?" responded my mother, and after a second or two continued, "Oh, oh yes. I then enquired of her if that was why she wanted to make sure we would buy the house before she told me the story. To which she repeated that we had nothing to worry about for she and her mother had lived there all their lives and nothing had happened to them. As a matter of fact, she assured me that she had never seen this Mr. Redcoat at all. And, that all of what she related to me was what her mother and father had told her.

"I then asked her how her father died, for I thought that the ghost might have had something to do with that. She explained that he was hit by an overloaded banana truck coming round Monkey corner. He died on the spot. I told her I was sorry to hear that and she explained that they had already gotten over it, for it had happened more than five years earlier. She said that being Christians, they saw these things as part of life. So they just prayed and went on with their lives; for, as she put it: 'The Lord giveth and the Lord taketh away. Blessed be the Name of the Lord.'

"I also enquired as to why they were going to Trinidad. She revealed that, with the death of her father Alfonso, they had no real close family here anymore as all of her mother's close relatives moved to Trinidad a long time before. And with her father's family gone, her mother felt it was best if they lived closer to her maternal relatives. Apart from that, her grandmother, that is to say Rhoda's mother, lived there, and she was an old woman and couldn't take care of herself. So

Rhoda, being her only daughter, had decided to move there to take care of her mother.

"This, she said, was the principal reason why they were selling this place. She said that they would not have sold it for a million dollars if it weren't for those circumstances. It had been in her father's family for generations and to sell it now really grieved her heart. She assured me that they were offered more money than we were paying them, but they wanted somebody like us to have it. Good people with a family and who love the land. So they knew that this place would be in good hands if they sold it to us.

"She told me that it hurt her greatly to part with this property, also because she grew up on this place, and her father, grandfather and great grandfather had worked very hard to make it what it was. She explained that she felt the pain even more when she thought of the fact that her great grandfather, who was born a slave, had worked his soul out trying to make this farm into a successful place.

"She then got into telling me of the many struggles each generation of her father went through so that they could keep this place. The challenges of making the crops successful over the years, especially when nature decided to wreak havoc on them, whether it was through continuous heavy rains, terrible hurricanes, or a severe period of drought. And then I remembered the reason why we started this whole thing. So I asked if it was because of the drought why they dug the hole under the house where Cammie had seen the ducks swimming, the second time that we came here.

"She, then remembering that this was the reason why she decided to tell me the story, explained that what she was about to relate was the only part of the story she really could say that she knew. She then shared with me this story:

Well, Mrs. King, this is an incident that happened when I was twenty-one years old. In fact it all started on the morning of my 21ˢᵗ birthday and it is something that causes me cold bumps every time I have to speak about it. It is the strangest thing that has ever happened to me in all my life, and began with a dream my mother had.

On that morning, she woke up and called me into her bedroom. I thought that she was going to congratulate me on becoming a full adult. As you know, that is the age when, according to the law, I became an adult and so, from then on, could do whatever I wanted without seeking her consent. I could now even vote. Instead, she said with the greatest conviction I ever heard from her, 'Dina, the man has given you the money and we are going to be rich, rich girl.' I, not understanding anything, thought that my mother was trying to start me off in a good mood, seeing it was a special birthday. She continued, 'Grandfather Thomas was right after all, we are going to be rich.'

When she mentioned great grandfather Thomas, I became puzzled. I didn't understand why she would mention his name out of the clear blue sky. Then I became a bit worried, for I thought something must have gone wrong with my mother overnight. She, seeing this expression of incomprehension on my face, tried to explain.

'It is the spirit, Dina. The spirit in the soldier uniform. He came in my sleep last night. He told me that you and I should dig for the money, because he has given the money to you,' she continued excitedly.

By this time, I was at a real loss, as my mother was not making any sense at all. I was doing my best to figure out if my mother had suddenly lost her sanity, or if she was talking in her sleep, not being aware of what she was saying.

'Mummy,' I said, 'you need to get up and drink a good cup of bush tea, and then you and I can talk.'

'Child,' she responded, 'you think that I am crazy. Well you wrong. Sit down on the bed and let me explain the whole thing to you, and you would see that I am in my sound mind.' With that, my mother sat up, held my hand and made me sit on the bed while she related her dream. She said that it appeared that she was sitting under a tree on the very spot where our house is. She said that she knew it was this spot, for at times during the dream, it seemed she was under a cocoa tree, and at other times she seemed to be under the house. Apart from that, she said she was sure it was on this spot, for she remembered that there was a cocoa plot on this spot before my grandfather and father had built the house here after the hurricane.

She said that in the dream, the time was about mid-afternoon. She was picking cocoa when this white man in a red suit with blue epaulets, just like my great grandfather had described, appeared at her right and called her name. When she turned around and faced him fully, he said that the girl is now here. We should go and take the money and release him from this burden of watching it, so that he could be free. She said she asked him what girl and he said 'Your daughter, Dina; today she is grown enough to have the money and you must dig for it together, and share it between the two of you.'

By this time, they were sitting under the house and my mother asked him where we should dig. He took a piece of stick he was carrying, and with the action of one throwing a spear, stuck it into the ground saying, 'Right there, right there is where the money is. You must wait until 12:00 midnight and then start digging. You must get rid of the dog for he can see me and would make noise. And please do not....' My mother says she never got to hear the rest as at this time, the dog woke her with its barking. Upon awaking, she lay and thought of her dream and realised that it was so vivid that she was sure it was a vision and not merely a dream.

She said that the more she thought of it, the more certain she became that it was indeed a vision. She became even more excited when she realised that, according to what my father had told her, great grandfather Thomas had described this man to a T, and it was he who had always said that Mr. Redcoat had maintained that the money was for the girl, that they would only get the money when the girl came. That he had even mentioned the very stick she saw in her vision. And finally, that my father had seen Mr. Redcoat on the very same spot.

Suddenly, my mother, seeming to remember something, grabbed me by the hand. And, without getting out of her night gown, literally dragged me out into the yard and under the house. And guess what? Mrs. King, as Mary made Jesus, sure enough, there it was. A piece of stick stuck into the ground as if someone had stuck it there with one spear-like throw. I was dumb for a while and just stood there half-bent in complete disbelief. My mother seemed transfixed. Her hand around my left elbow suddenly went very cold. The index finger of her other hand she put on her lips and just stood and stared in dumfounded wonder.

I do not know for exactly how long we stood there motionless. But I remember regaining full consciousness when the dog started to bark and there was this sudden gentle breeze blowing under the house. My mother, as if awakened from a trance, and, as if afraid of being overheard by someone although we were alone, whispered, 'He is here, he is here. But we have nothing to fear. He just wants to let us know that he is here watching.'

We came out from under the house and left the gentle breeze behind. And I couldn't but notice that while it was breezy under there, every tree in the yard was standing at attention. Not even one leaf was daring a half wink. This struck me as very odd indeed. We went into the house and sat in the living room a few moments in silence. As I sat there, my mind was racing and I wasn't sure whether I was dreaming, had gone crazy, or was just imagining things.

As my thoughts tried to put some reason to it all, I found that I was trapped in the dilemma as to whether this was real or not, and that my mind refused to think beyond that point. It seemed only capable of the continuous circle of: this is impossible, this could never be real. You have to believe it, remember the stick. There is no denying the stick now. And your mother; is she crazy? She most certainly is not.

My mind kept going round and round in this circle until my mother finally broke the silence. 'We must go and dig up the money, Dina,' she said resignedly. 'It was given to us and we must dig it up. The poor fellow's soul needs to rest in peace. You can't be ungrateful. And apart from that, you and only you could put the poor fellow's soul to rest. His soul needs to rest in peace.'

I was genuinely afraid, for I had heard from my father and grandfather many stories about evil spirits and voodoo, and the curse that may befall one who got mixed up in these things. And further, that dealing with the ghost of a dead person was seen as dealing in the world of evil. I went along with my mother's idea of *digging up the money. I couldn't help feeling that I was the reason why this poor soul was trapped on this earth, never to be allowed to enter into eternity the way the dead are supposed to.*

So the next day, we sat and planned when we were going to dig up this money and the tools we would need for this. We got fork, pick, hoe and shovel for the digging. But we had one major problem. What to do with Frisco our dog? According to my mother, the man had said that we must get rid of him.

After a bit of thought, my mother decided it was best to tie him at the front of the house for, to get under the house, one had to walk at the back of it, which could not be seen from the front. Consequently, if my benefactor decided to show up, our dog would not make him uncomfortable, for it would not see him in the first place. We tied the dog at the front of the house at six o'clock that evening.

At ten to twelve that Friday night, we were under the house, tools in hand, ready to demand our money from the earth. We had to wait the full ten minutes, which seemed like an eternity to me. My mother insisted that we would not break the ground until it was twelve midnight. She was afraid that if we didn't do it exactly as the spirit had commanded, we might not get the money at all. So to ensure that we got it right to the very second, she brought along our big alarm clock from the living room. She held it up to the pitch-oil lantern to count away the seconds and the minutes.

The night was absolutely still. There was not even the slightest of breeze. The owls, crickets, the croaking night frogs and the many other creatures of the after-dusk world all seemed to have taken the night off. It seemed to me that the atmosphere itself was waiting for something, not necessarily special, but certainly unusual, to happen. With all the night insects and other creatures in their hiding places, and the eerie silence surrounding us, I couldn't help but being reminded of the scenario in those western movies of old. Those where, when the little town heard that a bad outlaw was coming in their direction, and there would therefore be the spectacle of the usual showdown between him and the Sheriff, they, the townsfolk retreated to the safety of their homes, camouflaging behind blinds and curtains, waiting for the dangerous uproar. The night creatures around our farm seemed to have perceived the same pending danger, and unsure of the outcome, retreated to the safety of their habitats. At that moment, I truly envied those creatures their secured environs. But it was too late. I was already cast in the role of Deputy Sheriff.

At about a minute before midnight, I felt it, very, very gently at first, but then pleasantly stronger. It came whistling softly, quietly wrapping itself around us, almost as if caressing our arms and legs, while circulating in, and filling the entire space under the house. My mother looked at me directly with eyes and a facial expression which said not to worry, but he is here. She had already told me that she was told, that it is better not to speak when one was digging for treasure in the night under such circumstances.

I felt myself stiffen. My mind began recalling all the prayers I had learnt from the first moment of my childhood introduction to the Catholic church. The Hail Mary and others just flowed through my head as if on their own accord. It was as if my mind decided on its own that there was at that moment a dire need for salvation if not redemption.

While my mind was reciting these, I heard my mother's soft but firm and stern command, 'What you waiting for? Dig!' With that, I took up the pick and struck the earth in the area of the small hole that the stick had made three days earlier.

The pick went in as if the earth was mere loose sand and nothing more. My mother, by way of sign language, instructed me to continue digging.

As I broke the earth with the pick, my mother cleared it with the shovel. We worked without talking, our entire beings focused on the task at hand. This was so, as my mother would motion me to continue whenever I tried to stop or to say something to her. And all this time, the gentle breeze surrounded us, seeming happy to be in our company, whistling its soft and lonely tune as if trying to tell us a story, as if trying to convey something private and confidential to us.

After about five minutes, and just when my arms were beginning to tire, the pick struck something that made the sound of when metal meets metal. My mother signalled me to stop. Putting down the shovel, she began to remove the loose earth with her hands. Within a few seconds, the first surprise came out. I was so flabbergasted that my mouth dropped open.

My mother had discovered in the soil what seemed to be a small rectangular box about eighteen inches long and twelve inches in width. It looked black in colour. She cleared the remaining soil from around it and we pulled it out. After a bit of effort, we opened it and found what seemed to be a bag. As she tried removing it from the metal box, it simply disintegrated, revealing unbelievable contents. There was a teapot, teaspoons, sugar and butter bowls, a number of saucers, teacups, a kettle and a goblet. Even with the poor light offered by the lantern, I could see they were made of silver. Before I could say anything, my mother motioned me to silence by gently tapping her index finger on her lips.

She began taking them out of the box, handing me them to put out of the way of our work. As I took them, I spent a second considering each, and I remember thinking that this must be all a dream. It simply couldn't be true. After we had removed all the silver wares from the box, we stood for about a minute just lost in wonder. Then my mother motioned me to continue. Seeing my questioning expression, she quietly whispered 'There might be something else.' She was right.

I drove a few more picks in the earth. This time, I was full of renewed energy and vigour, and after the fifth strike or so, there it was again; the clash of metal against metal. My mother again stopped me. With her bare hands she began to clear away the loose earth. As she did so, we realised that we had discovered what looked like a chest. I became excited and motioned my mother to move and allow me to break more earth from around it. As we continued to dig and remove the loosened soil, we had a good picture of what we had uncovered.

It was a huge sailor's chest, of the type they made in 16th and 17th century Europe. It was so big that it took us a few more minutes of clearing earth before we could see the entire surface area. It seemed black in colour and was about four feet long and three feet wide and had a massive lock, huge hinges, and a look that said it was very heavy indeed. How deep it was, I would never know.

We started digging at the sides with the intention of getting it out completely. Our excitement was by now fever pitch. As we dug, more and more of the chest was revealed, including metal handles at the sides. But the more we dug, the deeper the chest seemed to be. Getting a little impatient, my mother motioned me to use the pick and break the lock so that we might see what was inside the chest and whether it was worth all this digging. To this day, it is the only time in my life I wish we had the wisdom to be patient. Believe me, Mrs. King; patience is really a virtue that is worth cultivating. This impatience was our first mistake in this exercise, but it was a cardinal one. One my mother will hold against herself for the rest of her life.

I did as my mother instructed, and with one blow of the pick, the lock was broken. We then opened the chest, which still lay in the hole. In it I beheld a sight of gold that I don't think anyone on this island, apart from me and my mother, has ever seen. Inside the chest there were coins and coins. My mother put both her hands in and pulled them out full of coins, throwing them out on the ground next to me. I did the same and then again and again. I then decided to inspect them by the light of the lantern. My mother threw out two more handfuls then came to join me. With the help of the lantern, we could see that these were indeed solid gold coins. I whispered to my mother, 'They are indeed real gold.' This brought my mother back to reality, but with that, the door to the world of Mr. Redcoat slammed shut for good.

When my mother heard me say that the coins were gold, she at first was speechless and just stared at me for about 20 seconds. And then she became ecstatic and shouted, 'You see what I told you! You rich, you rich! You never believed me, but Oh God, you rich!' As if by magic, everything immediately changed.

The gentle breeze suddenly became a strong wind, rushing around under the house like a mini hurricane. At the same time, there began this great noise as if someone was very hurriedly pulling some rather big and heavy chains, like those used on the anchor of a huge ship. Our house began to shake and rattle so violently that I was certain that it was about to come loose from its columns and just lift up and fly away. And as all of this was happening, we noticed that the chest was sinking back into the earth. We stood motionless, paralysed by fear and incomprehension of what was taking place. I wanted to scream, stop the chest from disappearing; just command the confusion to cease. But I did nothing, for it all happened so suddenly, without warning. And it finished so quickly that there was really no time to act. Within one minute and a half, it was all over. The mad wind had ceased and the iron chest had completely disappeared. All became still.

During that minute and a half, many thoughts flew through my mind. But what I recall most is my thinking that, 'Oh God, we are going to die.' For that brief moment, I saw clearly that Mr. Redcoat had lured us under the house to kill us. I somehow knew that we were doomed. But then it stopped and, without thinking, we rushed into the house and locked the door behind us. We rushed into my mother's bedroom and locked that door as well. It's only then I realised that we were both shivering like leaves. In another few seconds, we dropped to our knees and began to pray. I prayed with my eyes wide open, all the while expecting to hear the door being broken down and Mr. Redcoat coming in to finish us off. How long we prayed, I can't say. But when we couldn't remember any more prayers, we began to recite the psalms we knew. After this incident, the 23rd psalm in particular became a standard nightly recital during prayers in our house for many months following.

When we saw that Mr. Redcoat had not returned, we stopped praying for a while. It was then that we realised that our hands and legs were full of dirt. So we got up and after listening carefully to make sure that no sounds were coming from the sitting room, we cautiously opened the bedroom door. We went to the living room together and used the water in a bucket to hurriedly wash our hands and feet. We wasted no time in getting back to my mother's bedroom and lay on her bed still fully clothed, not totally convinced that Mr. Redcoat was finished with us for the night. We listened attentively to every sound, while speaking in whispered tones, for we were sure he would return sooner or later. He didn't.

The sun was already rising when we finally fell asleep, and this was only because of sheer exertion. We woke up around two and a half hours later. But even in that short time, I did not really sleep. I kept dreaming of Mr. Redcoat and replaying everything in my mind that took place under the house. My mother and I awoke at the same time and we just sat and looked at each other with the same worried and somewhat frightened expression on our faces. Our minds were turbulent with the unease of thinking what we might have brought upon ourselves. On my mother's suggestion, we knelt and prayed. After that, we got up and she slowly drew the bedroom curtains back and peered outside. 'It's quiet,' she half whispered, 'everything looks alright.' We then decided to make the next move.

I unlocked the bedroom door and slowly turned the knob and opened it. Holding it ajar, I peered out into the living room, with my mother trying to do the same over my shoulders. It was all quiet. We went out into the living room. With one glance, I ascertained that the only thing which was different from the evening before, was the dirt we brought in on our feet from under the house. No one had been in the living room. I now felt more assured and opened the door onto the veranda.

There was a bright sun, the birds were singing and there was a blue, cloudless sky. It was a typical Caribbean day. Thinking of the night before, I couldn't help feeling that this was the calm after the storm. But I still had another step to make. As I stood at the bottom of the veranda steps trying to imagine what awaited me, my mother, standing at the top, was looking at my tentative approach. 'Go ahead,' she urged, 'What are you afraid of? This is broad daylight, just check and see.'

When I looked under the house, everything was where we had left them, including the silver tea things that we had dug up and the gold coins we had removed from the chest. I ventured closer to the hole we had dug, half hoping, I suppose, that the chest might have reappeared. What I saw was the hole full of crystal clear water.

The trunk was nowhere to be seen. I rushed back to the veranda and told my mother. She went with me and we gathered the tea things and the coins and carried them into the house.

We then spent some time carefully studying these things and, though not being experts, we both assumed that they had real value. This proved to be correct. As we left the sitting room on our way to the kitchen to get something to eat, my mother suddenly began to lament over and over again, 'How could I have been so stupid? How could I have been so stupid?' She had already begun blaming herself for our loss. This was something she would do periodically over the next year, especially when she was sitting on her own for a while. I had to keep reassuring her that we had really lost nothing; that God works everything to his own purpose.

The truth is though; it took me a long time to really come to terms with what had happened that night. It seemed to me like a dream, something out of this world, and after all these years, it still seems that way to me. In fact, I am convinced that it was indeed something very unusual. We have moved on, of course, and since that incident, as far as I am aware, my mother has never seen Mr. Redcoat again. At least she has never told me of her having heard from him. I myself have never seen or heard from him. But I will always remember that night for as long as I live, for as I told you, it is the strangest thing that I have ever experienced.

Some months later, I thought of refilling the hole with soil, but never did. So from that night to this day, it has always been full of that crystal clear water. We have never really done anything much with the water and we have never tried bailing it out. The main reason for this is that my mother said my father came to her in a dream and said that water has healing powers. And you know what? It probably does too. Our dog is already 15 years old and has never shown any sign of sickness whatsoever. I attribute this to the water from that hole, for it is the only water he drinks. Also a few years ago, there was a severe and long drought. I used water from the hole to wet the crops, and you wouldn't believe the size of potatoes, carrots, bananas, melons and pumpkins we had that year. They are the biggest we have ever had, and my mother is adamant that they are the biggest she has ever seen.

Of course, now that it is going to be yours, you can do whatever you and your husband want with it. We have had a very good life here and I promise you that you would too. My honest hope however, is that you would love this place and take care of it so that great grandfather Thomas, grandpa Saga and my father Alfonso would not be too disappointed in me and my mother for selling it.

So there you have it, Mrs. King, the story of this place, as I know it. I can't say where Mr. Redcoat is and whether he has left for good. But I can assure you, I have never seen him, and you and your family will not have to worry about him.

My mother became silent, and for a few moments no one spoke. And then she said rather reflectively.

"I hope that we haven't disappointed them and that they are happy with what we have done with this place."

"You mean Rhoda and Dina?" asked Joan.

"If nobody else, you must talk."

"I am not talking to you Clementine," responded Joan.

My mother ignored the crosstalk and proceeded to explain.

"When Dina spoke of us loving this place and taking care of it so that her great grandfather, grandfather and father would be pleased, she said it looking up to the sky as if she expected them to hear her. I saw her wipe a tear from her eye. It was indeed a hard decision for them to make as regards selling this place. After she told me that story, I was even more determined that your dad should buy this place and that we should make our home here. I have not regretted that decision, even though I now know for sure that this man is living here with us. Or to put it more correctly, his spirit dwells here with us."

"But weren't you scared to buy something you knew was haunted?" asked Cameron.

"No, I thought that if they had lived here all those years and nothing happened to them, then why should something happen to us? And as I have always told you, my father brought me up not to believe in such things. So even though I believed her story, it did not have a negative effect on me. More than anything though, I felt it would be a wonderful thing to live in a place which was the product of a family history of hard work and determination."

"So did they ever get back the money?" asked Joan.

"Yes," joined Clementine, "what did happen to the money?"

"Well, as Dina explained, they never saw Mr. Redcoat again and never went searching for the chest anymore."

"And what did they do with the tea things and coins they had taken from the chest?" I asked.

"Oh, those were Spanish gold coins from the sixteenth century which are worth a fortune today. They sold a few of them and have enough money from them to live comfortably for two lifetimes. This incidentally is another reason why I so encouraged your father to buy this place."

"You mean we might be able to locate the chest and get the money?" interjected Cameron, not waiting for my mother to finish.

"No, not that!" said my mother, showing slight irritation at the question. "From the story she told me and the fact that they had sold a few coins and were now quite rich, I knew that they weren't selling this property for the money or out of fear for this Mr. Redcoat. They simply had to because of a change in their circumstances. Therefore, they wanted to sell it to people who could appreciate the history of the place, and they thought us worthy."

Our circle lapsed into silence for a few moments. Then, as if suddenly remembering, Daniel, my youngest brother, asked, "But Mom, you said you saw this Mr. Redcoat yourself. When did this happen?"

"Children," said my mother in a tired voice, "it is way past your bedtime and we could continue this another time."

She wasn't allowed to finish as protest went up all around.

"Mom, we are on holidays and nobody has any place to go tomorrow, neither work nor school," was the cry from Clementine.

"Joan is the youngest and look she is not sleepy," said Daniel. "Joan, you sleeping?" he asked, looking at her in a patronising sort of a way.

"You are only two years older than me," contested Joan, "so don't even bother."

"Clementine is right, Mom," said Cameron, "we need to hear this thing to the end."

Balgo, who had not said a word in a long time, joined the protest. "Aunt Tis," (he called my mother Tis because when he was a little baby and came to visit our home with his mother; my mother's sister, she, my aunt, would call my mother Sis. He, being an infant, could not say the word Sis properly but said 'Tis'. Over time, everyone joined him and started calling my mother by this name, "you can't just start something telling us that we have this ghost in the house and then send us to sleep just like that without an explanation. How are we to sleep?" he protested.

I saw my moment and took it gleefully. "Good for you," I said vengefully. "So who is the coward now? You all were just laughing at me; why you don't laugh now? Mom, you shouldn't tell anybody anything. Let Balgo, Mr. Most Brave, go home. It is already really late."

"I sleeping over," was his response.

"I wonder in whose room," I rebuffed.

"I never promised any explanation," said my mother, "you wanted to know what Dina told me and that I shared with you. Now it's bedtime and I have decided, so there is no use arguing with me. Is that clear?"

We all just looked at my mother for a few seconds as we knew that the only response to a command from her was to carry it out. My mother was the kind that, when she put "her foot down", no one was allowed to challenge her. This was one of those moments. As we started heading in the direction of the bedrooms, she, probably realising that she might have been a bit too stern and that our request for a conclusion of the tale was not unreasonable, relented a little and stopped us.

"Tell you all what. Why don't we continue this tomorrow morning, once you have helped out Marjory a bit with the cleaning and stuff? We could go down to the back garden with some lemonade and I can tell you guys how I met Mr. Redcoat. What you say?"

We all knew that this was my mother's apology for being too harsh, for this was her nature. It never took her long to realise when she was a little too rough with us and, once acknowledged, she never failed to take immediate steps to make amends. We happily accepted the compromise and went off to bed.

But most of the night, I did not sleep. For me, the very idea that I was living in a house haunted by the spirit of a dead person was inconceivable. I had a million thoughts going through my mind, not least of which was: how was I going to continue living in this house all alone when the rest of my family returned to the United States after the holidays?

I was not the only one tortured that night by my mother's tale. Joan ended up in my mother's bed, while Daniel slept with Cameron. Debra and Clementine shared one room and they slept with the light on all night. This I found out when I got up to use the toilet three hours later and saw light coming from the crack at the bottom of their door. And Tyrone, Mr. Most Brave, refused to go home, claiming it was too late and that he had already told his parents that he would be sleeping over. I was therefore forced to share my room with him.

The following morning, we all got up very early and dutifully did chores around the house to ease the load on our temporary house help, Marjory. She was more happy than surprised and seemed to enjoy telling us how she wanted certain things done. I am not sure whether this joy of hers had more to do with memories than with the fact that we were actually doing something around the house. For even while giving us her instructions, she kept telling us that we shouldn't do too much as we needed to rest and enjoy the holidays, for her greatest joy was to see "her children" happy.

Marjory had worked with my family since I was a baby and was like a second mother to all of us. She only left us after my family moved to New York to live a few years ago. But whenever they returned for a holiday, it was an unwritten law that she would come to work for us until they left. My mother was very grateful to her for all that she had done for us over the years. To show that gratitude, she had assisted Marjory's two children to get to the United States. They were now both working and studying and sent Marjory significant remittances that she did not now need to work.

But having watched us grow up and having spent most of her working life in our household, she felt it like a motherly responsibility to take care of my family anytime they were at home. She was always the happiest person when they came home. When the time came for them to leave, we all usually had to take turns in consoling her. She quite often would fall into a melancholy state, which would make us all very sad indeed. She never accompanied the family to the airport whenever they left for, as she said, she didn't want to embarrass herself in public.

That morning, Marjory made the breakfast call at 8:30 as usual, and we all gathered around the table. My mother came last and was fully dressed to go into the city. This surprised us all, for we had an agreement about the continuation of the story.

"Good morning, everyone."

"Morning Mom," was the chorus response.

"Marjory, how are you today?"

"Real good, Mrs. King them children help me with everything this morning. Debra even made the breakfast all by herself."

"Good, you spoil them too much. I am tired telling you to make them do much more around the house when the days come. They laze about the place too much. You are not their servant. I suppose it's useless explaining that to you, for is you who spoiled them in the first place, and what done gone bad in the morning, can't come good in the evening."

Marjory simply smiled as she always did in situations like these, winked at us, and pulled out my mother's chair for her to sit down.

"Marjory, I am not joking," continued my mother. "I really wished that you would enforce the same discipline on my children as you have done on your own."

"Oh, but Mrs. King," said Marjory in gentle and smiling protest, "but these are my children and I treat them just as I treat William and Mary."

"Only that you didn't spoil William and Mary, and these are spoilt rotten."

"Mom, you are going to town?" queried Joan.

"Yes Joan, if you must know. And Cammie, please get dressed after breakfast 'cause I would need your help in town as Tony will be occupied with some things here at home."

"But you…"

"But what?" my mother interrupted Joan, "The story, I will tell you later this evening. The shipping company called to say the barrels have arrived, and I am going to clear them today, for I am not able with the food prices in this country. So the story would have to wait until I get back."

So that was that, and we had no choice but to wait until my mother got back to hear the rest of this unbelievable and frightening tale.

Throughout the day, I had the strange feeling that we were all moving very cautiously in the house. It was as if we thought that someone was really watching us. I noticed that neither Joan nor Daniel stayed by herself or himself, but was always in the company of someone. Once on entering the kitchen, I came upon Debra asking Marjory whether she had ever observed anything strange in our house. In response, Marjory's face was a picture of total incomprehension. Tyrone did not go home but spent the day hanging around with me often repeating, "Man Tony, I have to hand it to you, you brave, you real brave. I mean to live in this house all alone with this zombie and thing. Man you real brave."

The idea that a spirit or someone unseen was looking over us, was not anything new to my siblings and me. Ours was a Christian home where my mother brought up her children in the fear and admonition of the Lord. So we were always conscious of a superior invisible being watching over us and judging all our actions. The difference in this case was that, while God's was the Holy Spirit, which we believed loved us because that is what we were told in Sunday school and by our parents; this spirit of Mr. Redcoat was that of a dead man; a spirit from the dark and unknown world of death and the grave, capable of doing us evil. All the stories we had heard from childhood about the return of the dead, were tales of their evil spirits returning only to seek vengeance, only to do evil upon those with whom they had a score to settle. So our fear was real, if baseless.

My mother spent most of the day in the city, and when she got back at around 4:30 in the afternoon, she was so tired that she simply took a bath and went into her bedroom. She fell asleep, further delaying the satisfaction of our curiosity. She awoke at about 6:30 and spent the next hour on the phone calling various friends and neighbours. We had dinner at 7:30 and after Marjory retired at about 8:30, my mom sat us all down in the living room and told the rest of her tale.

"So you were wondering if I was ever going to tell you the rest of this story, eh Jo? Well, nothing to worry about. I simply didn't want to frighten Marjory, and that is why I waited until she has gone to sleep. Remember she has also lived in this house all these years."

"You mean that Marjory knows nothing about the ghost?" asked Joan.

"Joan, you talk too much; you always talking when you should shut up," said Clementine.

"Ok that's enough; you girls are going to be civil to each other or I am going to send you to your beds. "So where was I?" she asked. "Where did we stop?"

"When you saw the zombie with Tony," was the prompt response from Daniel.

"She didn't say she saw it with me," I corrected.

"Oh yes. As I was saying last night, Tony was the one who caused me to see our permanent guest the first and only time I saw him. But by then, I had had enough evidence to know that he was still hanging around, surveying our daily lives.

"After we bought this property, we broke down the wooden house and sold it and began building this one. By the time it was finished, the first four of you children were already born and we asked Marjory to come and work for us permanently to help me with the kids. In those first days, I would be at one end of the house and hear things moving at the other end or in another room. I would naturally think it was Marjory or one of the children.

"But then one day, I heard dishes and other things moving around in the kitchen. I knew that Marjory had left five minutes earlier with the children for the Botanical Gardens, so I was alone in the house. I came out of my bedroom and listened, and sure enough, someone was moving wares around in the kitchen. I therefore thought that Marjory had returned for one reason or the other, and so called her. But there was no answer. I called again, but still there was no answer. So I went around to the kitchen. There was no one. Realising that I did hear those sounds and that there was no one in the kitchen sent a chill through my spine, and cold bumps came out all over my body as I felt my head raise.

"After that incident, I began to pay more attention to the noises that I would hear in the house and in particular at night. There were times when I would hear the glasses in the cabinet tinkling, or I would see shadows for a second that would immediately disappear. At other times, I would feel this gentle breeze flowing through the house while everything outside was still. All these told me that there was something unusual in this house.

"Then one day, your father bought a long mirror for me, which made it easy to check how I was dressed from head to foot. I decided to place it in the living room as my final check spot before leaving the house. About a week later, I woke up one afternoon to find the mirror cracked right down the middle. I did not know what to think. When your father saw it, he was very upset and started quarrelling about how much money it cost him.

"Two months later, he bought me another mirror and again I placed it in the living room. Three days later, the mirror was again cracked and exactly in the same way; right down the middle. Needless to say, your father almost flew into a rage. He demanded to know which of the children was so delinquent. I told him that I didn't think it had anything to do with any of you, and he looked at me shocked. 'Are you suggesting that the maid would do something so stupid?' he asked indignantly.

"I knew your father was very upset about those two mirrors and I also knew he would go out and buy me another one. So I decided to beat him to it and got myself a new one; only this time I placed it in our bedroom. That same evening when your dad came home, he brought with him a new mirror. This led to a long discussion as to why I thought I needed to buy myself a new mirror, and finished with him deciding against my advice to put the one he bought in the living room. He didn't believe my theory that there might be some other reason why the mirrors got broken. He insisted that there must be some straightforward and uncomplicated explanation, which lay in the misbehaviour of one or more of you children. So, plead as I might, he resolved to put the mirror in the living room.

"About a week later, there was the first Test between the West Indies and Australia in Melbourne or some other place in Australia. In those days, there was only coverage by radio. Your father, being the cricket fanatic he was, sat up all night listening to the commentary. This he did in the living room, using the big Phillips radio that we have since placed in the cellar. Yes, Cammie and Debra would remember that there was a time when there was no TV or stereo system in this house. The only thing we had as regards music and entertainment was that big

Phillips radio, and it wasn't bad at all. We could tune into the BBC directly at Bush House in London.

"But to continue with the story; it was about four o'clock in the morning when your father shook me gently, waking me up and in a whisper said, 'Come, I want to show you something.' I asked him what time it was and he said it was about three in the morning. With that being the case, I told him that it wasn't me who should go with him but that he should come to bed. He insisted, so I went with him. We went out into the living room and there it was, the new mirror cracked right down the middle, exactly in the same way the two previous ones were.

"I looked at it and immediately said, 'This has nothing to do with the children.' 'I know,' he said softly, almost in a whisper. 'I was here all night listening the cricket and none of them came out here, so I know it's not any of them.'

"I then asked him what happened and he said he did not know. All he knew was that he was listening to the cricket in the dark and must have dozed off a bit when he heard a sound of some sort. He said that he awoke and immediately put on the light and found nothing strange until he looked at the mirror and saw the crack. He was so shocked that he came and woke me up for he remembered me saying it had nothing to do with the children. He simply couldn't understand how the mirror got broken.

"He did, however, understand that it had nothing to do with any of you and became very concerned that there was something rather strange about the house, at least the living room. He was so disturbed by it that he suggested we think about moving out and finding a new property; he wanted to make sure that you children were safe. I spent quite some time trying to reassure him that you all would be fine and that there was nothing to worry about. But he was clearly worried for you children.

"That night or rather morning, I promised him that I would go to church and speak with the priest about the situation with our house. So the following day, I went and spoke to Father Isaacs. He said he wanted to see the house, and came home with me one evening to do so. After I explained that it was only in the living room that the mirrors got cracked, he went around examining the entire house. We then proceeded to discuss the history of this property as I knew it, and Father Isaacs and I soon realised that the living room was built over the spot where the hole dug by Rhoda and Dina was located. I then understood why my mirror in the bedroom never got broken."

"So it was he who broke the mirror?" asked Debra.

"Well, according to Father Isaacs, he is still watching over his money. The fact is that this living room sits exactly on the location of that hole. Now, if Father Isaac's theory is right, it means that he hovers in this area always, still looking over his money. The mirror, being where it stood, showed him a reflection of himself, which he obviously didn't like. He therefore wanted it removed. I am not sure that Father Isaacs was right, but there seemed to be some logic in what he said."

Listening to my mom, I couldn't help but feel that Father Isaacs was absolutely correct. I knew that there was indeed something strange as regards placing mirrors in our living room. In the six years my family had been away, I lost at least three mirrors that I had hung in that room. I would wake up in the morning, two or three days after having hung them up, to find them cracked right down the middle just like my mother had described. I never understood why, but thought it might be the sun, which came into the living room. So after the third mirror cracked, I surrendered and did not try placing any more in there. But looking back at it now, I realise that it could not have been the sun, for I had hung the third mirror in a corner of the living room that was not exposed to it. Yet it got cracked, and yes, right down the middle.

Therefore, my mother's story was for me, unlike my brothers and sisters, not simply a revelation. It was also an explanation. It was finally being able to see that I was not slightly mad, or strange or weird. That the strange things I had heard over those six years were not imaginations or the product of an unstable mind. It was reassuring to know that others before me, including the ultimate authority, my mother, had heard, and in some cases even seen, these things.

"So how did you finally see him?" asked Joan.

"Well," continued my mother, "over the years, these occasional strange sounds and shadows I thought I heard and saw continued. There was also the regular strange feeling that someone was looking at me, at us, and the realisation that there were many things happening in this house that I didn't and couldn't understand.

"Then came the time of Tony's exams and the incident which put everything into perspective. Tony used to be up all night, every night studying. On one occasion, at about 12:00 midnight, I came out of my bedroom to go to the bathroom. I knew that Tony would be at the dining table studying as always, and so decided to be as quiet as possible in my movements as I did not want to disturb him. As I stepped out of my bedroom, I looked down the corridor for Tony and saw him concentrating on his book. But lo and behold, standing over him, looking over his left shoulder was this white man in a red jacket with gold buttons and a navy-blue military-styled cap. At the very second I saw him, he looked and saw me and I knew that he realised I could see him. For that moment, time stopped.

"He was standing over Tony like a teacher or an instructor would, as if trying to ensure that Tony understood the work. But thinking of it now, I can see that he didn't understand the work himself; and so, was so intent on doing this, that he didn't hear me come out of my bedroom. Therefore, when I appeared, it was a complete surprise to him. I immediately knew who he was, for Dina's story came rushing back to my mind and I remembered that I had known on that day, that I would one day see him. How I knew this, I can't say; I just knew it, and, true to form, it did come to pass and there he was. In other words, it was as if this meeting between him and me was planned on that day, and it was only a matter of time before this meeting was held. That night was the date.

"He looked up and saw me and we both were trapped in that moment of time. We both didn't know what to do, how to escape. We stared at each other for about 30 seconds. In that time, I could see that he was dressed exactly as Dina had described, with the sword and all. I could also see from the expression on his face, that he had no intention of evil, but was just in an uncomfortable situation and simply needed the possibility to escape. I did not know what to do and my mind was travelling at a rocket's pace in its search of a solution. Then I remembered what your grandmother had said to me about seeing a ghost.

"According to her, she had the gift of seeing spirits and ghosts. She was born in a period when quite a lot of people had this ability to see the roaming spirits of dead people, and so knew how to deal with them. She had said that once they appeared unto her and didn't look evil, she looked the other way, thus allowing them to disappear. This is what I did.

"I lowered my eyes and looked away for a moment, and when I looked back he was gone. I don't know if Tony remembers, but that was the night when I told him that, once it was midnight, I don't want him studying at this dining table anymore. I wanted him to go into his bedroom. I remember him looking at me with the strangest of expressions, but I had to make a decision. Tony, do you remember that night?" she asked, turning her gaze on me.

"Yes, Mom; in fact I do. It was the night that you banned me from being in the kitchen, dining room and living room after 12:00 midnight, and I was really upset."

I did recall the incident. I was the sixth of eight children, and the five before me had all passed the Common Entrance with flying colours, and had gone to secondary school on scholarships. Unlike them, I barely made it and my parents had to pay for my secondary education, as well as my books. It was something they never did before or after, and my mother made sure that I never forgot it throughout my secondary school years. For her, it was an affront that one of her children was attending a second rate high school, and that he couldn't even get a scholarship to get there. So, for the five years I spent in high school, I was constantly reminded by my mother of my failure to live up to family name and tradition when I sat the Common Entrance.

This made me determine to make amends through the results of my O levels. So I studied day in day out prior to those exams, only to have my mother say to me that I didn't need to study at nights, but to go to my bed instead. I remember thinking that she wanted me to fail. That she was afraid that I would demonstrate that one did not necessarily have to go to the most prestigious school, as she preached, to attain the ultimate success as regards secondary education.

"It was not my intention to prevent you from doing your studies," continued my mother, seeming to read my thoughts. "But I hope you understand now that I couldn't very well have told you that I had seen a ghost standing over you, trying to read your books. Just imagine what that would have done to you and to this home."

"So what happened after you saw him," questioned Clementine.

"The truth is," continued my mother, "for many weeks after, I was worried about you all and in particular Tony. I was fearful that he, Mr. Redcoat, might begin to follow Tony around and might finally hurt him or cause him to hurt himself. But as can be seen, none of that happened. I find it interesting that he should appear in Tony's life, now that he is a young man and can understand these things without fear. But there are many things in life we don't understand, and in particular things from the world of the dead and the grave. I suppose that's why most people are so afraid of death. It's not only because they think it is the end, but more importantly, they really don't know what follows after. They really are in the dark and are completely ignorant of where it takes us." With that, my mother concluded her tale and we all headed to bed.

I wasn't so sure that my mother was right about the "without fear" as regards me being grown and understanding it all. It was indeed my fear that caused me to behave the way I did and that led to Balgo relating the story to them. As I lay in my bed looking at the invisible ceiling in my lightless room, my mind went back to my own encounter with Mr. Redcoat.

***

It all began on the Saturday evening of Kiddies' Carnival. I had gone with some friends into town to see the action. It was a very sunny day and we followed the bands around the city a few times, taking in the sweet steel band music and looking at the costumes in the various sections of the bands. But, with the sun blazing down in all its glory, it sapped my energy rather quickly and I decided to head home. I got home just before dusk, went to my bedroom to rest and soon fell asleep. I was awakened by what seemed to be someone struggling with me, trying to strangle me.

When I came to full awareness, my room was in darkness and I could discern nothing. I could however feel the presence of someone standing over me. In a second or two, the person began walking out of my bedroom. I remember not being afraid, for my thought was that it was my friend Bunda playing a practical joke. He would usually come to the house and hang out, and would sometimes make a fool of himself by doing things like that, just for the fun of it.

My family had left to live in the United States four years earlier, and since that time, I had lived alone in our house. From time to time, Bunda and other friends, as well as my cousin Tyrone and other family members, would come and stay at the house. Those were the days of very little break-ins and when crime in general was not a widespread phenomenon as it is today. So I never locked the doors at night, and always slept with my windows open. Close friends and relatives knew that they could pass by the house at any hour and it would be unlocked, once I was at home.

"Bunda?" I enquired as I got out of bed. There was no answer. I could clearly hear the steps of the person leaving my room, for whoever it was, was wearing what seemed to be slippers made of hard plastic which made a click, click sound on the floor tiles as he walked. I reached for the light switch, which was just above my bed head and switched it on. The room remained in darkness. I got up and started following the sound of the steps.

Our house had seven bedrooms, with three on one side and four on the other side of a long corridor which ran into the bathrooms at one end, and the dining room at the other. This dining room sat between the living room on its right and our kitchen on its left.

As the person left my room and headed for the corridor, he seemed to brush against the strip curtains hanging in front of the toilet, as I could hear the bamboo strips from which this curtain was made, colliding one with the other. I followed the sounds and started calling other names of possible persons who might have come to visit. People were always dropping in for one reason or the other, so it could have been anyone.

"Marylyn?" I enquired, but still there was no answer. By this time, I had left my bedroom and was following the footsteps as they entered the main corridor leading to the dining room. I tried the switches on the adjacent wall, which lighted the bulbs in the corridor. Again, there was only darkness.

The footsteps proceeded down the corridor quite tentatively, as if the person was in no hurry, just teasing me along, ensuring that I followed him. And followed I did, all the while calling different names,

"Aunt Marge? Bunda? Balgo?" But none of these names brought a response from my invisible visitor.

As the person approached the dining room, the footsteps turned left and continued into the kitchen and I followed. I was only able to do this without running into anything because I knew the house, and would usually walk in the dark without the use of lights. I could also tell from the sound of the footsteps, that the person was directly in front of me. In fact, I extended my arms several times, trying to grab on to the person but found myself grabbing at space. Still for all, I was not worried as it did not cross my mind that there was something amiss, or that this was something unusual.

On entering the kitchen, I tried the switch and again there were no lights. I continued to follow the footsteps until I banged my head into the exit door of the kitchen leading into the garden. And then it struck me.

Our kitchen had cupboards on both sides. It also had a stove, refrigerator, and the wash sinks, thus leaving only a central walking space between these. That space was not wide enough for two grown people to pass each other without colliding, much less not even touching and in the dark at that. I knew that I had followed the footsteps right up to the kitchen door, which was closed. So where did the person disappear to? Did he vanish into thin air? This was weird.

Looking through the louvers of our kitchen window, I realised that all the houses in the neighbourhood had light except ours. Now, there was no doubt in my mind; there could only be one explanation.

I ran out of the kitchen, back through the dining room, through the living room, out into the porch and onto the street, screaming at the top of my voice. I was running as fast as I could, for I was sure that someone or something would be following me. There seemed to be needles running through my entire body, and I could hear voices following me as I ran. My head felt like it was three times its normal size. I kept going as fast as my legs could carry me, escaping from what, I didn't know.

Our house was in an alley off the main road, and I ran down this alley until I got onto the main road where there were quite a number of people. As I approached these people, I stopped running and began to walk, my chest heaving as a result of my accelerated heartbeat. As I got closer, I recognised everyone there, including my first cousin Balgo. He was on his way to collect me for us to attend one of the carnival shows in the park that night, but had stopped to chat with one of the guys. I was almost out of breath and was really relieved to see so many people, but particularly Balgo. He was family. It meant I was saved.

As I got closer to the group, I signalled Balgo, and from that distance indicated to him that we needed to talk now. My frantic sign language must have made an impression on him for he immediately excused himself and came over to me.

"What happen, Tony?" he asked in a voice full of concern. "You look white like a sheet. Something frightened you."

"Oh Lord, Balgo, somebody in the house!"

"What did you say? Somebody in the house. In which house?"

"Our house." I said, with my chest still heaving.

"What you mean somebody in the house?"

"Believe me, Balgo, somebody in the house."

"How you so sure somebody in the house?"

"'Cause I just come from there and somebody is in there."

"And who is this somebody?"

"I don't know, but believe me, somebody is in there."

Tyrone was five years my senior and much taller and stronger. From since my early childhood, he gave the impression of someone who had no fear for anything, and who could and would challenge and beat anyone. With him around, my younger siblings and I always felt safe. That is why I counted myself very lucky to have met him of all people. And as usual he immediately took control.

"Ok, let's go and see who is this person."

"But I…."

"No buts! If there is somebody there, we need to go and confront them. You can't have strangers running you out of your own house. Come on, let's go!"

With that, he immediately set out for the house, with me following at what I considered a safe distance, so that if we had to run, I would had have a head start.

We entered the alley and I realised that lights were glaring from our house and the front yard was completed lighted. As we got closer, I could see that practically ever bulb in the house was switched on and all the windows and doors were wide open. There was this strong wind blowing the curtains outwards, yet the surrounding trees stood motionless, looking on as passive observers.

Tyrone entered the house while I stood in the road. As he went from room to room, I could hear him shouting that he had found no one. When he returned to the living room, I felt it was safe to enter the house. We went into the garden and from there into the cellar. Tyrone checked everywhere and of course found nothing. So we went back inside.

"There is absolutely no one here."

"I am telling you that there was someone here."

"Well, I am sure that you can see for yourself it is only me, you and God here, and no one else," he insisted.

"I swear to you that there was someone here."

"Who was it, a man or a woman?" he asked.

"I can't say."

"What you mean you can't say?"

"Well, I didn't see the person."

"You didn't see the person? So how come you know that someone was here?"

"Because I heard the footsteps walking through the house."

"You are really a joker; you are nothing but a big coward."

"Tyrone," I said. I always used his correct name when I wanted him to take me seriously. "I swear to you that someone was here."

"But how come you didn't see the person? Was the person invisible or something?"

"Tyrone, the house was in darkness and I only heard the footsteps."

"Anyway, let's check to see if anything is missing," he said.

I followed him and we checked every room. Not only was there nothing missing, but nothing was disturbed.

"Tony, are you telling me that someone was in this house and touched nothing, stole nothing, destroyed nothing?"

I had no answer to that, upon which Balgo burst out laughing. He collapsed on the couch and couldn't stop laughing all the while repeating, "You coward, you coward, I never met somebody so coward. Man, you too coward."

I knew I had not heard the last about my cowardice. Balgo was ahead, 1 to 0, and his victory would be celebrated many times. This was the way it was with us, and there was no way for me to escape it. Balgo had the upper hand this time around, and he was going to use it to maximum effect.

And so, there we were two years later and Tyrone having his moment in the sun. He didn't just tell a story of my cowardice, but demonstrated with the skills of a Broadway actor, the pitiful picture I was on that Kiddies' Carnival Saturday evening. Like most Caribbean persons of our generation, neither of us knew whether the stories of zombies, jumbies, duppies, ghosts and spirits were true. I had told him of my experience and he, having investigated and found no proof, made me into the little boy shouting, Wolf! Wolf! to the great amusement of my siblings. But with my mother's story, the turn of events caught us both and everyone else by surprise.

None of us had ever had someone confirm to us before, that they had seen a ghost or spirit. But here it was that my mother, the person we believed in most, and trusted unconditionally, had confirmed that my experience was not an illusion or a figment of my imagination. It was simply an introduction to a reality that we would, from that evening, ever be conscious of, and one I had to deal with on my own, after my family had returned to the United States.

If my mother intended to bring calm with her revelation, this did not work on me, and I slept with one eye opened for the next year I spent at home. Once I left for university, I never returned to live in that house. Needless to say, in that additional year I spent at home before going off to study, Balgo never came to the house once. Every time I met and invited him, he would promise to visit, but never did. Indeed, none of my siblings ever returned, and the house is now nothing but a shell as it has become totally dilapidated due to the absence of use, and the lack of care and attention.

Nowadays, whenever I return to the Caribbean, which is twice or three times a year, I most times avoid even visiting that house. But when I do, I can't help thinking how sad this sight must make Dina's great grandfather Thomas, her grandfather Saga, and her father

Alfonso. It must pain their hearts wherever they are, to see their efforts rot due to the superstitious cowardice of children of an enlightened age. That a spirit that couldn't beat them, the children of the age of the ignorance of slavery, has prevailed against their freed and educated inheritors. It certainly seems like Mr. Redcoat really won.

Richard A. Byron-Cox

When Japheth Met Lucifer

"Miss Phillips! Miss Phillips!" The shouting was coming from about a hundred yards down the road, and Lou Phillips knew from the first call that it was the voice of the neighbour, Old Jean-Jean. With stick in hand, her head-wrap barely dragged on, and walking as quickly as her old bones allowed, she persisted, "Miss Phillips! Miss Phillips! Oh Gawd, Miss Phillips! That ah evil."

From the first shout, a mountain rose in Mrs. Phillips' chest, her heart missed a beat and then began to race. Even though she had heard many of these "Oh Gawd, Miss Phillips" and quite often for the last three years, she had not gotten accustomed to them. The reason being, while she knew what they meant, she could never tell how serious the damage was with each new occurrence.

"Oh Gawd, Miss Phillips!" continued Old Jean-Jean, pausing to allow for her heavy breathing, "That boy wicked! He wicked to death!", a clearly out of breath and visibly upset Old Jean-Jean wailed.

"Miss Jean, please come in and sit down and tell me what happened", Mrs. Phillips said, opening the little galvanise gate to allow an almost collapsing Old Jean-Jean to enter. Lou Phillips, who was educated way beyond her time, was a married woman. However, for many people at that time, Mrs. was something one used interchangeably with Miss; the important thing was that you showed respect. "Please sit, Miss Jean, and tell me what happened", encouraged Lou Phillips, "Can I get you some water?"

"Is about de bad one again", said a still heavily breathing Old Jean-Jean.

"Sit down and take your time. I will get you some water to drink," said Mrs. Phillips as she went off to the tin bucket with drinking water.

Old Jean-Jean proceeded to make her complaint. "And is just dis morning I hear you beating him and, and, look what he did, Miss Phillips", said Old Jean-Jean, her chest rising and sinking after every two words. "You remember ah did tell you that ah was going to de river to wash two pieces ah clothes and come back? Well, Miss Phillips, when ah reach de river, ah hear a sound like a cat wailing. Ah looked further up de river and there was Japheth, dragging me cat on ah piece ah rope trying to drown the poor cat. Miss Phillips, when ah see that; ah drop de basin and scream. De moment he hear de scream, he let go the cat and dig out full speed. Ah was so frightened that I forget de basin and the river washed it way. That was me only basin."

By this time, Mrs. Phillips had brought Old Jean-Jean a big tin cup of water and, giving it to her, asked, "You know if the cat is alright?"

"Ah don't even know, for by de time he let it go, it was so frighten that it run off with de string round it neck."

Mrs. Phillips said more to herself than to Old Jean-Jean, "Lord, I'm tired with Japheth. I'm tired with Japheth. That boy is nothing but trouble."

Old Jean-Jean continued, "Ah know he is yo' child and you might not agree with me, but ah think that he is possess and you should take him down to Moses fo' he own good. I know that Mr. Phillips is a spiritual leader and all that, and it wouldn't look right for you to be seen going to ah obeah man with yo' son. But Moses is de only one could help that boy because he know how to drive out evil spirits and thing. And, and that boy is definitely possess with some kind ah evil spirit."

While Mrs. Phillips felt that Old Jean-Jean was out of place to tell her what she should do about her children; worse still, that she should take her son to an obeah man, she quietly confessed to herself that she had of late been thinking this might be the solution. Japheth had always been bad from the day he could speak; but for the last three years, from the time he turned ten, he had been just impossible.

Mrs. Phillips' troubles with Japheth began even before he was born. Of the twelve children she brought into this world, none caused her to vomit, and as much early morning sickness as he did. She had quarrelled with James, her husband, throughout her pregnancy with Japheth. Many a day she could not get out of bed due to just feeling too ill. On the night Japheth was born, the midwife nearly did not come to help her with the delivery due to the rain, thunder and lightning. Mrs. Phillips' sister, Pearly, had to plead and beg, and then the midwife only came after she was told that Mrs. Phillips' life was under threat. To cap it all off, the whole birth process took the better part of six hours, with Mrs. Phillips losing consciousness twice.

From that night and for the last thirteen years, Mrs. Phillips had known nothing but trouble with this son. When he was just seven and a half years old, she was summoned to his primary school. His class teacher, Marie Shorty, complained that Japheth had put a piece of broken mirror on the floor under the desk so that he could see the colour of the girls' panties, encouraging other boys to join him, thereby causing an uproar. Mrs. Phillips remembers vividly the expression on Teacher Marie's face when the latter declared, "I have never seen so much vice in someone so small. This child has no innocence!"

Mrs. Phillips knew that teacher Marie was saying that, in her opinion, Japheth was nothing but a little devil and she, Teacher Marie, would rather have nothing to do with him. While Mrs. Phillips understood this, it wasn't pleasant news to the ear. After all, he was the son of the village Pointer.

A year earlier, it was fisherman Buddy Boy who had come rushing with the news that little Jerome Gordon had been saved by him after going to Dark Rock with Japheth to fish. It transpired that, on the way too school, Japheth met Jerome, his classmate, and somehow convinced him they should go fishing. While seated on the rock waiting for the fish to bite, Japheth started up a conversation with Jerome.

"So you learn fo' swim yet?"

"No, but me big brother Bagga going teach me."

"You making jokes. Big man like you can't swim," replied Japheth.

"Bagga ah the best swimmer in the village so me go soon learn. Ah don't have fo' worry," said a confident Jerome.

But Japheth had already decided that it was time that Jerome learned to swim. Without warning, he got up and pushed Jerome off the rock, landing him in water at least two metres deep. One moment Jerome knew he was on the rock talking to Japheth, the next he found himself in the sea battling for his life, screaming, "Help! Help!"

between his sinking and taking in mouthfuls of water. Japheth, in response, sat on the rock encouraging him to learn to swim by slow-clapping and chanting, "Mek it Jerry mek it. Mek it Jerry mek it. Mek it Jerry mek it."

Jerome owed his life to the quick action of Buddy Boy who sat mending his fishing net on the other side of the rock. Upon hearing the childlike cry for help, he came running, sprang into the water and grabbed Jerome when he was about to go down a final time. He brought him up, pumped his stomach and took him home. Needless to say, Japheth took leave immediately upon the arrival of Buddy Boy.

Japheth was just as much trouble at home. His brothers and sisters allowed him to have his way, since to wrangle with him was to take on more than anyone could handle. As Old Jean-Jean continued her complaint, Mrs. Phillips remembered the time she had to go to work, weeding and moulding potatoes and carrots for Redman John over at his estate at Great Field on Saturdays. Every time she returned in the evenings, the flour, sugar and powdered milk were less than she left them. She ensured that she cooked before leaving, so that the children had something to eat and therefore did not need to use these. However, every Saturday she came home, it was the same thing; someone had used some of her already limited food supply. Determined to get to the bottom of it, on the way home with Hilly and Lilia one Sunday after prayer in the Praise House where her husband was the Pointer, she asked Hilly what he knew about the disappearance of these things. In doing so, she reminded him that Jesus does not like children who tell lies, so he would go to hell if he did not tell her the truth. Above all, she would give him a good licking if he didn't tell her what she wanted to know.

Now Hilly, eight years old and two years younger than Japheth, having often been at the receiving end of the vengefulness of his brother, would never have easily implicated Japheth on any matter simply on the threat of a whipping from his mother. But incurring the dislike of Jesus and then going to hell were prospects he didn't really look forward to. With Japheth still at the Praise House with his father, and Lilia the only witness, Hilly felt he could risk it. He gave Japheth away, explaining that he usually made coconut dumplings with the flour, and sometimes he mixed the powdered milk with sugar which they would eat.

Mrs. Phillips was not surprised. "So, why didn't you tell me before?" she asked. Hilly did not answer, for he knew his mother knew the answer to that. "It would be me and he when he come home today," she said in vexation. "Me and he! As a matter of fact, I go let yo' father deal with him. I am tired."

When Japheth, his other brothers and their father came home after having put the Praise House back in order for the night service, Mrs. Phillips, Hilly and Lilia were waiting for them in the dirt-floor kitchen where the family had their meals. In those days, most kitchens were built separate from the dwelling house. Most homes of the poor and underprivileged - the overriding majority in the Caribbean of that time, and to which class the Phillips belonged - were made of wattle and daub. These were constructions where the walls were made of sticks woven in a particular manner and then plastered with a mixture of cattle dung and earth. The roof was made of layers of grass, and the whole thing reminded one of the huts seen in some sub-Saharan African villages today.

When the others entered the kitchen, Mrs. Phillips told George to close the kitchen door. She ordered Manassas to hold Japheth while she spoke, for fear that he would try to escape. She then told her husband the whole story. Mr. Phillips sent George to cut a tamarind rod, upon receipt of which, he administered a serious licking on Japheth while chastising him about his greed and untruthfulness.

"I don't know what to do with you. You is the devil?" he asked rhetorically. "Why you can't be like the rest children and them Japheth? Why? You could tell me? I is a Christian man and spiritual leader, and you does behave worse than the devil in hell."

Japheth was just glad that the beating had ceased. He was in physical pain with minor bruises all over his body, for a tamarind rod is virtually unbreakable. In the muscular hands of Mr. Phillips, it was nothing short of a lethal weapon.

Mr. Phillips was a serious disciplinarian who believed firmly in the biblical principle of not sparing the rod and thereby not spoiling the child. He, like most Caribbean parents of that age, never wavered in the belief that corporal punishment was fundamental to the upbringing of children. He therefore administered the rod of correction to good measure.

This administering of the rod of correction to the delinquent he did, both at home and in the Praise House, as part of his duty as Pointer. He literally whipped his flock into righteousness when they sinned and fell short of the glory of the Saviour. This correction, administered through the use of his Pointer's leather strap, did not always go down well with some members of his congregation. It sometimes got him into trouble, as was the case with Brother Jacobs.

In those days, a Pointer was an important person, not just in the Spiritual Baptist movement, but in the community where he lived. In Pointer Phillips' congregation, Brother Jacobs was second in command, the de facto junior Pointer. But it seemed to Mr. Phillips that Brother Jacobs aspired to replace him and become Pointer himself. Mr. Phillips, not being one to entertain challenges of any sort, convinced Brother Jacobs that if he were to mourn a tenth time, he could rapidly become a Pointer and so have his own praise house. Brother Jacobs readily agreed.

It was therefore set for him to go on his knees for the tenth time, fast tracking his promotion to the office of Pointer. After he had completed the nine days and nights praying, eating only once a day under the supervision of Pointer Phillips, the Friday night came when he was to tell the vision he had while on his knees. When one mourns, he is supposed to have been given a series of dreams or visions which must be revealed to the congregation at the final act of the mourning process called 'Shouting.'

The Friday night came and the whole village came out to the Praise House to hear the revelations of Brother Jacobs. In those pre-radio, pre-television days in the Caribbean, the end of a mourning period was always a big event. In the small villages, it was a community affair, a religious pantomime open to public viewing. This particular mourning was special, as Brother Jacobs was the junior Pointer and a veteran mourner. The villagers therefore expected a lot from him. In the end, even the most demanding of them had to admit that they got much more than they had bargained for.

As Brother Jacobs told the vision he said was given to him while on his knees, he quoted scriptures to back up what he said the angels told him. As he proceeded, he began to make mistakes as to the places these verses were found in the Bible or what they said exactly. Each time he did this, Pointer Phillips administered the leather strap and the crowd would encourage, "Yes Pointer, give him the rod of correction!" After the third such intervention with the leather strap by Pointer Phillips, Brother Jacobs had had enough.

"Phillips, if yo' touch me one more time tonight, we go ha' big problem here!"

"Way yo' say?"

"If you hit me one more time, the praise mash up, fo' all hell go to break loose right here in the Praise House tonight!"

This second statement by Brother Jacobs was harsher than the first and said more forcefully and loud enough so that no one had doubts what he meant. Silence descended on the whole Praise House.

Everyone realised that the long awaited showdown between Pointer Phillips and his understudy was hovering in the vicinity. Mr. Phillips was now in a dilemma. He could hit Brother Jacobs for his ill-discipline and face the possibility of having a fight on his hands. Or ignore the insolence of his student and so lose his reputation and the respect of the community. It was unheard of that one should question a Pointer and in particular during mourning. Pointer Phillips decided to go with option one. All hell did indeed break loose.

Slap! Slap! The leather strap echoed around Brother Jacobs' head while Pointer Phillips said firmly, "I am correcting you…" He never had time to finish the sentence.

Bang! came a right fist from Brother Jacobs, accompanied by, "What the hell you think it is? I is yo' market goat?"

The blow caught Pointer Phillips in the middle of his face. It sent him toppling into a group of sisters, knocking over the wooden bench they were sitting on. People started to scatter as confusion announced its arrival. Some people rushed out of the Praise House while others pressed forward to see what had happened to Pointer Phillips. There were people shouting different things all at the same time. The Praise House lost all sense of order as confusion took over for a while.

A number of male members of the congregation rushed forward in the defence of their Pointer. For some minutes, no one could see Brother Jacobs as he was encircled by these men who rained blows on him.

Bang! Buff! Slap, came the sounds as Brother Jacobs fell to the ground.

"You too rude and out ah place! What you thinking 'bout fo' lash the Pointer?". Bang! Buff! More kicks and cuffs, " After all he do fo' you, you want fo' kill um." Bang! Slap! Buff! "You too big for yo' pants. You need fo' cut down to size. You too ungrateful."

The blows came in torrents from all directions. By this time, Brother Jacobs was not only on the ground; he was pleading for mercy. But little was shown. By the time they were finished with him, he was motionless, bleeding from different parts of the body. The picked him up and dashed him outside in the yard, still muddy from the early evening downpour, as if he were just a sack of rotten potatoes.

Mr. Phillips' face was swollen for days. He lost a front tooth, but his reputation as a worthy Pointer was not only saved but enhanced. His bravery made him even more authoritative in the eyes of all as a teacher and leader of uprightness in the community. This in turn placed greater demand on his family to be exemplary. Japheth was determined not to live up to those expectations, and the Pointer could not understand why.

"Japheth, you can't continue fo' embarrass me like that. I can't tell people at praise don't thief when me own son is a common thief," said an exasperated James Phillips.

Mr. Phillips went on and on, but Japheth wasn't hearing him. He was already planning his revenge. He knew that someone, either George, senior to him by a year and a half, Hilly or Lilia, the youngest in the family, had talked. He was going to make them pay for their mouths. He was tired telling them to see and don't talk. Lilia, he knew he couldn't touch, for she was everybody's darling. If he as much as clipped a hair on her head, his father would skin him alive. So he planned to put George and Hilly against each other in an effort to gain the truth. Once he was sure that it wasn't Lilia, then he didn't mind if Peter paid for Paul as regards the other two.

Japheth did not have to wait long to discover the truth and who was the culprit. Lilia, having seen the severity of the licking Japheth got from his father, felt sorry for him and on the next day told him of Hilly's confession.

Japheth knew that an outburst on Hilly now would secure for him another severe thrashing from his father. He realised that patience was the name of the game this time. He planned his action carefully, giving Hilly enough time to settle down and to believe that he did not know. Then one Saturday when Mrs. Phillips had gone to do her usual field weeding, Japheth put his plan in motion.

While Hilly and Lilia were outside playing, Japheth set to work diligently. First he got two handfuls of the tiny and fiery-hot red bird pepper, ground and kneaded them into a dough. He made a huge dumpling which he put in his usual Saturday baby-pot made with Mrs. Phillips' flour. When all was prepared, he made sure the food was cool enough so that Hilly could dive in the way he usually did. Hilly so loved to eat that his family nicknamed him, "Mr. Hilly, the greedy." This made Japheth doubly sure his plan would work perfectly.

"Hil and Lee," he called. "Ah mek ah baby-pot, come fo' some."

"Coming!" came the response.

It was Hilly who got there first. If his weakness for food could be described as terrible, then his love for coconut dumpling was unsurpassable. He simply devoured them as quickly as one could offer them to him. When he saw his calabash bowl with the nice big dumpling, he didn't wait. He immediately bit into it and chewed rapidly, swallowed and bit in again. He was chewing rapidly when he let out a scream, spat out the rest on the dirt floor of the kitchen and rushed to the kitchen bucket for water. He did not get a calabash bowl (Mrs. Phillips reserved her tin cups for visitors and special occasions), but dipped his face into the bucket and started drinking as quickly as he could. But as the hot pepper surged, he gave up drinking and began to scream.

"Oh J, me throat, me throat J, me throat."

"Serve you right, you talk too much!"

"Wha' happen Hil? Hil wha' happen to you?" shouted Lilia.

"Me tongue, me throat and me chest ah burn me."

"Japheth wha' happen to him? Wha' happen to him?"

"He talk too much and that is wha' does happen to people who talk too much," responded an unmoved and unperturbed Japheth.

"But is not talk he talking. Is cry he crying. J, wha' happen to him?"

By this time, Hilly was literally screaming and running to and from the drinking bucket while Lilia was getting more and more frightened.

"Japheth, wha' happen to Hilly? Wha' happen to Hilly?"

"He bite some bird pepper in the dumpling and that does happen to people who talk too much."

"Japheth, you have fo' do something," said Lilia, getting somewhat hysterical. "You have fo' do something fo' help Hilly."

"Well ah could get some ah Mammy brown sugar and let Hilly put it pon he tongue and that would help cool it. But Hilly go tell Mammy when she come home."

"Japheth, do something, we hav' fo' do something fo' help Hilly."

"Ah can't tek the sugar 'cause Hilly go talk. He go tell pon me."

"Ah wouldn't say nothing", interrupted Hilly, tears streaming down his face and holding his tummy as if he wanted to vomit.

"You sure you wouldn't talk? Ah ain't going to thief sugar fo' you and then you make me get licks fo' it."

It was Lilia who responded, as Hilly was by this time rolling on the kitchen's dirt floor. "J, Hilly is sick and he need help before he dead!"

Japheth got some of his mother's brown sugar and Hilly gratefully put some on his tongue. He continued to cry for more than an hour, with Japheth repeating time and again his one refrain. "This is wha' does happen to people who talk too much. Hilly you talk too much. That will teach you to see things and keep yo' tongue between yo' teeth."

Mrs. Phillips was to learn of Hilly's torture by Japheth months later from Lilia. When Hilly got sick after eating a rather spicy dish, Lilia suggested to the family that they should try treating him with sugar for she had seen Japheth use it and that it really worked.

"Ah could even talk to Moses fo' you," Old Jean-Jean was saying, bringing back Mrs. Phillips to the world of the present. "People say obeah bad, but it does have it good side too."

"Miss Jean, I know Japheth is wrong," said Mrs. Phillips, "and I will make sure that his father gives him a good licking when he comes home. I really don't know way to do with that boy anymore."

While Mr. Phillips was the village Pointer, this was not a job. As was the case with all other Pointers on the island, Mr. Phillips occupied his position by virtue of professing that he was a Baptist and having gone to mourn at Pointer Brooms, the required ten times. He also had the added advantage of being the only Shaker, the popular name the local Baptist religion carried at the time, in the village who could read.

The Spiritual Baptist was the religion of the poor and downtrodden. They were sometimes harassed by the police, for in a strict legal sense, theirs was an illegal religion, outlawed by the state. They were, and still are, a set of believers who, during their services, become filled with the Holy Spirit. This causes them to shake, shiver and sometimes jump, hence they came to be known as Shakers.

Despite the problems they had with the law, these people believed in their religion and continued the practice where and whenever they could. The Praise House (for that's what a Shaker temple was called in those days), of which Mr. Phillips was Pointer, was a wattle and daub structure. The floor was the uncovered bare dirt, and most people were so poor, they went to praise without shoes. That however did not matter, as you could not enter the Praise House with your shoes on. Inside was considered holy ground.

Even though he was a Pointer, Mr. Phillips had to find gainful employment and was rarely ever home in the day. Maintaining a wife and twelve children, not to mention the other six he had with four different sisters of his Praise House congregation, required money. He was a mason and carpenter who had learned his trade from his father. With the assistance of his sons, he also planted a little garden in his mountain lands, for, as he put it, "every little bit helps."

He did his best to bring up his children in the fear of the Lord, using the belt and his powerful Pointer's voice to great effect on them all. That is, save and except Japheth. He sometimes wondered whether Japheth had been sent to him to increase his faith and patience. Or if he was just simply the living recompense of the sins of his youth, which had finally caught up with him in the form of this son. Those who knew Mr. Phillips before he became a Baptist thought he was beyond redemption.

"As ah say, me basin washed away in the river," continued Old Jean-Jean, again calling Lou Phillips to the present, "and ..."

"I have a little one inside that I did buy when Lilia was born. I don't use it much and will give you to replace the one that washed away", said Mrs. Phillips, stopping what she knew was the desperation plea that would follow.

"George!" she called, "George! George! Way you?"

"Coming Mammy!" was the response. George appeared in torn trousers, wet from the knee down and his patchwork shirt ventilated at various spots by its many holes.

"George, go down the river by the area where Miss Jean does wash and see if her cat is tied up anywhere there." Turning to Old Jean-Jean, she said, "George will see if he find the cat and bring it back, and I go get the basin for you."

She came back with the basin and assured Old Jean-Jean once again that she will get full satisfaction when Mr. Phillips came home. With that, Old Jean-Jean departed and Mrs. Phillips was left to contemplate what to do with Japheth.

She had to admit to herself that she should have known that Jean-Jean's cat would not go scot-free after having heard Japheth, pretending to be unaware of her presence declared: "That blasted cat too thief and when ah catch it, ah go beat me food out of it." Japheth had become annoyed, for his mother had left his lunch on the box which served as a table in the kitchen. He arrived just in time to see a cat fleeing the kitchen, all his rice and fish gone, safely stored in its stomach.

Now, it is known that Japheth does the molesting, not the other way around. To molest Japheth is to invite trouble on your own head. It doesn't matter whether you are man or beast. One of his favourite pastimes from the age of four, was to stone every dog he met at any time. Even the family dog kept out of his way as he always had a ready kick to offer.

Japheth, knowing that Old Jean-Jean would complain to his mother and that there would be a price for his actions, did not go home all day but waited until he thought everyone was asleep. He then crawled under the house, which was built on wooden stilts, the way many were in those days on the island. But his father always believed in the old sayings, one of which goes "Moon does run until day catches it." When he did catch Japheth, he really gave it to him good and proper, or as Mrs. Phillips later explained to Old Jean-Jean, "He beat him fo' all who living and fo' all who dead."

After such a severe licking, which left him with some serious bruises on his buttocks, making having a seat an uncomfortable proposition for close to a week, Japheth did resist the temptation to misbehave for a while. He made sure he stayed away from Old Jean-Jean and her cat. But as was his nature, he couldn't resist for too long a situation, which allowed him to get the better of someone. Wasp was one person with whom Japheth had a score to settle for quite some time. About two months after the Old Jean-Jean cat incident, the perfect opportunity presented itself. Japheth just couldn't resist.

Wasp's real name was Mr. Thompson. He however was accorded such respect only when Japheth was forced by circumstances to recognise that Mr. Thompson was not his "sex and size", as people of that time said. In any other situation for Japheth, Thompson was simply Wasp.

Mr. Thompson earned the nickname Wasp from his peers because he had a long narrow body which was somewhat tri-sectional like that of a wasp. He was about Mr. Phillips' age, and was a popular man in the community as a regular in the rum shop, drinking and playing cards and dominoes with his peers or "The boys", as they referred to one another.

Japheth's particular dislike for Wasp stemmed from the fact that Wasp had always been heavily critical of him. He called him the worst names, making it seem that Japheth was a devil in the making. This all started after he caught Japheth stealing mangoes at his mother-in-law, Miss Millie. Wasp told Mr. Phillips and this meant another tanning of Japheth's hide with Mr. Phillips' broad leather belt. Japheth vowed to get even with Wasp, and the opportunity came when Japheth's licking over the Old Jean-Jean affair had kept him out of trouble too long for his liking. He was itching for something to do. When Wasp came along, Japheth saw it as nothing but a Godsend.

***

It all happened the weekend before Christmas. Wasp had just gotten paid by the banana company where he worked heading bananas by the bunch to put onto the lighters, which then took them to the steamship for the journey to England. Although Wasp was paid a pittance, he was one of the better-paid men in the entire village. Then again, he was paid regularly, once every fortnight, and so always had cash to spend more regularly than the rest of the boys.

On these payday occasions, Wasp liked to go to the rum shop and have a couple of drinks with the boys. His wife continually warned him of the danger of doing this, as he might lose the money. But Wasp liked doing it his way. He liked to see the envy in the boys' eyes as he took out his money to pay after having his drinks. He particularly liked it when the shop owner, Sourman would say, "Sorry Wasp, bring the money tomorrow. I don't have enough change."

That particular Friday, it was the close of work for the Christmas season. When they finished working, the Boss had called in Wasp and the other workers, opened a bottle of cheap whisky, and they had had a little celebration. Wasp made sure that he got his full share of the whisky. Not solely because he loved drinking, but also because it was the first time he was drinking whisky, and he was sure that it was also the last time. More than anything however, he wanted to ensure that he tasted it well so he could brag and boast to the boys that he had done that which they all dreamt about. He had actually drunk whisky.

By the time Wasp was ready to go home, it was later than usual. He therefore decided to take the shortcut through his mother-in-law's, Miss Millie's backyard to get to the rum shop instead of the main road, even though there was some rain, and the shortcut would be slippery. At this very time, Japheth was in Miss Millie's mango tree having his quiet feast. These mangoes were not only beautiful, they were really sweet. He would have liked to have brought Hilly to try them. But then again "Hil talk too much."

The moment he saw the figure coming in the dark, he became absolutely still, fearing being discovered. As the figure approached, he had no difficulty recognising the tri-sectional-body of Wasp. Japheth's fear mounted, and he thought he would wet himself. Of all people in the world, he had to be discovered by Wasp. This was really twice bad luck.

Wasp came right up and stood under the mango tree. For a moment, Japheth thought he would hear the chastising tongue telling him if he was not tired stealing, and that the same story that took place two years ago was about to be replayed again. His heart was pounding so loud in his chest that he was sure that if Wasp hadn't seen him, he would soon hear it and look up. How he wished he could compel his heart to be quiet, for it was bound to give him away. He could literally see Wasp telling his mother the whole story.

"Miss Phillips, ah catch that yo' son, the bad one, thieving Miss Millie's mangoes again. Way mek he so thief?"

He could also see his father taking off the broad Pointer leather belt, or ordering George to cut a tamarind rod. He knew that after that, he would not be able to sit properly for days to come.

But Wasp did not look up at all. He just leaned against the tree for a minute or two, cleaned his feet on the grass around the tree while muttering something to himself. He straightened his pants a little and continued on his way to the rum shop, having no clue whatsoever that Japheth was in the mango tree.

When Wasp was out of sight, Japheth allowed himself to breathe properly. He couldn't help thinking that God really answers prayers. He had had his fill of mangoes and decided it was time to go home. He came down from the mango tree and on getting to the ground, his left foot brushed something that felt like a bit of cloth. On closer investigation, he realised that it was a cloth purse, the kind like that in which his mother carried what little money she had. As far as he knew, she always had it tied around her waist or hidden in her bosom. He took it up and sure enough, it made a jingling sound. Japheth raced home. There he met George, Hilly and Lilia, as the others had gone to Friday night prayers. With the help of the light of the flambeau, he opened the purse, to find that it contained five shillings and fifty pence.

At first, he couldn't believe it, for he had never seen so much money before. He double-checked, holding the coins closer to the flambeau. And yes indeed, there were five shillings. Japheth just couldn't believe his luck and it set him thinking. He soon realised what had happened and decided to head for Sourman's shop to check the "happenings", as he put it. He got there in time to hear Wasp boasting about his whisky drinking at the company, and how he got a five-shilling bonus.

"Fellas ah, ah telling all yo'", Wasp was saying. "You all need to do like me and try and get ah wuk wid the company. The Boss, he nice until. You just can't beat the man fo' niceness. Ah mean, he could ah give me one, two, three, even four shillings bonus and ah would have been happier than Santa Claus. But guess what? The man so nice, the man gee me ah whole five shillings as bonus. Ah telling all yo', the fella really nice."

The others nodded their heads in agreement and Wasp could sense that he was getting the effect he wanted. Belly and the other guys were telling him how fortunate he was, and whether he could not put in a word with the Boss for them. All this time, Japheth was waiting. He knew that the moment he was waiting for would come sooner or later. And come it did.

As Wasp finished his third drink, he announced that he was heading home to see how the wife and children were doing, adding for good measure, "Dis is the best Christmas we going have. Wid dis big bonus, the wife can do whatever she want."

He then sank his hand into his waist, feeling for his purse. But alas, it wasn't there. He checked again, this time more closely. Out came the string with which he had tied the purse onto his waist for extra security, but no purse. Then he visibly froze. Suddenly he was not drunk anymore. It was as if someone had knocked the rum and whisky out of him and with that, knocked a good measure of reality back into him. Wasp's mouth opened to say something, but no words came out as he suddenly began a mad search on his person. At that moment, everybody stopped in midair it seemed, observing Wasp and his desperate search, which became more and more frantic by the second. But search as he might, the purse was nowhere to be found.

From that moment, the rum lost all taste for Wasp. His mind started to race with a million thoughts. Did he really lose the money? And if so, when and where? Was it possible that he dropped it and one of the boys took it up secretly? God forbid! But of all the thoughts and questions, the two that worried him most were what to tell his wife, and how bad would be her response. The whole village knew that Mrs. Thompson was not a woman to play with. She had such a reputation that they had nicknamed her Jezebel. Wasp knew that this nickname was justified, for he had many times been on the receiving end of the fruits of her anger. He didn't relish the idea of being exposed to this violence another time.

Japheth was ecstatic! Finally, he would get his own back on Wasp. Suddenly he needed to let someone know of his triumph. Let them know that Wasp had made the mistake and caused him problems in the past. Now he Japheth, is going to make Wasp pay. So Japheth raced home a second time. As he got into the yard, he shouted, "Hilly! Hilly! Come! Come! Ah have something to show you. Come! Come quick!" With that, he grabbed Hilly by the hand and they raced back to the rum shop.

They got there in time to hear the boys assuring Wasp that they hadn't taken or seen his purse; that he should not be afraid to go home and tell his wife what happened for she will understand. If Wasp did not know what to think, whether one of them took his purse or not, as regards the understanding of his wife, he knew they were dead wrong. Understanding was something that was removed from his wife as hell is removed from holy water. Japheth was also aware of this latter fact and, without waiting to hear much more, took Hilly and headed for Wasp's house.

"Hil, you ever see a big man get a good licking?" he asked.

"No."

"Well, thanks to me, you going see dat here tonight. You going to be sorry fo' Wasp when dey done wid him."

"Who you mean, Mr. Thompson?" asked Hilly, having never referred to him as Wasp.

"You know anybody else name Wasp?"

"Who going fo' beat him?" asked Hilly.

"His wife."

"His wife! Fo' what?"

"Shut up and watch. You ask too much question, as ah always say, you talk too much."

Someone must have told Mrs. Thompson that Wasp had lost the money. When he arrived home, he was greeted at the gate with a broomstick across the head and a second across the shoulders. The third was administered to his waist, and then the blows just came in a torrent. Wasp made no attempt to defend himself, apart from trying to shield his face with his hands. Mrs. Thompson beat Wasp until there was no strength left in her to strike another blow. When she was finished, she sat down near to her husband who was lying face down in the yard as lifeless as a corpse, and wept like a child. That was the only thing the remaining strength in her body allowed her to do.

Japheth watched with pleasure, while repeating now and again "Tom drunk, but Tom no fool." This was a statement Wasp was known to repeat time and time again when told that he had drunk too much.

Hilly could not believe what he was seeing. He could not comprehend it all. "How could Miss Thompson beat she husband so, Japheth?" he asked.

"The man too stupid, that is why she beat he up. He just too stupid," said Japheth. As they headed home, Japheth told Hilly that Wasp got what he deserved and that will teach him a good lesson not to talk about everything he saw. He further advised Hilly that he should let Wasp's experience be a lesson to him and therefore learn to keep his "trap shut".

When they got home, Hilly had great fun in relating to George and Lilia the whole story, describing all the "ouch and auch" of Mr. Thompson as he received the blows from his wife. "Georgie, you should ah been there, it was something else, we left Wasp lying down in the yard like a dead man!" he concluded.

***

The following Sunday, Mrs. Phillips was coming from church with Hilly and Lilia when she met Wasp on the way.

"Good morning Mr. Thompson, and how are you today?"

"Good mawning Miss Phillips. Well, as you see, ah not too pram pram."

"My Lord, Mr. Thompson! What happened to your hand and face? You had an accident?"

"W….ell, yes. You know how it is in the banana business. And then again some ah them bunches so big that you have to be always careful."

"I know what you mean," said Mrs. Phillips, in a most sympathetic voice. "You need to be more careful in the future. How is Mrs. T and the children?"

"Everybody alright, praise Gawd."

It was Lilia who was later to tell her mother what really happened to Mr. Thompson, based upon the story Hilly had related to them. Hearing this, Mrs. Phillips questioned Hilly as to what he knew about the whole affair. He, seeing no problem for himself and in particular Japheth, as they had been only observers, told her the whole truth.

"When did this happen?"

"Friday night when you and Papa been ah praise."

"How did you manage to see this?"

"Japheth carry me fo' see it."

"Where did this happen?"

"At Mr. Thompson house after he loss de money in de rum shop."

As she continued her interrogation, it did not take long for her to put two and two together and realise that Japheth knew much more than Hilly about this matter. Her suspicion grew a couple of days later when she heard through the grapevine, that Wasp could only give his wife and children boiled bush yam to eat on Christmas Day, as he had gotten drunk the weekend before, losing his entire pay. All the men who were in the rum shop at the time swore that, had he dropped the money in the shop, they would have seen it and would have given it back to him. They all had wives and children and knew that Christmas was one time you didn't want your family to be hungry.

Mrs. Phillips finally concluded it was Japheth who had stolen the money when Old Jean-Jean came with the news that she saw Japheth spending money buying bodyline. The puzzle was solved. It was

Japheth who had stolen the money. She called Hilly for a second set of questioning.

"Hilly, you said Japheth called you to see Mr. Thompson wife beat him even before she started?"

"Well, we went to de shop first and then we went to de house and wait until he come home and then he wife start to beat he."

"And Japheth knew that Mrs. Thompson was going to beat Mr. Thompson before she did it?"

"He tell me that this going to happen and want me fo' see it."

Mrs. Phillips, speaking more to herself than to Hilly, said, "So it is really Japheth who stole Mr. Thompson money? That boy is the devil in hell. Let him wait until he gets here. When his father is finished with him, he would be crippled."

Mrs. Phillips was truly disturbed by this latest misbehaviour of Japheth. He had sunken to the lowest to steal money and beside that, from a poor and desperate family like her own and above all, during Christmas. This was something that deserved the sternest of beating and she was going to ensure that her husband administered this to Japheth.

"Just wait tell he get here!" she almost shouted.

But Hilly, being afraid of Japheth's revengeful anger, awaited him outside the gate. When Japheth arrived home, Hilly explained that he could expect a licking from his father because of the money he stole from Wasp. It was there and then Japheth determined that he was already 14 years old and no one was going to beat him anymore. He therefore would have to move on if he didn't want the Pointer Phillips/ Brother Jacobs fiasco that took place at the Praise House, to repeat itself at home. And so it was that he left home and started his independent road in life.

***

His father woke up every night for a month, hoping to catch Japheth sleeping under the house, but never did. After the first two weeks had passed, his mother prayed that he would come home. By the end of the month, she had virtually forgiven him all his sins and only wanted his return. Her husband, on the other hand, felt that it was good that Japheth was gone. "Let him go and face his trouble he self. He feel that he is man, so let him go and fend fo' he self."

Japheth was least concerned how they felt about him. With the help of a couple of crocus bags he had stolen from home, he made his bed every night under the school house. This was located a little way out of the village since it served two villages, and was placed halfway between them. Using Wasp's money to feed himself, he went swimming, fishing and just hanging around between his and the neighbouring village each and every day.

He saw Hilly and George almost daily, as well as other members of his family from time to time. He maintained his distance from the others. Some of the villagers encouraged Mrs. Phillips to have one of the bigger children go and drag Japheth home. But her husband had spoken. Apart from that, Mrs. Phillips was sure that it would take at least two of the bigger boys to accomplish this task. Japheth remained free and independent.

Japheth was happy with his newfound freedom and did exactly what he wanted to. He had money and could buy what he wanted. For the first time in his life, he didn't have to think about the threat of the broad leather belt, or the unbreakable tamarind rod. No, now he was the master of his own fate.

He had never had a ready-made pair of pants and so spent 20 pence of the money to purchase one. In truth, Japheth never had new clothes, for they were always the 'hand-me-down' from his senior brothers, in particular George, and were always full of patches. It was a great joy for him to have completely new pants. Not only that, they were ready-made, really rare in his village, as all the clothes were made by the children's parents. When there was a wedding or some other special occasion, they were made by the village tailor and seamstress. Japheth's new pants were a pair of 'one-stitch-cool-breeze', the latest style in the country, something his village had only heard about, but had never seen.

With the purchase of his pants appeared another problem. Where to wear it? This was however soon resolved. It was the holiday season and there were always lots of activities in all the villages. He found out that there was going to be a New Year's fete at the Lom Bay school hall on the Friday night, the last day of the year. It was therefore going to be one of those really big fetes where a large crowd was bound to attend. What better place to wear his one-stitch-cool-breeze.

Lom Bay was three villages and nine miles away. It had a reputation as a rough and violent place, even by Japheth's standards. Most people avoided it. In fact, normally, the idea of going to fete in Lom Bay, when you were not from that village, was simply out of the question. But not for Japheth. He had his new one-stitch-cool-breeze, was dying to wear it, and there was no place better than a fete to do this. Then again, he had never gone to a fete before due to this Praise House business of his father. Come what may, he was going to Lom Bay if that is where the fete was.

Japheth had no new shirt to wear with his trousers, and so got Hilly to bring him his Sunday Praise House shirt. This was his best shirt. Each of the brothers had one which they were only allowed to wear to Sunday prayers and nowhere else. This was part of what Caribbean people of that time referred to as their "Sunday best." So, dressed in his blue Sunday-shirt and his one-stitch-cool-breeze, Japheth set out at 1:00 p.m. on the nine-mile walk to Lom Bay. There were no cars in those days, and only the rich had donkey and horse carts. Like most villagers, the Phillips had a couple of donkeys, but Japheth had left home. If he wanted to use one, he would have had to steal it. He therefore had no choice but to foot it to Lom Bay.

There was however an advantage in the village being far. Japheth got to show off his ready-made one-stitch-cool-breeze to all the girls on the way. Never mind he was bare-footed, he felt great just to see the envy on the faces of the boys and young men he passed.

He made sure that he had three or four stones in his pocket for, as he put it, "You never know when you will meet an uproarious dog on de road". The truth was that from the first day that Japheth found out that he could throw a stone hard enough to hurt a dog, all dogs had to be prepared to run, once they were within his range. It is because of boys like Japheth that it is said that a dog in the Caribbean would prefer to meet a thousand men than one boy. But his journey to Lom Bay went off without incident. Of course, there were a few mango and other fruit trees that, under other circumstances, he would have raided. But he was going to his first dance and beyond that, he was wearing his brand new one-stitch-cool-breeze. He wasn't going to stain it up for anything. The fruit trees could wait.

When he got to the school hall, it was already a hive of activity and the band men were setting up their instruments. In those days of no electricity and therefore no electrical instruments, The Blue Birds were a band of exceptional popularity. It comprised two box guitars, an accordion, a contrabass, two trumpets, a bugle, two trombones, drums and a saxophone. They could be heard tuning up and Japheth could feel the excitement rising in him as he watched the arrival of many people from the surrounding villages. This confirmed to him that his villagers were right in saying that the Old-to-New-Year fete was a big thing where everybody went. With the Blue Birds being one of the best bands in that part of the island, this added to the air of genuine excitement all around. The Blue Birds were so good that when other bands were considered lucky if people paid ten pence to get into their fetes, people gladly paid fifteen pence to get into a Blue Birds' fete. Japheth of course had his fifteen pence set aside.

They weren't quite ready to start the fete, so Japheth walked around, taking in the scenes and all the activities. He noticed that there were quite a few fellows in the one-stitch-cool-breeze. Most of them also had shoes and those that didn't, had at least a pair of gunslingers on. Japheth thought that he should have bought a pair of gunslingers when he bought the pants; after all, a pair was only 15 pence and he had the money. Anyway, it was too late now. As he walked around, Japheth saw all those 'fancy girls' from the different neighbouring villages and wondered whether he would get to dance with one of them. He had never danced with a girl and thought that this might well be his opportunity.

He went and bought a bodyline to eat while he waited. He promised himself that he was going to get a shot or two of rum, once it was dark enough when the barman couldn't easily determine his age, as he didn't want people asking him too many questions. Besides, someone might recognise him, seeing that his father was the village Pointer, and would have put many a man and woman from the surrounding villages on their knees at one time or another. Mr. Phillips was therefore very well known in the Baptist community and Japheth wanted to play it safe. This was not because he cared about embarrassing his family. It was because he feared that someone might think he was still living at home and ran away just to attend the fete.

They could therefore spoil all his plans for a good time by getting an officer from the village police station to send him home.

As he ate his bodyline, Japheth considered his options carefully. He was underage, and if anyone there knew and disclosed this fact, he would not be let into the dance. He couldn't risk that. He therefore retreated to the far end of the school yard, hoping to avoid anyone that might recognise him. He chose this particular area of the yard for it was not far from a dung heap and people did not choose to hang around such places. He contemplated what was the best way to enter the fete without calling too much attention to himself; specifically he was concerned about his age. He also thought of what he would do once inside. He decided however, that the second question was not so important right now. What he really had to do was ensure he got in. He determined that it was best to try to enter when the crowd was big at the door and the doorman would not have the time to carefully observe those who were entering. But would rather be intent on collecting fees and ushering everybody through.

His plan worked like a charm. When the music started, the crowd began to gather at the entry and the doorman was busy trying to deal with everybody as quickly as possible. When Japheth reached him, he was more than glad to accept the fifteen pence from somebody who had the sense to have the exact money so he didn't have to make change. Japheth was in his first fete.

The place was superbly decorated with pretty-coloured balloons and paper hanging from the roof. The band was on the stage and the fellows were really making the place sound sweet. At the other end of the hall, away from the stage, there was a bar. Japheth knew he had to wait until there was a big rush at the bar to get his two shots of strong rum. Otherwise, he could be hassled by the barman about his age.

He decided to walk around and take a look at everything, starting with the stage. He was fascinated by the band, its shiny trumpets and trombones, the beautiful uniforms of the members, with their red bands around their waist and their blue gallon hats. He loved how the musicians seemed to put their very being into the music. He so admired it all, that he found himself wishing he were a member of The Blue Birds. He was so taken with the band that he spent the better part of thirty minutes just admiring them. By the time he turned around to move on, the hall was ram-packed and people were already dancing. Japheth decided to find a corner of his own so that he could get his bearing in the place before he made his next move.

He found a spot not too far from the stage and stood there looking on. He watched as young men approached the young girls while the band played something slow and got them to dance. He thought and thought what he had to say to get one of these girls to dance with him. He noticed that many of the young men who found favour with these young women, were wearing as he was, the one-stitch-cool-breeze. Unlike him, they were all wearing shoes. His heart sank as he wondered what to do. He looked in the direction of the bar and saw a large crowd. This was the time to try and get his double shot of rum, but as he made to move off, trouble struck.

As Japheth made to leave his corner, a young lady dancing with a rather strong looking fellow, stepped on him with her high-heeled shoes. The heel was so fine and sharp that it caused Japheth instant pain, and he howled. The young woman looked around.

"Jesus! You mash my toe with yo' kips kops," said an annoyed Japheth.

The young lady immediately responded, "Me name is not Jesus!" And looking down, she realised that Japheth had no shoes. "And why the hell you don't put on shoes? Go go put on yo' shoes!" she defiantly instructed.

Japheth, by this time, was holding his toe, trying to ease the pain. When he understood what the young lady had said, the pain instantly began to subside and his anger began to rise. He felt like boxing her in the face right there and then, but looking at the young man who was with her, he realised that he would have to make a fight of it. Then again, he had heard that young men do not go to fetes in Lom Bay alone. They always had their backups in case of fights. Who were this strong man's backups, he couldn't tell. But he remembered from stories he had heard many times while hanging around Sourman's rum shop, that to get into a fight in such a situation without having your own backup, was like committing suicide. He had to be careful.

Japheth decided it was best to go and get his double shot of rum and think about his options of dealing with her. He limped off to the bar, got his rum without much problem, drank it in one go and had another. As he finished the second, the rum started taking effect. As this effect increased, Japheth became sure that he had to get even with the fresh young girl who mashed him and thought it hard to say she was sorry. Well, something had to be done and he would show her! The question was how. He had to think this out carefully. As bad as he was, he couldn't very well beat three or four men, much more a whole village, assuming she was from Lom Bay. He went to a corner and thought of it. The more he thought, the louder he heard the girl saying "Go go put on yo' shoes!" And this hurt him. He had to do something. He had to do something.

As he stood and thought, the voice just kept shouting, "Go go put on yo' shoes! Go go put on your shoes!" And, suddenly it came to him. He knew what he had to do and that to do it, he had to get outside and get to the dung heap. But he had a dilemma. If he went out, he might be forced to pay to get back in. Worse still, he might not be let back in at all. And, if he really did what he planned to do, it would certainly mean the end of his first dance and not only that; he would most likely be running all the way from Lom Bay to his village. However, come what may, he had to teach that young girl a lesson. So he stepped out of the fete.

He went straight to the next door rum shop, bought a box of matches and proceeded to the dung heap. Searching by the light of the matches, he found the flat pressing iron without handle that he had seen thrown away on the heap earlier in the evening. He then got a piece of dry banana strip and put both in his pants pocket. When he got to the entrance, the doorman insisted that he had not seen Japheth before and forced him to pay another fifteen pence entry fee. Japheth did not protest, for the doorman could have refused him entry altogether because of his age. He couldn't risk that as he had important things to do inside.

He went back to his corner to arrange himself for action. First he located the young lady who was a little way away from the corner. Using the dry banana strip as string, he strapped the flat pressing iron onto the sole of his right foot and stood patiently waiting for his moment to strike. How he prayed that the band would play one of those waltzes which force people to move around the room. But ten, then twenty, and then twenty-five minutes passed and they didn't. He was getting impatient when he saw her heading his way in the company of another young lady. Japheth knew his moment was about to arrive. As she got closer, Japheth stepped out of his corner and made himself ready. When she was in striking distance, he made his move.

"Good night Miss."

The young lady, recognising him, replied, "Me tell you go put on shoes."

"Dat is what ah want fo' tell you, Ah been go put on me shoes. How you like it?"

As the young lady attempted to look down, Japheth slammed his right foot on her left foot with such force that the banana strip broke and the pressing iron came loose from his right sole.

"Oh Gawd! Oh Gawd! He break me foot! He break me foot!" screamed the young lady as she fell to the floor gripping her left foot.

Japheth heard or saw no more. By the time the young lady fell to the floor, he made his dash for the door. He got out as fast as he could. Once out, he set off like a bullet from a gun, running like mad. Three hundred yards into his run, he glanced back but no one was following him. He however kept his foot on the gas and for the first time that day was very glad that he wasn't wearing shoes or gunslingers. He was told that you had to practise to walk in them. He therefore didn't want to imagine what it was like running in them.

Although it was clear that he wasn't being followed, Japheth didn't stop running until he had gone about one mile. He began wondering whether to return to his village or head somewhere else. He soon realised however, that if he went to a village which he didn't know, it might be the village of the young lady, as he didn't know her and consequently didn't know where she was from. He decided that the safer thing to do was return to his own village.

For the next two weeks, he lived in fear that the men from the girl's village might somehow find out about him and ambush him. To minimise the possibility of this happening, he went to the mountain lands of his grandfather and hid out for a week and a half. When he went back to the village, he immediately found Hilly and was really relieved to learn that there had been no talk about him in the village of late. No one had come looking for him. He was still mad at the young lady however, for she had brought his attendance to his first fete to a very premature end. He didn't even have the time to ask a girl to dance. It was indeed a shame.

***

For the next two years until he was sixteen, Japheth got into no major trouble i.e., by his standards. He got into countless fistfights and broke the legs of a few dogs well with his stone throwing. But by and large, he did not cause his mother or anyone else any major headache. Then came his seventeenth birthday and he decided that he was a real big man now. After all, Papa and Mammy Phillips had lost control over him the day he left home. Added to that, he had long begun working for his own money and had built his own little wattle and daub at the edge of the village on government land. From the day he attended the fete, he had grown accustomed to taking his shot of rum now and again. And although he wasn't recognised as part of The Boys, he had of late been allowed to freely order his rum at Sourman's.

Having decided that at seventeen he was a grown man, Japheth now considered what he must do to signal this fundamental change in his life. After a little thought, he decided it was time to get a pair of shoes. He had never forgotten the scorn in the young lady's voice and eyes when she told him that he should put on shoes. He also remembered the envy he felt when he saw other young men wearing shoes. Yes, it was decided, he needed some shoes. This would be his present to himself this Christmas.

It was the middle of November and Japheth was working ploughing lands for Mr. Clarke. He resolved to save all of his money to ensure the purchase of his shoes. So from then until he got paid on December 20th, he did not spend any money. On the day he got paid, he took his money, went to his wattle and daub and dug up the tin pan where he kept the rest. And even though he knew by heart how much it was, he still counted it again, and then counted it again and then a last time before putting it back in the cloth purse he had stolen in the market the last time he was in Town. As he had said to Hilly, he stole it because the woman like she wanted somebody to steal it.

"Hilly boy, Town is ah busy, busy place, and you have to have your head on in Town or people could rob you blind. Imagine that a set of people in de market and instead of attending to one body at a time, she want to call everybody over to she so that de other women way selling can't get any customers. She too greedy. So in one engagement, she rest down de purse and turned she back to show ah fella something. Ah eased round, tek it up, and out of town like a racehorse."

"Japheth, you really did that ah Town?"

"You know me 'fraid anything or anyone?"

"No. So how much money you get?"

"Hilly, ah tell you ah lot ah time already; five is me lucky number. When I opened the purse I saw the five shillings, I couldn't believe my eyes."

"But Japheth, suppose she ha' children fo' feed?"

"Fo' she bad luck Hilly. She crave all and lost all."

Japheth smiled as he recalled the story. He felt that he was really lucky, for now that money was really useful. Without it, he would have never been able to get his pot and other little things for his wattle and daub. He was also able to have two pants and three shirts made by the village tailor, Tinman, all thanks to this money. And with the little he had saved, he could now go into Town to buy his shoes. He will wake up at five and head to Town. He should get there by nine, have enough time to buy his shoes and get back home by six in the evening.

***

Christmas Day came, and Japheth got up early, took his bath in the cold river and put on a one-stitch-cool-breeze. He then took his shoes out of the box. It was a black in colour, leather kick-and-stab, for that was the style. It wasn't that it was his intention to go anywhere, but seeing he had never worn shoes before, he felt the need to practise. With some effort, he got his shoes on and began pacing around the wattle and daub, being careful with each step. This was not simply because he was learning to walk in the shoes; he wanted to make sure that he didn't damage them by hitting them against anything. He practised two or three more times the rest of Christmas Day, taking breaks to do his cooking, eating and sweeping the yard. After all, it was Christmas. Close to dusk, he made a final practice. He simply couldn't run the risk of embarrassing himself when he finally went public.

On Boxing Day, Japheth decided that he would visit his family. He knew he would be welcomed for Hilly had said that their mother had indicated that he should come. She had convinced his father that everybody should be home and the family should be reunited for the Christmas. Japheth thought that this was as good as any day to appear home in his one-stitch-cool-breeze trousers, money jingling in his pocket, and above all, his new pair of kick-and-stab. Not even his

106

father had ever worn shoes, so Japheth knew that his would give them the shock of their lives.

After having his bath and getting dressed, he took his shoes in his hand and walked barefooted until he had crossed the river. Having crossed, he put on his shoes and, with his hands in his pockets, walked slowly and carefully in the direction of his parent's home. But he never got there. On his way he met Belly.

***

Dressed in his Sunday best, Belly was heading to Sourman's rum shop to get a bottle of rum to take to the bay. There, some other fellows were going to cook, eat, drink and have a good time. These were "The Boys" from Sourman's shop. This kind of activity Belly liked, as it gave him a good excuse to overindulge in his favourite pastime, eating and drinking to his heart's delight and his stomach's content. Indeed, his love for eating is what caused the villagers to rechristen him Belly.

When Belly saw Japheth, he was genuinely impressed, in particular with the shoes. He stopped dead in his tracks; his mouth dropped open, he stared, and after recovering himself a little said, "Japheth! Ah you that? Me almost no recognise you boy. You dress fo' kill. Way you get shoes from?"

"Way you mean? Me buy them ah town."

"You find money; an' plenty too?"

"You could say that again," said an extremely pleased Japheth.

"Way you going now? Come go wid me man. Ah going down de bay to meet them boys. We going cook and drink something together fo' celebrate de season."

"Me going see me old people. As you know, me live pon me own now, an' de old man say he wan' fo' see me. So ah need fo' go and see what he want," replied Japheth.

"Well you could go wid me, have ah couple, and then go to see them. After all, dis is Christmas, and you is a drinking man?"

"Yes man, me ah drink since me left home, 'cause now me open an' close me own door."

"But Pointer was ah drinking man and people say sheep can't bring goat. So you going or you can't go fo' see them smelling ah rum?" insisted Belly.

"Boy, you know that me is me own man. Me open me own door and spend me own money. Phillips can't tell me one thing." Japheth always referred to his father as 'Phillips' when he wanted to underline his independence from him. In his view, this showed that he was just as much a man as his father.

"So you coming wid me or what?"

"Of course man. Look, tek dis and buy another battle ah rum," said Japheth, taking some coins from his pocket, "Ah go wait here fo' you."

"What happen, you quarrel with Sourman? This is Christmas man. People don't quarrel on Christmas. Lewe go in and wish de man de best fo' the season."

Japheth agreed with Belly that regardless of their differences, he should forget that and go and wish Sourman season's greetings. He was not surprised that Sourman was quite open to him, and even gave him two free drinks of strong rum. This was a reflection of the Caribbean people and culture of that time. They never kept malice against anyone for long.

Having bought the rum, they proceeded to the beach. Belly knew Japheth would not be very welcome as he was much younger than all of the others and was not part of The Boys. On approaching the others while still some distance away, he announced, "Look who ah meet on the way with a battle ah good strong run to offer anyone a drink. So guess what? Ah tell him to come with me because nobody drinks alone on Christmas, Boxing Day worse. So ah bring him along and we bring three battle."

By the time they got close enough, no one was really listening to Belly. Everybody was watching one thing and one thing only.

"Yes, the boy find gold and no ask me way," said Belly, realizing the serious preoccupation of the others.

"Season's greetings everybody," said Japheth.

"Season's greetings one body," came the chorus response.

"Fellas, young Phillips find gold this Christmas," said Belly.

"Belly only joking," replied Japheth.

"Must be jokes," joined in Mr. Todd, "but way you get money from fo' buy shoes?"

"But Todd, you always want to know people business. Ah tired telling you somebody going burst yo' face fo' you," interjected Sammy, who was smoking his cigarette, quietly looking on.

"Man, all yo' stop the foolish talk and open one ah the rum; all morning ah want a drink," said Mother Bakes. His real name was Fredrick Small. Mother Bakes was a nickname given to him because of his all-around plumpness, the likeness of a fried dumpling of unusual large size.

With that the drinking got underway. Along with Mr. Todd, Sammy who was a shoemaker and Mother Bakes, the group included Mr. Williams, also called Willie the Rounce, Mr. James whom everybody called Jamesie; Mr. Lewis Jackson nicknamed Butch, Maurice whom everybody knew as Pig Snout, thanks to his rather long and fleshy lips, and John Palmer whom everybody called Sprat as he was very small in stature. The food was already boiling in the big biscuit tin on the fireplace, made of three stones and fuelled by dry wood. Things began to swing after three or four good shots of strong rum. This was evident, as The Boys began to sing carols and folksongs. Butch was on his box guitar, Mr. Todd had his quatro, Mother Bakes on his boom drum, Willie the Rounce had his bugle and Jamesie had his mouth organ. There was more than enough music for a party. As the rum soaked in, the music got better, with the singing frequently punctuated by shouts of "Fire one man! Fire one!"

Now there are some drinkers who, when they have had a few drinks, tend to lose control of many parts of their bodies, in many instances their tongue first. Mr. Todd was such a person. He was the kind of man who, after having a few, would start making fun of his peers, cursing and carrying on about all sorts of things. After consuming five or six shots, he was fully charged and decided to target Japheth. Big mistake!

"So way you really get money from fo' buy shoes?" Todd demanded of Japheth.

"Todd, shut yo' big mouth and play the quatro." It was Sammy the shoemaker who answered, even before Japheth realised that Mr. Todd was talking to him. "Leave the boy alone! He don't trouble you." Sammy, while never having had a run-in with Japheth, knew, as the entire village did, that even though he was still only a teenager, molesting him could lead to unpleasant consequences. Indeed, they all silently thought to themselves that while they were glad for the extra bottle of rum Japheth brought along, Belly was quite mad to have encouraged him to come along. This meant trouble, especially with a doltish chatterbox like Todd around.

"So you going tell we where you get the shoes?" Mr. Todd insisted, ignoring Sammy.

Japheth looked at him but did not respond.

"You little boys these days too thief and lie and nobody can't…" He wasn't allowed to finish, for the response came at him like a bullet.

"Who you calling thief and boy?" responded Japheth hotly.

"So you not ah boy?" demanded Mr. Todd in drunken defiance.

"Todd, shut yo' long-mouth self and play the music," intervened Sammy. "You no weary talk? You must learn to give yo' mouth ah rest. You swallow ah parrot or something?" With that, Mr. Todd held his peace and the music and drinking continued.

Then the food, which was a cook-up of rice and peas, pork, chicken, beef, manicou, iguana and a host of other things, was ready. Everybody had their fill and after the eating, they returned to the serious rum drinking. All seemed well and Mr. Todd even handed his quatro to Japheth to have a go.

The merry-making continued until all the rum was finished. It became apparent that somebody had to go back to Sourman's to get a couple of bottles. After the group spent some time looking around at each other, hoping that somebody would volunteer and realising that this was not going to be the case, Todd took it upon himself to decide who should undertake the task. His nominee was Japheth.

"You is the only boy among we big man so you have to go," he commanded Japheth.

"Well come and mek me go!" challenged Japheth, clearly already angry and virtually daring Todd to take him on.

Again Sammy stepped in. "Todd, Jesus Christ! Fo' Gawd sake, why you don't behave yourself? I go go fo' the rum, gee me the money." Everybody except Mr. Todd trooped monetarily, and Sammy set off while the others continued to play and sing.

As they waited on Sammy's return, the singing moved from Christmas carols to folksongs and then to the old-time three-beat calypsos. Aided by the strong rum, they imagined themselves something close to a heavenly host. Suddenly Mr. Todd got up and wanted an excuse; he said he had a call from nature. As he was passing Japheth, whether by accident or design, he stepped on Japheth's kick-and-stab. This was the crack that led to all hell breaking loose.

"What happen, you blind? You don't see me foot there."

"Way you don't move yo' foot when you see people passing?" came the response.

"You consider yo'self people?" replied Japheth defiantly.

"What you mean by if me ah people?" asked Todd rhetorically. And turning away from Japheth, he continued to the others in the most contemptuous of tones. "Dis is the problem wid them little boys that believe if them have on a pair of shoes, then them is big man."

"Me tell you already no fo' call me boy. You say that you is big man and you can't even buy ah battle ah rum. What kind ah man you be? Ah shame you no have no shame."

"Gee me me quatro," said Todd, yanking the instrument from Japheth's hands.

"Yo' quatro is dead left. You never buy ah thing in yo' life. If not fo' Phillips yo' pickney and them stay hungry fo' days."

Now that was the worst thing that Japheth could have said to Todd. There was a rumour that due to Todd's negligence of his wife and children, Japheth's father, from the goodness of his heart, had virtually given life to Mrs. Todd and the children. In particular little Joshua Todd, who was a virtual carbon copy of Japheth, or as the villagers put it, he was "the spitting image of Japheth". No, this was not something that Todd could accept, and from a little upstart at that.

Without warning, Todd took his quatro and banged it over Japheth's head. The instrument, being made of very thin plywood at the base, went straight over Japheth's head. The arm hung down from his neck looking somewhat like a clumsily tied huge wooden tie, while the keys at the end of the quatro's arm looked like a pendant attached to an oversized unusual chain. Japheth was stunned for a few seconds, but only for a few.

"You must be crazy? Ah see from the time ah come here you want trouble. Well dis is trouble! Dis is trouble." As he spoke, he was ripping the remains of the quatro from around his neck. By this time, Mr. Todd was running down the beach doing the best he could to get away. The others started shouting, trying in vain to convince Japheth that he should forget it and let Todd go, as he was only going to get himself into trouble if he retaliated. But Japheth was not listening. It was as if he had gone mad and deaf at the same time.

He took two empty rum bottles and banged them against each other, breaking both. The others began to plead with him to give Todd a chance. They were all speaking at the same time, but none daring to touch him, none trying to physically restrain him. Japheth started running after Mr. Todd and fell down. He got up and started again, and fell down again. He dropped the broken bottles, hurriedly kicked of his shoes, retrieved the broken bottles and started out again in pursuit of Todd with whom he caught up in less than two minutes.

Mr. Todd was running and falling, getting up, running and falling. This was obviously the result of having had too much drink. Japheth caught up with him when he had fallen for the sixth time. Mr. Todd, realising that there was now no escape, began to plead.

"O Gawd….Japheth… na kill… me." Mr. Todd was by this time breathing like a horse that just did 5 good miles "Japheth do….Gawd go bless you …..do…do I beg you do…..na kill me."

"Kill you," Japheth said, his heavy breathing caused more out of rage than tiredness. "Me na stupid. But me see like you have a problem with you breathing, so me ah go help you." And with that he held Mr. Todd's nose and using one of the broken bottles cut away the front soft lower part of his nose from his face. He cut it from left to right so that one could raise Mr. Todd's nose from his face like when raising the bonnet of a car. Mr. Todd screamed as the blood poured down his upper lip and into his mouth. Japheth started back the way he had come, leaving Todd in the sand bleeding profusely from the nose. He passed the others running towards Todd, but he paid no attention to the worried, horrified looks they all had on their faces. He ran back to the spot where he had kicked off his pair of kick-and-stab, collected them and headed straight for his little wattle and daub.

By the time the rest of the gang got to Mr. Todd, he was bleeding so much they thought that Japheth must have finished him off. They were more than relieved when they saw that this was not the case. As they grabbed Todd and were hurrying to get him to the village nurse, Sammy came running from the other end bringing with him the bottles of rum he had bought. When he got to them, he exclaimed, "Same very thing ah always say; somebody, whether sooner or later go burst Todd face 'cause he love people business too much, and he no listen when you talk to him."

"Me always tell Todd that he talk too much," said Belly.

"You Belly should shut up!" responded Pig Snout, "Ah you who bring that vagabond boy fo' Phillips here in the first place. Everybody know that Japheth is ah vagabond, but you had to go and bring him here."

"Why you don't shut your one-eye self, anybody talking to you?" shot back Belly.

"Me might have one eye but ah could see better than you because ah not that stupid to bring a troublemaker like Japheth here."

"You better shut yo' mouth your one-eye self before you end up like Todd and lose yo' nose," said Mother Bakes. With that no more was heard from Pig Snout.

"Man, we need fo' find that Japheth right now and give him a good cut backside. We can't allow him to treat ah big man so," suggested Jamesie.

"Fellas, forget Japheth, we need fo' help Todd right now or he go dead," said Sammy.

"Sammy is right," said Mother Bakes, "Lewe get some sea water, dash it on him and then go by Sourman and find something for dress he nose."

"No," said Sammy, "we must carry him by the village midwife so that she could dress him up."

While they were deciding what to do with Mr. Todd; Japheth, shoes in hand, was making rapid progress to his wattle and daub. The Boys got Todd to the midwife who seemed to have had some premonition that she would have such a problem on this holiday. When they knocked at her house, she came out, invited them in, where they found that she had everything laid out, including thread and needle to stitch up Mr. Todd's nose.

***

With the start of the New Year, seventeen-year-old Japheth became the bad-John supreme of his village. There were various stories how Japheth had single-handedly beaten the hell out of Belly, Mother Bakes, Willy the Rounce, Sammy and the others, ending by cutting up Mr. Todd's nose. Nobody doubted that Japheth was the new bad-John of bad-Johns. News started going around to the other villages that it is not so easy to try and tackle the people of his village, as they had a bad-John who was not afraid of the devil himself.

Word of Japheth's bravery and strength spread far and wide. It was said that he could conquer anything and anyone. He could drink more rum than anyone and never got drunk. He could go a whole week without sleep and never feel tired, and he could do the most unusual things without any negative effect on him.

With all the acclaim surrounding his name, Japheth felt the need to live up to expectations and so changed his behaviour to suit. He would beat up anyone who dared challenge him, curse old women, something which no one in the village had ever done before, disrespect his father, the village Pointer, which was another of those unthinkable and impermissible things, and would molest others when he felt like it. So people feared Japheth, but most admired him for his exceptional bravery.

What the village admired most and what to them was the ultimate proof of Japheth's true bravery, was his prowling at night. Now, this was a time in the Caribbean when everyone was afraid of darkness and what might be waiting for them in the uninhabited and unlighted areas of the islands. This was still in the time when the majority of Caribbean people were largely uneducated, and superstition about darkness ruled supreme among the ordinary folk. No one went walking in the night unless this was an absolute necessity, and when they did, it was never alone.

It was not that Japheth was immune to these superstitions. It was more a case that his village thought him a super brave person who was not afraid of anything, but had the strength to conquer everything, including the evil spirits of the dark. Japheth, so as not to give birth to any doubts about him being the king of the braves, felt the need to maintain this image. He set about doing just that.

He made it common practice to be the last to leave Sourman's shop, in the night and always alone. As the bad-John of the village, he could enter Sourman's shop whenever he wanted. He would go to the rum shops in the neighbouring villages and then walk home very late in the night. Rumour also had it that he would very often sleep in the open, not worried about what danger might befall him. But what the villagers found most impressive was that he went fishing at nights and returned by using the shortcut through the village cemetery. This was something not even his father, the village's most righteous man, would have thought of doing.

In those days, there was no electricity. Ninety-nine percent of all people could not read nor write, and their greatest fear was that of darkness. Theirs was a society which taught that darkness was synonymous with evil. So these deeds of Japheth were nothing short of exceptional. It put Japheth in a special class all by himself; in a place where not even his father could reach him. Respect was due him, for he was the bravest of the brave. He continued to enhance this reputation by going to fetes in other villages and coming home at four in the morning. He would think nothing of teasing and laughing at obeah man Moses. In the eyes of other villagers, this was tantamount to playing with death, for Moses was a man who could talk to the evil spirits, and who would actually chase black cats in the night. But Japheth was not worried by any of these special powers of Moses.

Japheth developed a love for going to fish at night as he found that the fish bit better and more at that time. Night fishing therefore became a hobby for him. Apart from catching fish, he could quietly drink his rum, smoke his tobacco and dream about going to places like England and America. He had heard that in these places, they had winter where something cold called snow fell from the sky. He had also heard that in winter, smoke came out of one's mouth when he spoke, even though he was not smoking. He also dreamt of going to Cuba, for he had heard that they need cane cutters there. And he wouldn't mind seeing what a steamship looked like, for this is what one had to take to get to these places. So night fishing became somewhat of a passion for Japheth and he went three or four times a week. At first he was apprehensive of the dark, but after a week or two, he soon dismissed this, and would even sometimes laugh at the foolishness of the villagers. This was until the night he met Lucifer.

Japheth usually went fishing about 9:00 p.m. when most of the villagers were about going to sleep. He would fish until around 12:00 midnight, sitting on the rocks waiting for the fish to bite, while he smoked his tobacco and took shots of his strong rum. At midnight, he would gather up the fish he caught and go home. His was a bamboo fishing rod and quite a thick one too, for he didn't want it to break while pulling in something he caught.

On this particular night, the fish bit rather slowly, and it was about 12:30 before Japheth caught anything. However, once the first one bit, things got better. In fact things got so good that Japheth had about 5 or 6 pounds of fish before too long and determined that it was time to head for his wattle and daub. He gathered up his fish, put them on the line as he always did, and started the mile and a half journey home. As always, he took the shortest route, which was through the cemetery, usually dead silent at this time of the night. He hadn't gone far after entering the cemetery, when he heard the first sound. It came from a small bush in the cemetery, and Japheth simply ignored it and continued walking. He had only gone about three metres more when he heard it again. This time, it was much louder and somewhat aggressive. He turned around, for the sound came from behind him, and there it was; about 500 feet behind him, the biggest pig he ever saw.

The pig was white in colour and seemed to be eating something it had dug up from the grave it was standing on. But it didn't eat the way a pig usually does. It ate rather like a tiger attacking its prey. Suddenly, all the stories Japheth had heard from his parents and grandparents about appearances of the devil on earth invaded his mind. He distinctly remembered them saying that Lucifer usually comes in the form of a pig. Japheth froze. Immediately, his heart changed pace and began drumming like an engine, and he heard himself say in a cold whisper, "Oh Gawd, Jumbie."

Now it all came rushing back to him. The warnings of his mother and father how he was evil, and one day before too long his evil is going to catch up with him. He could hear his father reminding him that God does not sleep, and that he would pay for all the sins he had committed, and all the wrongs he had done to others. He heard Old Jean-Jean saying that disobedient children will be beaten with many stripes. Worst of all, he remembered obeah man Moses promising to put a curse on him. All of these and a thousand other incidents of people praying for the Almighty to strike him down, passed through his mind in less than 30 seconds. He knew that his time to pay up had come, and decided that the devil will have to catch him running.

He took off at top pace running as if crazy or being chased by a thousand tigers. He ran until he got out of the cemetery and was in a banana field. When he stopped, he realised that he was sweating from head to foot as if he had just had a bath. His heart was vigorously protesting the size of his chest cavity, and his knees were wobbling terribly. He looked around and was relieved to find that the pig was nowhere in sight and everything was still. He thought to himself, "It was only ah pig; true it was quite big fo' ah pig. But still it was just ah pig and nothing more." His relief was to be short-lived.

As he left the banana field and was near to the next corner, he could hear the sound again and as he approached the corner, it got not only louder but heavier. As he rounded the corner and looked ahead, there it was, an unbelievably huge hog, about three hundred feet ahead, standing on its hind legs, ripping the green bananas from a tree in a small field directly in Japheth's path. This time, Japheth felt his heart definitely stop, his throat was instantly dry and he could feel the sweat pouring down his body. His mind began to wander as he couldn't understand how it got in front of him. Did it use a short cut? But he knew all the shortcuts and indeed was using the shortest of them all. Then he remembered, while living souls walked or ran, spirits flew or just appeared and disappeared. He realised then that he was in serious trouble. Now he had no doubts whatsoever; this was the devil, and he was looking for a confrontation with Japheth. This Japheth knew he couldn't win and therefore needed to avoid. The question was what to do?

Japheth stood motionless, praying for the deceleration of his heart. He stood for a full minute, forcing his brain to function, demanding that his thoughts be straight. The hog stopped ripping at the bananas for a moment, looked straight at Japheth for about a half minute as if sizing him up, then returned to the bananas with even more aggression. Japheth at first decided to turn and run, but he realised that would be stupid. He would be running back to the cemetery which is where he first saw the hog, and God knows how many more of them would be waiting for him there. Outside of that, he would be going in the opposite direction of his wattle and daub. Home is where he wanted to go. Then again, two hundred yards from the end of the small banana field stood his parents' house and his best bet, indeed his only realistic chance to save his life, was to try and reach their house and hope that his father would open the door for him. No, turning and running would not do. The only way was forward.

He began to inch forward, but with each step, the hog would give a grunt, and as he got closer, the grunts became louder. But Japheth kept walking. When he had gone about two hundred feet, the hog left the bananas and came and stood in the middle of the path that Japheth had to use. Japheth stopped and the hog, standing on its hind legs, stared at him, then went back to attacking the banana tree. Japheth took a few steps forward, and again the hog stepped into the path and just stood and stared, only this time it grunted as if to threaten or warn

Japheth. This was the devil in person, thought Japheth. He knew that he was going to die, for there was no way to turn, no road to escape. And suddenly he began to cry and pray at the same time.

In his prayer, he asked God to spare his life so that he could have the chance to change and live righteously like his mother had always wanted. He promised that he would stop doing all the bad things he usually did, including giving up smoking and drinking. Japheth prayed with his eyes open, for fear of closing them and having the hog do him something evil. But at the end of all his praying, the hog was still there and daring him to pass. He realised this was the moment of decision.

Japheth started considering his options while the hog seemed content to just wait and let him make his move. He racked his brain trying to remember how his father had said one should deal with these situations. Now he wished more than ever that he had gone to prayers more, and that those times he was forced to go that he had actually listened when his father was giving the lessons. Alas it was too late; he however determined that he would apply what he remembered.

He eased the fishing rod off of his shoulder and started unhooking his fish from the line, all the time never taking his eyes off the hog. He put the fish on the ground, wrapped the line around the rod, took a deep breath and started walking directly up to the hog. As he started walking, he saw the hog leave the banana tree and step in the middle of the path. Japheth's knees began to wobble and he could feel the sweat running down his face in such streams that he almost thought it was raining.

He remembered that his father had said that, when you are beating an evil spirit in such a case, with each lash, you shout zero, for if you start counting, then as you call the number, the spirit multiplies by that number. So on reaching the hog, he began to beat it with all the strength he had, while shouting "Zero! Zero! Zero!" after each lash. But as Japheth beat the hog, the bamboo fishing rod began to shatter; he struck the hog until the rod finally broke and then he took off. Thus began the race between him and the hog to get to his parents' house first.

As Japheth raced home, crashing into banana trees and anything else in his path, he began shouting at the top of his lungs; "Pointer Phillips! Pointer Phillips! Save me! Save me! Oh Gawd, Pointer Phillips! Save me!" He prayed and prayed that they would open the door for him.

It was Mrs. Phillips who, always a light sleeper, first heard the screaming and woke her husband. He got up in a hurry, lit a candle and was lighting a second when there was a thunderous pounding on the door with more shouting "Pointer! Pointer! Save me Pointer! Pointer Phillips; please, for Gawd sake, save me!"

Mr. Phillips opened the door and Japheth collapsed into his arms. He quickly closed the door and in a moment there was a sudden strong breeze which severely shook the house as it passed. For the rest of the night, they spent their time attending to Japheth in an effort to revive him, and on their knees praying for protection and deliverance from whatever was chasing him. They woke up the other children, and the entire family formed a circle around Japheth, praying while he lay in the middle of the floor totally unconscious and unaware of it all.

The next morning, the Phillips woke up to find a significant number of the banana plants trampled. Mr. Phillips inspected the walls of the house and found that all was basically intact. He went back into the house to meet Japheth explaining to his mother and siblings how he met the pig that changed into the huge hog. When Japheth started detailing how the hog would sometimes appear in front of him and other times behind him, Mr. Phillips realised that this was no ordinary pig. In fact, this was no pig at all. He turned to Japheth and in his most religious of voices declared "Boy, you don't realise that it is the devil you saw?" Turning to his wife, he said "Lou, the boy came face to face with Lucifer himself, only that he was in the form of ah pig."

Japheth's father, with the help of his wife, encouraged his son to repent of his sins and follow the ways of the Lord. He cautioned him that, "You get away this time by the skin of yo' teeth; next time you would not be so lucky."

"Yes, Japheth," Mrs. Phillips continued. "You were spared because your family is a God-fearing one and your father is an honest servant of the Lord."

Japheth listened and made the expected promises. He joined the rest of his family in prayer, all in a circle and on their knees. At the end of it all, Mrs. Phillips said she felt lighter and she believed in miracles, and that Lucifer had appeared unto Japheth to make him turn from wicked things to righteousness.

***

Two weeks later, Old Jean-Jean came calling, all excited and looking as if she had the most urgent of news. "But Miss Phillips, ah think them say yo' son changed his life since he meet the devil in the cemetery. But it no seem so at all," she said shaking her head negatively.

"What has he done now?" demanded Mrs. Phillips.

"He was down by Sourman beating poor Moses with a stick. Is a lucky thing that yo' husband was passing and stopped him before he killed the poor man."

"What are you saying, Miss Jean?" Mrs. Phillips enquired in a most unbelievable tone.

"Yes, yes, and when yo' husband asked him why he was beating Moses, he say he was told that is Moses who set the evil spirit on him that night. That boy is no good, no good," old Jean-Jean repeated, all the while shaking her head negatively from side to side.

Mrs. Phillips got up and went to the window. As she looked out and saw the banana field from which her son was rescued from Lucifer, turning to Old Jean-Jean with tears in her eyes, she said, "And to think he had a personal encounter with Lucifer. Lord, what to do with Japheth?"

Sattou's Pain

And

Mr. Penniston's Burden

"Goal! Goal!" shouted Jumbo, as the ball rebounded from the goalkeeper's chest. "Goal! Goal!" he continued as we all raced up to the goal mouth to press the point that he had indeed scored as the goalkeeper looked to be standing behind the line, when the ball rocket

ed into his chest from Jumbo's right foot. Tempers began to flare and arguments broke out as our opponents refused to concede what we thought was rightfully ours. I rushed forward, fully committed to helping my team defend its right. As I got to the goal, I remembered the breadfruit tree and, even in my excitement, I looked back for it. Sure enough there he was, his quart of white rum in hand, the old straw hat shielding his face from the sun, his eyes trained on me. When will he ever leave me alone, I thought. When will this spy ever leave me alone? I felt like going straight up to him and demanding whether he wasn't tired spying on me, and if he had nothing better to do than be my grandfather's news carrier. Instead, I backed away from the melee, leaving the others to settle whether the ball had scored or not. As I glanced back at the breadfruit tree a second time, I saw him remove his straw hat, smile, and take a sip of his white rum. I prayed that someone would cut down the breadfruit tree and, by God, I meant it. Mr. Penniston's spying was simply overbearing.

***

"So, who told you boys about my fights?" Sattou asked, smiling slyly, "Of course it is Gracie. What else did she tell you bad about me?" he continued, still smiling. "But no, I don't get into fights any more, 'cause life has taught me some lessons. Getting into fights is a bad, real bad thing. You can even lose your life. So I don't want any of you boys fighting, you hear me?" he asked in a raised tone of voice. We all nodded our understanding. But he, not being sure that he had gotten through to us, wanted to emphasize his point. "Now listen," he said, "I told you that, for I know violence is a dangerous thing, real dangerous thing. A matter of fact, it so dangerous that there was a time I really saw death in the face. Yes partners, I swear to God I almost dead." He suddenly looked around as if wanting to make sure that we were alone. Having ascertained that this was the case, he continued.

"Partners, the third time I stowaway, I ended up in Santo Domingo and only God save my life. You see this hand?" he said, holding up his left palm, "Well, I can't bend it in the middle the way you all can. Look, look," he commanded as he got up and moved around, showing it to each of us in turn. He revealed a terrible scar in his palm, directly on that line where the hand folds to make a fist. "Now you make a fist. Go ahead, make a fist." We did as instructed and he, as if celebrating the winning of a point said, "See, you could do it but I can't. And you know why?" he said, pausing for effect. "Yes man, violence, that's why. That man could ah chop off my neck and I had to put my hand to take the chop from the cutlass and save me life. Or your uncle Sattou would ah been a dead man today. Believe me, ah dead man."

He said all of this with a very serious and convincing expression on his face, which all but frightened my brothers and me. To think that Sattou The Great almost lost his life was virtually inconceivable to us all. "So how did that happen?" I asked. "Who did this to you and when did this happen?"

"Well, when I was twenty, I stowaway on a big boat that came here to collect produce; you know, bananas and things to take to England. It carried passengers as well, and a fellow arranged the thing for me, after I give him a five dollars from the money I saved doing all kind ah work, including digging potato rows and yam banks for Pa. The man used to steer the lighters taking bananas out to the big ships, and he managed to arrange it as if I was one of the men unloading the bananas from the lighter. I got onto the big ship and hide away between the cargos until we left port. I was thinking about going to England and if I didn't get through with that, to go to Aruba to work in the oil refinery. In them days, they paid good money over there, and plenty people from this island went there to work.

"When the boat pullout and was way out in the ocean, I eased out of my hiding place and mingled with the crowd and the sailors. That is when I bounce up this white man and me and he became friends. His name was Patrick Belvedere but he tell me just call him Pat. He was a Yankee, and you know them Yankee, they always have plenty money. So every evening, we would go to the bar on the boat and drink and thing. Well, the boat sailed for two weeks, stopping in various places to let off and take on people and produce. Then we reached Santo Domingo. The Yankee told me that we have to go ashore as the girls there are the prettiest in the whole world. Now, I had no sailor papers or anything like that, for I was a stowaway, and my intention was

131

England, not no Santo Domingo. But he said that we would be there in Santo Domingo for some time, and I agree to go see these girls. So we left the boat and head ashore. That was a mistake and I ended up getting this hand and I still ain't reach England yet.

"Anyway, to continue the story, he decided to take me to a place called the Coconut Club, a place he usually go to when he is in Santo Domingo. He said the girls there were the most beautiful and charming. So we left the wharf and we went walking through some small alleys, turning left and right, left and right. During all this walking, I saw so many beautiful girls, that I thought that it was enough for us just to be on the streets. There was no need for us to go to any club." Sattou stopped suddenly, for just then my mother walked in.

She gave Sattou such a look of sanction and warning that he was forced to ask, "What is it, Gracie?"

"I hope you haven't forgotten who you telling your stories to?" she enquired.

"Gracie, what you worry about? You know I will never say anything out-ah-de-way to the boys," he assured.

"Sattou," my mother responded, "the correct word is 'improper' and not out-ah-de way."

"Ok, ok, but, I mean you worry too much. Even if I was to say something out...ah...., I mean improper, your children are so well brought up they wouldn't even understand."

"So you say. But you very well know that little donkeys have big ears."

"But, but Gracie, you don't believe that I could tell the children anything wrong?"

"Satt, I am simply telling you that you should behave yourself and watch your tongue. Believe me, these children are small but they are not stupid. They are way ahead of where we were when we were their ages, so no bad behaviour, ok?"

"Gracie, no need to worry really; girl you worry too much for nothing. You will grey before your time."

"Well alright," my mother said, her face breaking into a smile. "you know how to always get your way," and before Sattou could respond, she turned on her heels and exited the sitting room, shaking her head and muttering, "What can anybody do with you? You always must have your own way."

I was glad my mother had left, for I couldn't wait to hear what led to Sattou almost losing his left hand. For years, we had waited impatiently for him to come home from overseas so that we could finally meet this, my mother's childhood champion of adventure, whom she adored and sometimes referred to as "Out-ah-place Satt".

He had arrived earlier on this, the first Saturday of our summer holidays. My mother was as excited as a little girl expecting a long-promised Christmas doll. They hugged, did a little jig and hugged some more before she finally introduced us to him, presenting us as, "My four trials and crosses." She said because of him, she always wanted a boy, and the Lord more than obliged her, and she now understood what old people meant when they say, "Careful what you wish for. You might well get it."

"Don't tell me," said Sattou, "let me guess. Pointing to me, he continued, "I am sure you are Charlie, right, you are just as I imagined."

"Yes, I am Charles," I said.

"Yes, you are my high school boy. So how school?"

"Good," I said, still not believing that I was finally talking to the Tom Sawyer of my mother's family.

"And you here are Chris and Colin," he said, pointing to my twin brothers who both smiled as he tapped them on the nose, looking them straight in the eyes. He then turned back to my mother and playfully asked, "Now, where is he, where is he?" pretending to be searching for my smallest brother who was standing behind my Mom, his face buried in her skirt.

"Come on Ali," said my mother in a voice, the tone of which was somewhere between encouraging and mildly commanding, "say hello to your uncle Sattou."

Ali looked out from behind his hiding place and in his usual shy manner said in his infant voice, "Hello uncle Sattou." This made my Mom and Sattou laugh as she assured him, "Al is like that with everyone at first, but in an hour or two, Satt, you will not know how to shut him up."

Sattou had gifts for everyone, which he duly passed out. He then went into the kitchen with my mother where she was preparing lunch. My twin brothers and I remained in the living room inspecting our gifts. We called him uncle Sattou when he was in fact our first cousin. But he had grown up with my mother as a little brother. His mother, aunt Shirley was fourteen years my mother's senior, while he was a mere three years her junior. So they grew up like sister and brother rather than aunt and nephew. This growing up together was the source of all the stories my mother told us about "Sattou The Great." By the time I was ten, I had heard so much about the exploits of Sattou that I thought him the bravest, strongest and smartest person in my maternal family.

My mother painted him the eternal adventure seeker and stuntman extraordinaire in childhood. She assured us that he could do four continuous no-hand flips without any problem. She further assured that one of the neighbour's boys tried it and almost broke his neck. And there was the time when he climbed the soursop tree at the back of the house to pick a soursop. On approaching the fruit he wanted, five wasps flew from a neighbouring nest and landed on his face. Instead of panicking, he simply picked them off, crushed them in his hand and went on to pick his soursop. My mother said he was the only boy in the village who caught a live congo snake; and when diving, he could stay under the water longer than any other boy she knew. But he became Sattou The Great long before he did any of those and many other stunts. He became Sattou The Great at the tender age of seven.

Being the youngest in a large household, he was spoiled rotten by my maternal grandparents, as he was their only grandchild for many years. He did not know who his father was. There were whispers that he had gone to England during the wave of West Indian migration to the motherland just after the war. Wherever he was, he never showed up, leaving Sattou and his mother to the mercy of fate and the goodwill of my grandparents. Sattou therefore grew up like my grandparents' last child and first grandchild at one and the same time. But having heard the whispers that his father had run away to England, he decided that he would go there and bring him back.

One morning when he was age seven, after my grandmother had dropped him off to school, Sattou left the school and ended up down the bay. In those days, the roads from the town to other parts of the island were either very bad or non-existent. A lot of travel was therefore done by using small boats, which plied along the coast, carrying goods and passengers. Seven-year-old Sattou somehow got himself onto one of those boats and reached the main port in the city. He then somehow got on to one of the lighters and reached the big ship in which he intended to go to England. He didn't get to England because his luck ran out when he got to the ship and none of the adult passengers would claim him as their child. He was swiftly despatched to the police station where my grandfather collected him a day later. From that day, he became Sattou The Great. Indeed, my mother still marvels at his bravery in undertaking that mission, and more so that he almost succeeded with it.

And here we were after lunch listening to Sattou The Great in person. I simply couldn't believe it. He began the Saturday afternoon by trying to get to know us better. So while my mother did her various chores, he sat with us asking little questions. We, of course, were more interested in hearing from him and began to ask him about many of the stories our mother had told us, to which he responded with great pleasure. As he spoke, I observed that he was very much like my mother had said. He did everything with a laugh, seemed carefree in all his actions; and gave the impression that he was really in love with life. He made me feel that he was as free as the wind and as rich as the earth. His joy seemed boundless and seemed to be coming from an overflowing eternal internal reservoir. I remember thinking that it was no surprise that my mother loved him so much. Who wouldn't?

With my mother gone, Sattou turned back to us smiling and said, "So, as I was saying, this white man Pat and I went walking through these alleys. After a while, we came out into a broader street and Pat said, 'There she is', pointing to a beautifully painted wooden place. As we approached it, I saw marked above the high door, "The Coconut Entertainment Club." At the door, we met two brown skin fellows, and Pat gave each a US dollar. As we began to enter, one of them step in front of me, blocking my entry while saying something in Spanish. Pat, using his left hand, simply brushed him aside while informing, 'He is with me.' Two seconds later we were in.

"Man, I can tell you, I never see a place like that in all my life. Never, never. There were nice girls all over the place. Some dancing, some serving drinks, some sitting around tables chatting; but partners, girls like peas. There were people smoking cigars and drinking all kinds of fancy drinks, and there were pretty lights everywhere, all over the place. And don't talk about music. There were some fellows playing banjos, guitars, drums and other instruments, and as they played, so them women danced. You think people here could dance meringue and cakewalk and thing? Jokes you making. Them Santo Domingo women is the best thing I ever see."

"They could dance better than our carnival dancers?" Chris wanted to know.

"Man, our carnival dancers can't dance. And guess what? Them Santo Domingo women have better costumes than anything I ever see here. Partners, them costumes pretty for so, and don't talk about colours, colours for so. Our costume designers will learn a thing or two from them women over there. Take what I tell you."

"So what happened?" I asked, wanting to make sure that he continued with the story to the end.

"Well, we found a table in a corner of this big club. Even before we could sit down, two women came over to take our orders for drinks. My friend asked what I wanted to drink. I, wanting to give the impression that I was a man accustomed to drinking, said, 'Man, anything you drink Pat, I drinking.' That was a stupid mistake on my part. The man called for two coconut rums and we drank that. Then he called for two more and we drank that. We relaxed a little, with him telling me to enjoy the place and get up and dance if I feel like it. Then he called for two more drinks and after that one, I started to feel tight. But you know white people already, when them having a good time, them having a good time. So he told me to drink without fear because he had enough money to pay for everything.

"By the time the fourth round ah drinks arrived, two girls came and asked if they could join we, and Pat readily agreed. This led to more drinking. Pat could talk Spanish, so he was conducting all the conversation. I didn't know one word ah Spanish and them girls could only talk a little English. After a while, Pat took one of the girls and started to dance. Partners, you ever see a white man dance meringue? It is the funniest thing in the world. Tell anybody I tell you so. And with the rum in me and I feeling a little tight, man, when I saw this man dancing, I laugh until I nearly collapse. But he didn't mind at all. In true white people fashion, the man just continued to jump around the place with no rhythm or rhyme whatsoever.

"After he danced about three or four songs, he came to me, give me some money and tell me he had to step out with the young lady for a while. He called the waitress, give her some money and told her to give me anything I want. With that, he hooked arms with his dance partner and they went through a little back door of the club."

"Weren't you scared to be in there alone?" interrupted Chris.

"Me, scared? Na, I was taller and stronger than most of them people in the club. Scared? Na, no way."

"So what did you do after you friend left?" I asked.

"What you mean, what did I do? I continued to drink my rum and thing, and that was the mistake I made, 'cause I got drunk. Boys, rum is not good and when anybody ask you who told you so, tell them your uncle Sattou, 'cause I know, rum is not no good," he said, trying his best to appear very serious.

"And what happened after," I asked, getting impatient to hear the rest.

"Well, boy, I get so drunk that I fall asleep right there at the table. Next thing I wake up and it was broad daylight and the people cleaning up the place. I had a headache and had to think a while before I pieced it together, worked out where I was, and remembered how I got there. Rum really bad, take what I tell you."

"So you mean you slept at a table all night with all that music and people dancing and thing?" asked Chris.

"Boy, I tell you, I was stone drunk. That is why I tell you rum is no good. Anybody could ah lift me up and carry me anywhere and I would not know. A matter a fact, they could ah kill me and I would not know."

"So why the girl didn't wake you?" I asked.

"Girl, which girl?" he responded.

"Remember you said that two girls came to your table and one went out with the white man. Well what happened to the one who stayed with you?" I reminded him.

"Oh, she? Well, partner, when Pat took her friend and started to dance, I wanted to invite her to dance too. But I didn't know how to say that in Spanish and couldn't bring myself to use sign language. Then again, I was already tight like wedge, and with them white people wiggling, say they dancing, I got more interested in watching them than in the girl. Next thing you know, she get up, tell me she coming back in a while and partner, I never see she again. Boys, I telling you as your uncle, woman is not simple to deal with. Not simple at all. Never forget that."

"So you really mean that a girl left you and walk off?" asked Colin.

"That is another thing you should know, and when you become big men, you must never forget," said Sattou.

"What?" demanded Colin. "That we shouldn't get drunk?"

"No, no," responded Sattou in a rather hurried manner, "you need to know that there are many stupid women in this world. Now look at me, a beautiful man like me. And look at you boys, beautiful boys like you and…"

"I am not beautiful," I said, remembering what my mother had told me. "I am handsome. Only women are beautiful," I said matter-of-factly.

"Well, Charlie you know what I mean, and I sure you would agree with me that the four of us are handsome, very handsome. Not so?" There was general agreement on this point as Sattou waited for some sign that he was not incorrect.

"But you were telling us about your hand and how it managed to come so," reminded Chris, "so tell us."

"Yes, I am coming to that, but I had to tell you how everything started, not so? Yes, back to the story. Now I was so embarrassed, for there I was, waking up in a bar with people around me, wiping tables and mopping floor and thing. I scrambled up me self and hit the road

141

before you could say Jackrabbit. I decided to see if I could find my way back to the wharf and the ship and so began to walk.

"I can tell you that Santo Domingo is a nice place, and man, them woman pretty for so. And them people could talk, especially the women. Now at that time, I didn't know a word of Spanish so I didn't understand. But just to listen to them talk make me decide I was going to learn Spanish. And the music boy, the music of that country is something else, really something else..."

"But how did you get the hand?" I interjected, trying to mask my impatience.

"Yes, yes, tell us about the hand, how did you get it?" Chris supported.

"All right, all right. Well, as I walked looking for my way to the wharf, I came upon this market place with all kinds of ground provisions, fruit and things. Partners, everything in the place pretty and smell real good too. And all of sudden I felt hungry. Then is when I remembered that I didn't eat ah thing since the day before. So I went to the nearest stall and asked the fellow to sell me a coconut water. Now I couldn't talk Spanish so I had to communicate with the fellow through sign language.

"When I done drink the coconut water, the fellow say something and I asked what he say. He put up one finger and I realised that he was asking for his money. So I shoved my hand in my pocket and feel for my money. Partners, nothing. So I shoved my hand in my other pocket and partner, me heart immediately started to beat real fast. I checked and rechecked each pocket to no avail. All me money was gone. I didn't have a cent, and this is when all fall down.

"The fellow started shouting, 'Me denero! Me denero! Dame me denero!' So I put up my hand…"

"What was he saying?" interrupted Chris.

"He was asking for his money," responded Sattou and continued, "so I put up my hand to tell the fellow now, wait let me explain, and at that moment I saw the cutlass coming. In that split second, I saw that it was sharpened back and belly and was heading straight for my neck. I ducked, but he attacked so suddenly and so quickly that I couldn't get my hand out of the way in time. I felt a sharp pain and blood spouted on my face and clothes and all over the place. When I looked at my hand, it was hanging on by the skin only."

"Ah!" gasped Chris as he put his hand to his face, "Jesus, Jesus, uncle Sattou, Jesus." Looking up, he continued "Oh, please I…, I…, I….," and then he started to vomit. Sattou sprang to his feet, lifted him up and took him outside. Chris vomited some more, while Colin and I stood around watching Sattou holding him. In a few seconds my mother came rushing out.

"What happened? What happened to Chris? What happened to him?" she demanded, as she took him from Sattou. Colin and I looked at Sattou and then at our mother. We were very relieved to see that she too was looking at him. Christ was always seen by the rest of our family as the softest child. Many of our relatives used to often say that my father needed to toughen him up. Not that he was effeminate in any way. It was rather that there was a more caring and emotional side to him, which was absent in both Colin and me. He was always more considerate of others than we were. At school, he refused to hit or fight anyone for any reason whatsoever. Everybody said that he was a copy of my maternal grandmother, morally speaking, for this was her creed how one should live one's life.

My mother was always very concerned about her four boys, but Chris was her baby, even if he wasn't the last of her children. For Colin and me, Chris was a constant source of embarrassment and disgrace for many years, especially in the teenage period, for he simply wasn't rebellious. He was always well-behaved and first in his class. He therefore was the standard by which we were judged. He was just by nature a very quiet soul.

"Mummy, I am alright, I just suddenly felt bad inside, but I am alright now. I will go in and clean up the living room. Thank you, uncle Sattou for…"

"Don't worry about the cleaning up, Chris," said my mother, "I would do that. Sattou, watch this child carefully for me please; he is very sensitive to a lot of things."

"Gracie girl, these are my nephews, you think I go wait for you to tell me to take care of them? They are me own, how could you think that I would…?"

"Sattou, don't misunderstand, I am not saying that you would deliberately upset the boys. I am telling you that this one, Chris, is a little softer than the others, and you need to look out for him more. You understand me or not?"

"But mom, you know I can take care of everything and…"

"Sattou, don't listen to that child; he will tell you that he can do everything, but he is softer than the other two. So what they can take, he can't, never mind what he says."

"But mom," protested Chris, "I…"

"Ok, ok, just be careful and don't get sick anymore," said my mother. With that, she took her leave and went inside to clean up. We remained outside with Sattou.

"Ok, I think we had enough for today and I don't want to upset Gracie. So let's forget that story and move to something else."

"No, no," I protested, "let Chris go inside, Colin and I want you to finish this story."

"No, I think your brother would want to hear the story and we could continue another time, so let us stop here."

"Chris doesn't want to hear the rest of the story," I insisted, "and we want to know what happened after the coconut man chopped you."

"Uncle Sattou, I want to hear the rest of the story too, so let us continue. I am alright now, really, and there is no need to worry."

"And then you are going to vomit again and cause mommy to come out again," I said.

"Charles," said Sattou, "stop treating your brother like that or I will not be telling anybody anything. He is your younger brother and you always take care of the younger ones. Do you understand me?"

"Yes uncle Sattou," I said meekly.

"Good. So what do we do now, continue or wait till later?"

"No, uncle Sattou, let's finish now," said Chris, "I want to know what happened after the market."

"Ok, once Chris says he is ok, I suppose we could continue," said Sattou. This brought tremendous relief to me, for I was fearful that I would never know the end of this adventure. It is not that the dramatic episode with the cutlass didn't affect me. It was rather that these stories transported me into a different world. I somehow knew they were fundamental to my education. But with the adult members of my family, one never knew; they had a way of sometimes starting these tales and never finishing them. I thought this one was too good not to know the end.

"Well, blood was pouring from my hand," continued Sattou, not taking his eyes off Chris, "but the fellow was still waving his cutlass as if he intended to chop me again, or anyone who intervened on my behalf. I, with the blood pouring from my hand and barely conscious of the market women screaming in horror, held my left wrist and backed away from him. As the pain began to hit me, I started to look around wondering what to do. Some people started coming to me and I could hear one shouting "Ayuda! Ayuda! Ayudale por favor." Then I began to feel faint, and in the approaching daze, I saw him. I must have collapsed, for I remember nothing else until I came through in the hospital."

"You mean you fainted?" I asked.

Sattou did not respond to me but was looking at Chris who had cringed and put his hand over his mouth. "You want to vomit again?" he asked.

"No uncle Sattou, I am alright; tell us what happened," came the not too convincing response.

"Well, when I awoke, I was lying in a hospital bed and I had the impression that everything was spinning. At first I couldn't figure out why I was there in this really strange place, and I was trying hard to get control so that the spinning would stop. Then I saw Pat. He was standing over me and I could see he looked very concerned. There were also two women and a man, all dressed in white clothes. As things slowly became clearer, I heard Pat asking me how I feeling. As I made to answer, I moved my hands, and then was when I realised that my left hand was all wrapped in bandage. My memory came back and I had a sudden fear that I had lost my hand and said, 'Oh God no.' But Pat told me not to worry as they had stitched it back on. I was happy to hear that, for I thought it meant I would have normal use of my hand again.

"The fellow in the white clothes was a doctor and he sat down in a chair next to the bed and explained everything to me. He said I would not lose my hand but that I might not be able to use it like before. He was right. All the time he was talking, Pat was just standing there

147

looking remorseful as ever. The two ladies were looking at me, their eyes full of pity as well. And there I realised how close I came to death."

"Yes," said Chris, "it is a lucky thing that is only your hand."

"What you mean is a lucky thing that is only his hand?" interjected Colin. "Would you want anyone to chop you on your hand?"

"If it wasn't his hand, it would have been his neck and he would have died," defended Chris.

"Yes, he is right," supported Sattou, "if my hand wasn't in the way, that man would have chopped my neck clean off, believe me."

"But them people in Santo Domingo real wicked," I said, "you mean to say a man wanted to kill you for a coconut water? Did the police do him anything? Did they lock him up and charge him?"

"No, he wasn't locked up," replied Sattou.

"So, you mean that he tried to kill you and nothing happened to him?" I almost shouted incredulously.

"Well, wait partner, the story isn't finished yet. If you wait you go hear. As a matter of fact, I ain't tell you the best part yet. Just have patience and you go hear story," said Sattou, and he proceeded. "Well, Pat was really a good friend and went and got my travelling bag from the ship. He even went out and bought me pyjamas and soap and things like that. He said it was his fault that I almost lose my hand and he should have never left me alone in the club that night.

"I tried to explain to him that I had only me self to blame, 'cause if I didn't drink the fellow coconut, then he wouldn't attack me. But Pat insisted, for he said that if I didn't go with him to the club and had remained on the ship, none of this would happen. He said another ship was leaving in five days and he wanted to leave with it but he knew I couldn't get out of the hospital in time, and he would stay in Santo Domingo until I could leave the hospital.

"I didn't try to convince him not to leave as I knew no one in the country. I couldn't even talk the language and, with my hand in such a condition, I couldn't work. So the question to me was how would I survive on my own?

"From that first day in the hospital though, I noticed that one of the two women in the white uniforms, a pretty brown-skin girl, showed so much concern for me that I was really surprised. And guess what? She looked just like Gracie. Just like Gracie."

"You mean like Mummy?" asked Chris.

"Yes partner, just like your mother. And partners, I like her right away. And guess what? I soon find out that she like me too. The second day she came in to work, she tried talking to me. Partners, I didn't know one word of Spanish and she only knew a few words in English. But she had such a nice smile and looked so much like Gracie, that I decided that she and I must be friends. So I asked her if she would teach me a little Spanish and she immediately agreed.

"Well, partners, after three days, me and she come friends. I told me partner Pat to ask she if she go agree to let me stay by her for a short while when I come out the hospital seeing that he had to leave. I told him of course, that he might have to give her a raise. He agreed to ask her and believe it or not, she said yes. But he had to force her to take the money. Partners, when you talk about a Good Samaritan, Maria is a first class Good Samaritan."

Sattou stopped and seemed to be in deep thought while my brothers and I waited. He seemed not only to be in thought, but to have left us and to be some other place. He came back after a minute or so and said slowly, "I hope she found a good fellow and got married, 'cause if there is one woman on this earth who should get a good husband is Maria."

"So what happen after?" I asked.

"Well, in about two weeks, I moved in with Maria and her mother and…"

"No, I mean with the coconut seller, what happened with him?"

"But that is what I coming to. Charlie, you must not be so impatient, wait and you go know everything. So now, as I was saying, after Pat left and I came out the hospital, I moved in with Maria and her mother. They took the best care they could of me. I can tell the three of you that Christian people is good people, and them people was Christian. They feed me, dress me hand, introduce me to their friends, wash me clothes, teach me Spanish and did many other things for me. I can't done thank them.

"Maria mother had a little shop where they sold rum and other things, and as me hand got better, I started to help her with it. This was good for me in many ways and I was able to contribute a little to the household. I would go into town with her to buy goods for the shop and through these experiences, I learn a good bit ah Spanish and learn a lot ah things about Santo Domingo. That place is something else. You know is two countries they have on that island? Yes man, you have Santo Domingo on one side and Haiti on the other side, side by side, just like how you all have the neighbour over there. But in Haiti the people talk French.

"But all the while I was living with Maria and her mother, my mind was on Mr. Coconut Man. From my trips to town with Maria's mother, I knew where his market was. I made a promise that he wasn't going to get away with chopping me. Once my hand was better, it would be me and he. My friend Pat had told me he had gotten the police and went to the market trying to locate this man. Interestingly enough, no one seemed to know him or anything whatsoever about him. I know that he was right there among them, but no one wanted to say. So I decided that I would have to deal with him me self.

"At first, I plan going to the police and taking them to the market to identify him so that they could lock him up. But after a while, I realise that that plan can't work. I was a foreigner, I did not speak the language, and I was positive that none of the other vendors would back me up in an accusation against him. So I had to find another way of making him pay for what he did to me. Ask your mother, I, Sattou The Great, I rather dead than he get away with doing me wrong. I had to teach him a lesson."

"What lesson you wanted to teach a big man like him?" asked Colin naively.

"Well, I decided that a fellow like him should taste me hand. So I sat down and partners, I work out a plan. One evening I went to the market, waited until he left for home and followed him. I keep him in sight but make sure that he didn't see me. The fellow walk about two miles before he reach a little village. He then ducked in a little place by the roadside. I went close enough to see that it was a rum shop. There was plenty men in there and all of them talking loud, loud, loud. You know rum shop men, them always talking loud and rowdy.

"I waited outside the rum shop for about an hour. The man came out and walked up a little bushy track not too far from the rum shop and disappeared in the dark. I went home, for I was sure that Maria and her mother would want to know where I was if I stayed out any longer. A week later, I went back to the market and again waited until he left and followed him. The fellow took the same road and duck in the same rum shop and although I waited for two hours, he never came out, so I had to head home.

"I lay-waited him a third time and decided to see where he goes after the rum shop. He came out about three hours later and head up the same bushy track. I followed him for about ten minutes but he kept walking, so I knew he had to be heading home. I turn around and headed home to Maria and she mother. When I got there, I almost got into trouble. I met Maria bawling. She said I find some girl friend and I went to see this girl. Partners, if is one thing I could tell anybody, is that Santo Domingo women real jealous. Partners, Maria made so much noise you would ah think I kill somebody.

"About a month later, I manage to convince Maria that is not no woman I was going to look for, but I had something to do. I promised her that I would not be going out in the night for a long time to come after this. So she allowed me to leave the house. Partners, I head straight for the rum shop and a peep inside. There was me boy, drinking coconut rum as if it going out ah style, playing dominoes and talking at the top of his voice. Well, I say to me self, 'Tonight is your night of reckoning. Tonight is judgement night.'

"So what did you do?" I asked, getting excited.

"Well, partners, I walk way from the rum shop and went into the little track he does use to go home and waited. I made up me mind to wait until thy kingdom come if I have to. All the time I was planning what I am going to tell him, and how I was going to tell him 'cause my Spanish was not so good. But I wanted to make sure that he understand me.

"I don't know how long I waited. But after a long time, I looked and saw him coming into the track. I stood up behind a banana tree and waited. When he was right upon me, I jump out from the behind the banana bush and I started.

"'Tu me puedes recorder?' I said. Partner, he jump and I repeated the question, 'Tu me puedes recorder?' 'No, no, no' he began. So I held up my left hand to my neck and he immediately turned around and started running back to the rum shop. But I grabbled him. and start to thunder some blows on him. He fell down. Is then I grabbled him by he left hand and wring and wring until I hear 'Cracks!' and he let out a scream; then I let him go and ah take off, home I coming."

"You mean you broke his hand?" asked Chris incredulously.

"Yes, his hand was broken," confirmed Sattou.

"But why did you do that, uncle Sattou?" questioned Chris.

"What you mean why he did that," contested Colin. "The Santo Domingo fellow chopped him first."

"Yes Chris, I had to let him know you don't just chop people like that and think you can get away with it," ascertained Sattou.

"So what happened after?" I asked, trying to give the story some momentum.

"Well, a month and a half later, I sneak up to the market and I saw he had his left hand in a sling just like I had mines a few months earlier. I said well, he getting a taste of his own medicine now.

"I waited a good six or seven months and then I went down to the same rum shop and peep in. And yes, there was me boy, playing dominoes, drinking rum like it going out a style, and shouting as usual. I step away quietly to me shortcut and waited. Only this time, I went a little higher up and stood behind some bushes. When me boy came up, I sprang out. I thought he would ah get a heart attack. The fellow make one big scream and then he try to run. I grabbled him by he left hand. He try to fight up with me, but ah drunk man can't fight. So I wring he left hand and wring it partners, until it say 'Cracks!' and I take off, home I coming."

Sattou stopped for a while, for Chris had put his hands over his ears and was looking at the ground. I silently prayed that he would not start vomiting again, for that would have surely meant the end of the story. "You alright Chris?" he asked, a look of worry and concern on his face. Chris answered by nodding his head. "You don't look alright to me; we can stop here today and tomorrow when you feel better we will continue."

"Oh no, uncle Sattou, I am alright, really I am fine."

I am sure Chris only said that because he knew that Colin and I would have crucified him if we didn't get to hear the rest of the story due to his weak stomach. He removed his hands from his ears, sat up straight, and was unblinkingly attentive. Sattou seemed reassured and we moved on.

"Over the next few months, I only went into town when I had to shop with Maria's mother. Six months after I last broke his hand, I went back to the rum shop a couple of times to look for him, but he wasn't there. So I say to me self: he can't stop drinking rum, no way. So I waited another two months and then went back and peep in the rum shop and he still wasn't there. It was about nine months since I didn't see him and I decided to visit the market where he use to sell. But partners, he wasn't there either. Well now, I had a problem, where to find Mr. Coconut Man.

"There were quite a few of these small markets in the town and I decided to look around one or two of them to see if he was in any of them. One Friday evening, I went to this small market on the other side of the town and found him selling there. I made sure that he didn't see me as I waited outside and followed him when he left. Sure enough, on his way home, he changed course. Instead of continuing on the road that led to the rum shop, he took a left. I followed him. He walked for about twenty minutes and then ducked into a small board place. My instinct told me that it was a rum shop. I start to look for some way to hide to lay-wait him. I didn't find any place so I decided to wait right there on the road.

"Partner, he came out the shop staggering as usual and began to walk home, with me following. I was hoping that he go take some kind of shortcut so I go fix him. But guess what? He didn't do that. He just keep walking the straight road. But it seemed that something tell him look back or that he felt my presence, you know how you could sometimes feel people walking behind you? However, whatever it was, the fellow turn round and, partners, he saw me.

"So what did he do? What did he do?" demanded Chris in a voice full of excitement, anxiety and impatience all at once.

"He freeze," said Sattou, tensing his body and changing his voice for added effect.

"And then what?" demanded Chris. "What happened?"

"And then he put his hand in his pocket to take out something. I thought he was going for a knife, so I start thinking real fast what to do. But then he said, 'Señor ven aqui, disculpa que su mano he cotado.' He then started to plead with me to forgive him while handing me a little bag. When I realised it wasn't a knife he had, I was relieved and took the bag. I opened it and it was ram cram with money. 'Toma eso' he said, 'pero me hand, no break me hand no more por favor.'

"I was surprised to hear him talk English and I responded in English. However, before I could get in three good words, he said, 'No speaker English Señor, no speaker English, only no break me hand no more, por favor Señor.'

"I took the money, looked at my left hand then looked at his left hand. I look him in the eye. He continued, 'Señor, Señor desculpa, desculpa Señor.' There were tears in his eyes now. I looked at my hand again and looked at him and strangely, I felt sorry for him and didn't want to break his hand again. I said bueno and left.

"On my way home to Maria and her mother, I checked the money and realised that I had more than enough money to pay my passage home. Right there and then, I decided that I had had enough of Santo Domingo and it was time for me to move on to England or Aruba. So I began to plan how to escape.

"But uncle Sattou, escape from what?" asked Chris.

"Partner, is not escape from what, but from who. I know I couldn't go home and tell Maria and she mother that I leaving."

"But why not, I thought they were your friends?" continued Chris.

"Of course they were my friends. Maria loved me to death. That is why I had to sneak away because Jesus Christ, if she and she mother did know that I was going to leave, there was no way that them was going to allow me."

"So tell us how you escape," I encouraged.

"But wait, so you never saw Mr. Coconut Man again?" asked Colin.

"No, I never saw him again, for from that night, I only had one thing on my mind, and that was how to left Santo Domingo."

"So how did you escape Maria and her mother?" I persisted.

"Well, that is another story all by itself and partner..." Sattou's voice trailed off as my mother came out.

"Boys, time for dinner and then bed. I know it's holidays, but you have to get up early to go to church tomorrow. So come on, get going. Go and wash your hands." We all raced off.

After dinner, we went and washed up, put on our pyjamas, said our prayers and went straight to bed. I hoped, for the life of me, that we would be able to continue with Sattou's story the next day. When I went out into the living room to say good night to him and my parents, I heard my mother saying, "So what you think? I pray none of them becomes as bad as you, God forbid. And I hope you haven't been telling them any of those..." I didn't hear any more for, upon my entrance, she stopped. They all bade me goodnight and I went back to the bedroom and my bed.

About an hour later, my mother came in to make sure that we weren't still up reading. She put out the lights. I fell asleep thinking about Sattou and the story he had told us. I had dreams of the comical actions and different expressions on Sattou's face as he told his tale, and I found myself in some of the many strange places and among many of the strange people he told us about.

Sattou reminded me of my maternal grandfather whom my brothers and I loved greatly, and whom he called Pa. We would fight each other to sit closest to him when he visited our house. He had these fascinating stories of the First and Second World Wars, and of the devil in a human form called Hitler. His stories about the Battle of Britain, the exploits of Kitchener, the triumph at Normandy, the ultimate surrender of the Germans, and the role of our island as part of the Empire in it all, made me feel small, yet great. Real great because we, the people of a small West Indian island, as he put it, had helped to beat the hell out of that great evil called Hitler. He told us how Churchill had taken the Empire through it all, and that all of us had a lot to thank Churchill for. He said the British Empire was the greatest in the world and there was nothing like it, and that we were part of it. Yes, I felt great, really great.

For me, our grandfather was a living history book. When he spoke, I most times saw these places through my mind's eye and virtually wished that I were there. It is not that my grandfather glorified war. Rather it was that he tried to explain in the best way he knew how, what commitment it took to achieve victory, not just on the battlefield of war, but on the general battlefield of life. He and Sattou told us about these places, people and things we had never seen and heard of before. They took us into a world, where we longed to be, hoped to be, virtually prayed that one day we would be.

There were however differences between the tales of my grandfather and those of Sattou. Indeed the tales themselves and the styles and manner they related them were different. Their stories had different characters and were of different times. And while my grandfather's emphasis was always on teaching us something he considered important, Sattou was clearly more intent on making us enjoy it all, in demonstrating his bravery, strength and cleverness to us. So, his were tales of his own life, events where he was the main character. In telling them, he relived every moment, transmitted every detail, from an unusual heartbeat to every scream and shout.

He was the Tom Sawyer my mother had told us about, the boy she grew up with and idolised, and made into the hero I wanted to be. All of his great exploits which she took great pleasure in detailing were trophies I also wanted to win, and considered myself at the right age to do so. After all, Sattou himself was but a boy when he did all those wonders.

The following morning, we were all up early as was the case every Sunday morning. The only way any of us was allowed to stay at home and not attend church, was if he was "at death's door", as my mother put it. We went to church to attend Sunday service in the morning, then went back at 3 p.m. for Sunday school in the afternoon, and finally to Sunday night service. I have always wondered how is it the Catholic Church has not seen it fit to canonise somebody from the English-speaking Caribbean. I have never seen people who were so drilled in religion from childhood to the grave, the way we were.

We had breakfast and went off to church with my mother, leaving behind my father and Sattou whom we did not see, for he was still asleep. Service lasted from 8:00 to 10:30, and by 11:30 we were home. We went straight to see Sattou.

"Good morning, boys; how is everybody doing?"

"Fine, fine, everything fine", I said. Sattou looked at Colin and Chris and they both nodded their agreement.

"And how was church? I hope you pray for me."

Nobody answered.

"Now, don't tell me you boys forget to pray for your uncle soul. How you expect me to reach heaven?" We were all looking at the ground now, the guilt of our negligence as regards Sattou's future eternity, suddenly too powerful to face. "Alright, so you all forgot. Ok, I forgive you this time, but next time you have to remember to pray for me so that I would make my path right with the Lord."

"Yes, you need to do that, and without delay, for no man has the lease on his life," said my mother, entering the room. "You boys know that the first thing you must do is change your clothes when you come from church. So get to it and don't let me have to tell you again; and wash your hands, for lunch will be soon." We all ran off and were seated at the dining table in less than ten minutes. As we ate, my mother, father and Sattou talked about what he was going to do. Whether he was going to finally settle down, or he wanted to continue travelling. He said he was still determined to get to England or Aruba; that our island was too poor for him to make a living, and so he wanted to try his hand somewhere else. I wanted to ask him why England or Aruba, but could not. In those days, children were not allowed to speak around the dining table except when asked a direct question by an adult. So I resolved to ask him later.

After lunch, Sattou went into the sitting room with my father, and we promptly followed. My father demanded of Chris and me if we forgot we were to do the dishes. As we got up to leave, my mother came in and assured him that she would do them. This was a great relief. I was therefore able to sit and listen to my father and Sattou discuss their early days of knowing each other, and all the things they did at that time. Needless to say, I was fascinated by it all. In all of the stories they recalled, Sattou was always the good and unwilling villain, forced to do the wrong thing to get the right result. The time flew, and when my mother announced it was time to get ready for Sunday school, I thought she must have made a mistake. But she was right. So I reluctantly got dressed and headed off to the church once again.

We got home from Sunday school to find my mother and father asleep in their room, as was usually the case. I decided that the important thing now was to steer Sattou around to finishing the tale on Santo Domingo. We found him in the backyard reading the Bible. He looked up and began to explain that he knew his life was sinful and he had to make a change and continued, "Speaking of change, why is it you boys are still in your Sunday school clothes? Go and take them off right now!" In that moment, I think we all saw my mother in Sattou. Rather than trying to explain, we raced off and were back in record time.

"Uncle Sattou," I said, "so how did you leave Santo Domingo?"

"What?"

"You remember you were telling us about your left hand and the time you spent there."

"Oh that you mean; yes that was a good time. I will never forget Maria and her mother. They were good people to me, real good people to me. So what you want to know now?

"Well, last night you promised to tell us how you escape from Santo Domingo and came back home."

"Oh yes, well you see, is not Santo Domingo I had to escape, it was Maria and her mother. Partners, I could tell anybody, you see when them woman from Santo Domingo love you, well boy, them really love you. I knew that Maria and her mother would never let me leave."

"So how did you escape?" I pressed.

"Well, I coming to that. Partners, once I got the money from the fellow, I start to think how to get home here to our island. I think and think for two days, the Saturday and the Sunday. By Monday morning I made up me mind what I going to do. So that Monday I went down by the wharf and find out when I could get something coming here. I spend half the morning asking, then I find out that it have a boat going my way on Sunday in the next two weeks. I decided to take that boat 'cause it was leaving at the beginning of December and I wanted to reach home for Christmas. But before I could take the boat, I had to resolve a problem. How to get my passport from Maria?

"You see, when I was sick in the hospital and had to move to Maria's place, I give her my passport and everything for safe keeping, and never ask she back for them. Now, if I go and just ask for me passport just so, it was bound to look suspicious. So I had to think how to deal with that. Partners, I sat down whole week and think and think, where she could have my passport. Then it struck me. The only place this could be is under her mattress or under her mother mattress. The question now was how to get the opportunity to search for it. Then I hit on it.

"That Saturday just before I did my regular task of closing the shop for the night, I took a good dose of Epsom salts. Man, by middle night I was running to the latrine so often that Maria and her mother knew before I tell them, that there could be no discussion 'bout me going to church with them that Sunday. Partners, as soon as they were out of sight, I went to work. I searched under the four corners of Maria's mattress with no luck at all. So I decide to try the mattress of her mother. Still no luck. Partners, I start to worry, 'cause if the passport was not under the mattress, then where could it be? I then search the two bedrooms, every corner, every nook and cranny, but I didn't find a thing. I started to despair, for the passport seem lost. I could not believe that after planning this thing so good, taking so much Epsom salts that kept me running to the latrine, even while I was doing the search, that I can't find the passport.

"Church was only for two hours and I know that Maria and she mother were coming back soon, so I needed to find the passport. I sit and I think and think; but think as hard as I could, I didn't know where else to look. So guess what? I decide to pray, and partner I go on my knee and beg God to help me to find the passport. As soon as I get up off me knee, something tell me I was right, I need to look under the mattress again. It didn't make sense to me so I didn't want to do it. But yet this thing keep saying to me: Search the mattress again, search the mattress again.

"So I went into Maria's bedroom and decided to take the entire mattress completely off the bed. But again I didn't find anything. I put back on the mattress and make up the bed, all the time thinking how stupid I was to search a place I did done search already. When I done make up the bed, something keep telling me, 'Search under the mother mattress again.' So to avoid the temptation, I decide to go out in the yard. While I was out in the yard, I get a latrine call and had to go. But even while I was there, I had the voice telling me, 'Sattou man, search the other mattress, search the other mattress,' and that is exactly what I finally decide to do.

"So I went back inside she mother room and took off the entire mattress. Lo and behold, in the middle of the spring bed, there was a brown bag. I grab it up and open it and there was my blue British Empire passport. Partner, I felt happy, real happy, for I know where me passport was. I put it back in the bag and quickly put back on the mattress and make up the bed for I knew they could arrive from church anytime."

"But how come you put back your passport after searching for it so long and knowing that you were going to need it to travel home?" I asked.

165

"Good question, but I had to do that, 'cause I had to wait two weeks for the boat. I am sure that Maria mother would ah check the bag before that time and she would ah miss the passport. So it was better to leave it there for the time being and take it when I was ready to leave to avoid all suspicion.

"With the Sunday approaching for the boat to leave, I start to think of a stunt to pull so that I didn't have to go to church that morning. Maria and she mother live more than three hours away from the wharf and to get a ride on Sunday in those days was not at all possible. I knew that I had to leave early as the boat was leaving at 1:00 p.m. in the day. Little by little during the week, I wrote a long letter to Maria thanking them from the bottom of me heart for everything they did for me. And during the week I was thinking what stunt to pull. But think as I may, I couldn't come up with a way of escape that wouldn't look suspicious. I didn't want to use the Epsom salts again because I couldn't do that and then go on a boat. The other thing is that Epsom salts does not only cause belly wuking, but belly hurting too.

"Sunday, I put on my clothes and head to church with Maria and she mother. They usually sit up front and I would sit at the back. But that Sunday, I didn't stay for long. As soon as the people settled down, I eased out and home I coming at top speed. I rammed a few things in me travelling bag, got me passport and took off walking as fast as I could. When I was gone about a quarter of an hour, I remember that I did not leave the letter of thank you and some of the money that I had taken from the coconut man as a gift to show my gratitude to them. I rushed back and left them on Maria dressing table in she bedroom. And then I hit the road again heading for the wharf. As soon as I was out of my neighbourhood, I start to run. I run most of the way to the wharf.

"What did the neighbours say when they saw you leaving with the bag?" ask Chris.

"Partner, there I was lucky, 'cause most people was at church and I was able to slip away without anyone seeing me, 'cause that could have indeed been a problem. By the time I reach the wharf, I was soaking wet with perspiration from hustling in all that hot sun. But I made it on time, paid the fare, got on the boat and was on my way home after living in Santo Domingo for almost two and a half years.

"Once I got on the boat, the evil that I did overcame me, and I felt very sad indeed. I had left Santo Domingo without saying even goodbye to Maria and her mother who had done so much for me. I believe that what happened to me on the boat on my trip home was sure punishment for this bad thing I did to them." By now, Sattou was in a real sad mood and we could tell that he was feeling truly guilty for what he had done. We all held our heads down, preferring to look at the floor, giving this moment of guilt a chance to lift itself from the atmosphere.

After a few moments, Sattou asked, "So partners, you want to hear what happened on the boat or not?" The response was immediate and universal, and so Sattou proceeded. "Well, partners, we set sail and I was sharing cabin with a fellow from Grenada whose name was, oh, but wait, what was his name again?" said Sattou, pondering for a moment. "Oh yes, his name was Tunenus. He say he went up to Santo Domingo to cut cane and was returning home for the Christmas. It was from him that I first heard about the hurricane. He said it is forecast to hit the West Indies and he hope it don't hit Grenada. He was praying that he could reach home before it hit the boat. Well, I thought is joke the fellow joking, so I go up on deck only to find out that quite a few people know about it and that the question was not if it would hit, but when it would hit. Immediately I saw death facing me. I knew it was for all the wrong things I did and especially the wrong I did to Maria. I was sure that she and she mother pray on me and God heard the prayers and now I must pay the price.

"Well, the boat was to take a week to get to Grenada. After four days, the weather start to get calm and we noticed that the sea began to get still. On the fifth day, the Captain announced that we have to stop in Martinique as the hurricane was now in the West Indies. By the time we got to port in Martinique, the wind was tossing the boat all over the place, howling bitterly and causing the sea to rage. Swells were breaking over the bow of the boat and everybody was ordered to their cabin by the Captain. When I reach my cabin, I meet Tunenus vomiting like a dog. I got a bucket for him to vomit in. Then I started to pray silently. I asked for forgiveness for all the bad things I did and especially for what I did to Maria. I promised God I would never do that again if he spared my life.

"We reach port in Martinique and we had to spend three days there until the storm and the sea quiet down. Then we take up anchor and sail on. With the storm past, I start to pray to reach home in time for Christmas. A rumour started on the boat that the hurricane mash up Grenada real bad and I felt real sorry for me partner in the cabin. He said he live a Guave, and he sure his house done mash up. I told him that he mustn't be so pessimistic but pray and hope for the best. I also promise to pray for him and his family.

"Partner, when we reach Grenada, the whole place mash up. And when I say mash up, I mean mash up. When the boat started to approach the port and Tunenus look out and saw that everything blow down, he started to bawl. I tried my best to cheer him up. When we reach port, I shook his hand, said goodbye and promise to pray for him and his family. But my heart was low and I felt a chill, which told me that there was no good news waiting for him when he reach home. I came off the boat and went around St. George's walking. I could do that, for the Captain said that he had no idea when we leaving as we have to get water and fuel and food and other supplies. With everything mash up in Grenada, all them things was going take a long time to get.

"As I walked, my heart started to sink deeper and deeper. The store windows were broken, there were huge trees lying on the ground and pieces of roof, galvanise and thing all over the place. I met a fellow who told me his name was Willy. He said in the city was bad but in places like Guave, where they had plenty wattle and daub, it was worse.

When he mentioned Guave, my heart went out to me partner Tunenus, and I whispered another small prayer for him.

"I walked around a little more and looked at the people as they tried putting things back together. There was so much destruction all around that my heart could not take it. I returned to the boat and lay down in my cabin and thought how blessed my island was. The hurricane made St. George's into a waste and, even though I was really sorry for the Grenadians, I was thankful to God that he had save our island 'cause if it had hit us, things would have been worse here. We have much more people than Grenada and this island have plenty, plenty more poor people and plenty, plenty more wattle and daub.

"We spent five days in Grenada before we could get all the supplies the boat need and then set off to come home. The trip from Grenada was to take three days and we were to reach here Christmas Eve day. But it took a whole week. The evening we left Grenada, within four hours the winds became strong again and the boat had to battle a storm. Partners, there were waves taller that this house, and the wind tossed the boat like a small kite in the sky. The boat engine shut off and we started to drift in this bad weather. Some people start to bawl, saying: this time we really dead. I really thought this was the end of the boat and so made up my mind to meet my God. I thought it was my fault that the boat was having these great problems. I remembered that Haiti was the next door neighbour of Santo Domingo, and I was sure that Maria and she mother gone over there, got a powerful voodoo man to cast an evil spell on me, and the perishing of this boat was the result.

"We drifted for five days, including Christmas Day. But by the third day, which was Christmas Eve day, the wind had quiet down and we drifted while the engineer tried to get the engine working again. That Christmas Day is the worse I ever spend in all my life. When I woke up that day, I had a heavy feeling in my stomach. This was Christmas and I was spending it on the sea and in a drifting boat at that. We had cold milk and biscuit for breakfast and the Captain promise that we would get something better for Christmas lunch. As soon as he done talk, the wind started to blow again. With every passing minute, it got stronger and stronger and before you know, the boat started to dance again.

"The boat dance and drift for a good three hours. When 12 o'clock came, I didn't see no food, so I say is cook they still cooking it. Then 1 o'clock came and partner, no food. So I start to wonder, for I find the food taking too long to come. At about 2 o'clock, the Captain came and say that due to the bad weather the pot can't stay on the fire. Every time the cook put it on and the boat dance in the wind, it keep tumbling over. So he say he order the cook to give everybody two smoke herrings and twelve salt biscuit and some more cold milk. He then wished us all a Merry Christmas and went to the wheelhouse. Partners, I can't describe how I was feeling at that moment.

"When I got me two smoke herrings and me twelve salt biscuit, I went back into my cabin to eat. But then I remembered how at home

171

Pa used to kill a whole pig and sometimes a sheep or a goat for Christmas. And how Ma used to cook so much food for Christmas lunch, all the meat we use to have and thing. And here I was, eating bare smoke herring and some dry biscuits. I burst into tears."

Upon hearing Sattou say this, my brothers and I began to laugh, for we found it funny indeed to imagine a man like him crying for anything. "So you really cried tears?" I asked, my voice and manner clearly indicating that I thought he was spicing up the story to make us laugh.

"So you think is joke I joking?" came Sattou's serious reply, backed up by a short and intense stare that asked: how dare you doubt me? He continued, "I cried for a while, but even when I stop, I couldn't eat the smoke herrings and dry biscuits. No Sir, not on Christmas Day. Any other day, but not Christmas Day," he said this, shaking his head negatively. "And I know why it happened to me and I was wrong, so I couldn't vex with anybody."

I never got to hear how Sattou finally reached home to our island, for before he could finish his story, my mother came out and ordered us to wash up and get ready for Sunday night service. When we came back from service, we were ordered to bed. On Monday morning, Sattou took his bus and left. He said he was going to see Pa, as he called our grandfather, before going off to Trinidad to see Shirley. He promised to return to visit us boys again before the summer holidays were over.

I was sad to see him go, taking with him the world of strange characters and happenings, of places bustling with activity, and where adventure waited around the corner. This world that kept my nerves and pulse in a suspicious mode, ready to start running like an anxious horse at the crack of a whip, or take sudden flight like an alert wild bird at the slightest movement. He left, leaving me in a world of this little island with no bright lights, no strange people, and where no adventure ever took place.

I had six weeks holidays, and the only real excitement I could look forward to, was going to my grandfather's farm in the country. There I usually spent two weeks living the life of village royalty. My grandfather was seen as a 'big shot' in the village as he had one of only two 'wall houses', and had lands enough to employ labourers. He had served in both the First and Second World Wars and was well respected for the fact that he had travelled abroad and spoke proper English. These were the days when most West Indians were too poor to travel abroad, and when the means of communication in our part of the world were a thousand times slower, and a thousand times less than they are now. Indeed, when my grandfather had left the island for Europe, he had done so by ship, as there wasn't even an airstrip.

My grandfather owed his prestige in the village also to the fact that he had an education at a time when the vast majority of the village inhabitants could neither read nor write. And he had done what many men of his time who went to England did. He got married to a British white woman and so "raised his colour", resulting in my mother and her siblings all being "brown skin with good hair" as the villagers described them then.

These things, as inconsequential as they might seem these days, bestowed upon me a rite of passage in the village. We were "brown skin", educated, and had a wall house. Then again, we were from Town and only spend any length of time in the village during the summer holidays. This incidentally led to the majority of the boys in the village referring to me as "Town Bwoy."

My rite of passage also brought its responsibility. I was expected to be more cultured than the village boys, for while I didn't represent the cream of our society, which was the preserve of the local whites, I was expected to be more British than the real English. After all, I was removed, if only partially, from the indignity of the black skin, and the scorn and contempt it represented. Therefore I had to embody all things white and British.

And there were people in the village who made sure that I lived up to these standards. I mean black people who accepted that they were inferior to me and my family, simply because we were brown skin. They would remind me that I am "above this or that" and that I shouldn't "bring down" myself and my family. I was therefore always very alert to the presence of grownups and never allowed a "false action" when around them.

My real torture in the village as regards keeping me in line was Mr. Penniston. He was white and lived on the outskirts in a small community called Hartshire, inhabited entirely by local whites. They did not generally interact with the people of the village unless there was a real need to. He, however, had regular conversations with my grandfather, as his farmlands bordered ours, and they would quite often meet on their way to and from their farms. Looking back at it now, I am sure that Mr. Penniston conversed with my grandfather first and foremost because grandpa was married to a British white woman. Local whites were inferior to the real thing.

I did not interact with Mr. Penniston but he seemed to be always around whenever I dropped my guard and just be a boy like any other in the village. My grandfather would soon find out of my indiscretion and would sometimes give me a lecture about always remembering who I was and what I represented. At first I did not know how my grandfather knew of my discrepancies, and thought he must have a sixth sense. Then one day I had gone river jumping with some of the boys. Having mis-stepped on one of the slippery stones, I fell into the water and was soaked from head to foot. Not wanting to be scolded by my mother who was on the farm that day, I kept on the wet clothes until they became dry again. Two days later my grandfather scolded me, explaining that I could have caught a serious cold.

"I am tired telling you not to follow these village boys when you come down here. You are always getting yourself into difficulty. Penniston is right, you are from different surroundings from these boys. You can't expect to do everything they do. These boys go and steal his mangoes and other fruits and…"

"But grandpa, I never stole Mr. Penniston mangoes and…"

"I know that and you wouldn't dare do that and let me find out!"

"But I never did anything wrong to Mr. Penniston," I protested.

"He never said you did him anything wrong, but he is always seeing you doing things which are unbecoming of you. After all, you are an intelligent boy; next year you will be in high school. You must live up to what is expected of you. You understand?"

"Yes sir."

So there he was, the big Macko who made sure that I was held accountable for all my misdeeds. He was able to do this, owing to the fact that he sat under the big breadfruit tree at the end of the village's ball ground, drinking his liquor in the evening, which was the very time I went to play cricket, football or pitch marbles with the village boys. I, like all boys, paid little mind to home training on the ball ground, unconscious that I was giving Mr. Penniston the information needed for his regular dossier to my grandfather. Once I discovered this, my trips to the ball ground became less enjoyable. I was now always looking over my shoulder at Mr. Penniston under the breadfruit tree. I was all but checkmated, as with the day of the football match. But that would all change the holiday Sattou came.

***

It was the Friday morning of the end of my second week in the village. Before going to the farm, grandfather and I went to the village's police station to call my mother to inform her that I would be returning to town a week later. She in turn informed us that Sattou was coming to the village that said Friday, and that we should meet him at the bus stop in the evening. I was overjoyed and couldn't wait for evening to come to see Sattou. To think that he actually kept his word and had returned so soon was unbelievable.

He arrived with his usual flamboyance, and when he descended from the bus, all in attendance paid him much more than a casual glance. He hugged me, shook hands with grandfather and we got on the donkeys and headed to the house. Sattou spoke from that time until it was my bedtime at 9:00 p.m. He told of his latest trip to Trinidad and of Aunt Shirley. Grandfather kept the chatter going by asking numerous questions, in particular about aunt Shirley who was a first daughter.

I did not know what time they retired the night before, but they were up early the next morning, and by 6:30 we mounted the donkeys and headed for the farm. As we rode, my grandfather and Sattou spoke about the things that happened in the village when he grandfather was a boy. How his father worked for the former owners of the land as a common labourer. He told of a life of fishing in the river for mullet and sucker, of catching ground doves, stewing them with brown sugar and devouring them with roasted breadfruit. He told of eating mangoes and sucking cane until he thought his belly would burst. All of these tales left me certain that even though they lacked the material things as boys have now, they were really, really happy children.

When we arrived on the farm, grandfather showed Sattou around the watchhouse, explaining the different improvements he was able to introduce since Sattou was last there. He told him of his plans for the further development of the farm and his hope that I would one day become a good farm manager, as there was money to be made from the land. He said I was the only one of his grandchildren who had shown any interest in the farm whatsoever, and he was placing his hopes in me to continue with the farm. Sattou felt the need to go on the defensive and so offered:

"But Pa, you were the one who always said that I was like you; that I had to seek my fortune in foreign lands and not here on this island. You said that England was my place."

"Yes, I did say that," admitted my grandfather, "but I may have been wrong.

You will one day come to understand that the older you get, the wiser you become. Many of the things I said thirty years ago when you were a boy, I have come to realise were not correct."

"Are you saying that you didn't know what you were saying all those years ago?" asked Sattou.

"I am only saying that age brings reason," responded my grandfather, "age brings reason. Anyway, we all have to do what we have to do, and I suppose you will find your way one day, the same way I found mine."

Sattou sat in silence for a few moments and then continued. "Pa, I have to know, and if you and Shirley wouldn't tell me then I must find out for me self. I must…"

"Satt, I can't tell you what I don't know. Only Shirley knows the truth and she is your mother. She should tell you. Did you try asking her about it this time when you were in Trinidad?"

"Pa, you know I was never close to Shirley. I am closer to Gracie by far, and I am sure if Gracie knew she would ah tell me."

"Satt son, as I said, the only person who knows the truth is your mother. I have asked her many times to tell you. At least that she owes you. Gracie, I or anyone else can't help."

"Pa, and this is why I want to get to England and find him, 'cause he knows."

I realised that this conversation was a little beyond me, and so took my leave of them and went visiting the workers carrying out their various tasks. I returned some- time after midday and we had buljowl with green banana and coconut dumpling for lunch. This was washed down with lime swank made with the cool river water. After such a heavy meal, we all fell asleep in different crocus-bag hammocks, strung up between the branches of the various fruit trees surrounding the watch house.

I awoke around 4 p.m. and found my grandfather and Sattou sitting with a bottle of white rum taking a couple of shots, which they chased with river water kept in a calabash. The talk was about their travels, and I sat up and began to listen. But it wasn't long after, that grandfather instructed me to take Sattou down to the river, and show him the sweet potato piece that was just planted. I was glad of that, for finally I had Sattou all to myself. I thought that I could encourage him to tell me how he finally got off the boat and got home after the storm in Grenada.

The new sweet potato piece was at the river's edge which was the border between our farm and that of Mr. Penniston. As we walked, Sattou talked of the different types of mangoes he had enjoyed as a boy growing up on these lands. He said mangoes were his favourite fruits and in particular the big meaty Julie mangoes. Then he stopped.

"Look Charlie!" he said, "Look at them beautiful Julies! Man, them is what I talking 'bout! I must get a few ah them to take to Shirley."

I looked to where he was pointing and realised it was across the river at the Julie mango tree of Mr. Penniston. I immediately advised Sattou of this fact, adding that we therefore better forget them.

"Who say so?" he asked in the most innocent of manner. I could see he didn't understand and was somewhat surprised.

"Well, we can't pick any, 'cause...", I began.

"What make we can't pick any? Boy, joke you making. Is your uncle Sattou you with, and if I say we must could get a few, then we must get a few."

"But that is Mr. Penniston's land and his mango tree. He is a fellow who don't give away anything to anybody."

"Man, he can't mind some Julie mangoes, I sure of that. Come with me."

"Uncle Sattou, Mr. Penniston is not a nice man and if he catches us he might do us something and he is bound to tell grandfather."

"Do who something?" This response made me realise I committed a serious error which forced the situation to the point of no return. Sattou seemed determined now to prove to me that fear was something I should forget, once I was with him. He then informed me that taking a few of Mr. Penniston's Julies was no big deal for him, whether Mr. Penniston was there or not. "Penniston is a bad-John or what?" he continued. "Well, if he is a bad-John, all bad-John does meet them breaker. Come partner, nothing to worry about. We go pick a few Julies and Penniston wouldn't mind." Without another word, he started jumping from stone to stone. Before I could make sense of it all, he was on Mr. Penniston's side of the river, bellowing an order to me to hop across. I simply complied.

When I got across, Sattou was already up in the mango tree. I looked up to find him sitting on a branch, wiping a pretty Julie on his trousers. He bit into it and then shouted down to me, "Charlie, man them Julie sweet for all who dead." My heart was in overdrive, for I was sure that Mr. Penniston was somewhere around and would hear us. Sattou finished his mango while surveying our lands on the other side of the river and remarking how beautiful it all looked. He then shouted down at me, "You could catch?"

"Yes," I assured him.

"Ok, I throwing down some for we to carry over." I whispered an ok but Sattou would have none of that. "Boy, what you whispering for, you could catch or not?"

"Yes uncle Sattou, I can catch."

181

"Good, then look for these coming down."

He had sent down about seven which I had put in a small pile at the foot of the mango tree when I heard a rustle in the bushes behind me. I turned around and came face to face with Mr. Penniston. I froze for a second and then, as if released with all the power of a space craft, I dashed for the river, forgetting anything about trying to hop across. I just plunged in and began to swim for the other side. I did not look back until I was standing dripping wet, on a stone in the middle of the river.

"Come down yo' thief," I could hear Mr. Penniston shouting. "Come down and ah taking yo' straight ah barracks so that them lock yo' up! All yo' too thief!"

"Is who that, Pen O?"

"Yo' thief yo', who you calling Pen O? I is not yo' sex and size," shouted back Mr. Penniston, "and yo' better come down right now or ah knocking yo' down out ah me mango tree!" With that, he bent down and was obviously looking for something to use as a missile. He found two stones and was about to take aim when he was interrupted.

"Ay Pen O, careful how you pelt stone because somebody might have to save you when you drunk and fall down in the river again," shouted Sattou.

"What yo' say?" shouted back Mr. Penniston, his right hand frozen in midair.

"You hear what I say, so careful how you pelting stone."

"Ah who dat, Sattou?" questioned Mr. Penniston, his anger obviously subsiding.

"That you should find out before you start to call people thief," responded Sattou.

"Man sorry, man, sorry."

After that, I heard no more for the shouting had ceased and their voices were not audible above the sound of the river. I saw Sattou throw down a few more Julies which Mr. Penniston caught and placed on the same heap that I had started. He then got down from the mango tree and they shook hands and stood conversing. I was most astonished as they seemed to be very good friends.

Sattou seemed to have forgotten about me for a moment, and I stood on the stone looking on at their exchanges. After a while he looked around, saw me and waved me over to them. When I got there, Sattou showed some annoyance with me.

"Why you had to go and jump in the river like that? You crazy or something?"

"I, I, I didn't know that you and Mr. Penniston are friends, and the village boys always say…"

"Well, Sattou," interjected Mr. Penniston, "yo' know boys already, and them here in the village could be ah little troublesome sometimes, and so ah have to keep them off. But Charles here, he is ah nice boy. So don't get vex with him."

I couldn't believe what I was hearing. Was Mr. Penniston calling me a nice boy? Well, well, what really was happening to his head I thought.

Sattou was however very worried about my wet clothes and so, after a bit more short exchanges with Mr. Penniston, we gathered up the Julie mangoes and took our leave of him. As we said goodbye, he assured me, "Charlie, you could come anytime and pick mangoes here, anytime yo' want ok?" I nodded my understanding and we began our stone-jumping back to our side of the river. With each jump, I felt this pain in my left knee and by the time we got back to the watchhouse, my knee was badly swollen.

All the way home to the village, my mind was occupied with the seemingly casual, almost friendly, relationship between Mr. Penniston and Sattou. While I accepted that they may have known each other since Sattou was a child, that still did not explain Mr. Penniston's evident respect, one might even say appreciation for Sattou. I decided to approach Sattou about it.

"But uncle Sattou, I didn't know you and Mr. Penniston were friends?"

"Who? Oh, Pen O. Well, I know him since I was a boy."

"He seems to like you a lot," I said.

"Well, I don't know if he likes me."

"Well, he treats you like a friend," I volunteered.

"Well, Pen O, like most white people, can behave strange sometimes. He does cause you any trouble?"

"Well, he doesn't like the boys in the village," I responded.

"He didn't like me either, when I was a boy growing up here in the village."

"So is since you became a man he changed towards you?" I asked.

"No, with me it was a bit different."

"How come?"

"Well, that we could talk about another time. Right now we need to find some remedy for your knee before it swells more. Pa has soft grease in the house?"

Sattou left early on Monday morning without returning to the Penniston issue. I thought, "Just like all adults," they start a story and usually never finish it.

***

It would take another five years for me to find out the reason for this casual relationship between Mr. Penniston and Sattou. But in those years, my grandfather never once rebuked me because of something told to him by Mr. Penniston. Mr. Penniston himself completely changed towards me and was now less formal and always pleasant with me. He would often invite me to pick mangoes or whatever fruits I desired from his lands. I was convinced that this was all to do with Sattou. But what it was, what was the reason for it, I didn't know and no one else seemed to know. I tried speaking to both my mother and grandfather about this, and they simply confirmed what Sattou said as regards Mr. Penniston's dislike for him during childhood, and then his later change of friendliness towards him. Beyond that however, no one was able to explain.

Then came the summer of the year I finished secondary school. After my exams I went to the village with my grandfather. One evening I went down to the river to take a swim and as I was about to undress I heard, "Charlie, Charlie! Look over here." I looked over to the other side of the river to see Mr. Penniston beckoning to me. I jumped the stones and got to his side and he began, "I didn't know that yo' down here. When yo' come?"

"Good day Mr. Penniston, how are you? I came down yesterday."

"So yo' school close and thing?"

"Yes Sir, we finished exams."

"Well, I hope yo' do well. But I sure yo' would do well, yo' is a good boy."

"Yes, Sir, I hope so too."

Watching him from close up, I could see how much he had really aged. He wasn't frail, but his body was wrinkled and his hands shook noticeably. He was completely bald and the lines in his face were deep like small gutters. I was told that he was about my own grandfather's age, but his body was much more wrinkled, and one could easily have thought that my grandfather was much younger than he was. As I stood thinking these thoughts, he asked, "How is the old man doing? He down village or he up here with you?" I assured him that grandfather was up at the watchhouse and that he was alright. He then invited me to sit with him for a while in the shade of a mango tree so we could have a little chat. I agreed.

"How is The Magnificent?" he asked, while taking out a petty quart from his shirt pocket. "Well, yo' know I does take me little grog every now and again. People does say rum bad and them could be right, but if it wasn't for me grog, I might ah never appreciate The Magnificent. So when last yo' hear from him?" I looked at him with enquiring eyes, "I mean Sattou," he confirmed.

"Oh, but is Sattou The Great we call him. He is fine. He is in Canada, but my mother says that he will be going to England soon."

"Yes, that is my Sattou, just like his father, always want to go to England. Yo' know, I call him Sattou The Magnificent for he is more than great, he is ah magnificent boy and me best grandchild."

I wasn't sure that I had heard right and questioned rather automatically, "Your grandchild?" for certainly I couldn't have heard right.

"Oh, I see no one has told you. I don't blame them. We never owned him, and your family is too proud to force themselves on people who don't want anything to do with them."

"But why did you say your grandchild?" I repeated.

"Because he is me grandchild," he affirmed. Raising the petty quart to his lips, he took a large drink, wiped his mouth with the back of his hand and continued. "I hope you have a little time, 'cause I going tell yo' the whole thing. Yo' are old enough, so nothing wrong in me telling yo'. Sattou is the son of my first son and your aunt Shirley. So yes, he is my grandson." He stopped and looked at me expectantly. I remained silent just looking at him for I knew not what to say. He continued, "They were young people growing up in the village together. She was about seventeen; how old yo' be now?" I told him I was seventeen and he continued, "Yes, she was about yo' age and he was twenty-two. When she get pregnant with Sattou, I and the wife was very upset for it was an embarrassment for him to have pickney with somebody black, even though Shirley was half-caste. We did know that he wanted to go to England. So we told him if he disowned the child we would send him there. So he denied having anything to do with Shirley and we shipped him off to England. Some people think is Aruba he gone, but he gone ah England." He stopped again and I could hear myself breathing rather hard.

"Yo' grandfather is a good man," he said, after taking another sip of his white rum. "'Cause he could ah throw Sattou and his mother out on the street. But he kept them and took care of Sattou like his own child. I don't think they told Sattou, when he was a child, who is his father. So he grow up treating your grandparents like his parents, and Shirley like his sister, rather than his mother. I did not like Sattou, for I felt that he was an embarrassment to my family. In them days, we white people just didn't mix with black people, and yo' family is half black. So I avoided having anything to do with him or his mother, and I ban me wife from having anything to do with them.

"But yo' know, as he grow up and I look at him, the boy was the spitting image of his father. I know that I did he and his mother a terrible injustice." With this last statement, Mr. Penniston stopped and took another large sip from his petty quart and kept silent for a while. I wasn't sure whether I was required to say anything, but decided it wiser to hold my peace, and so I just sat and waited. But my brains were working overtime.

After a while Mr. Penniston continued, "But even with the wrong, some might even say evil that my family did yours, yo' grandfather and the rest of the family never show us a bad face. They continue to talk to us as if nothing happened. But deep down I thought that they hated us and in particular me. I could not be more wrong.

"Sattou was a little devil when he was a boy. He did not get into a lot of trouble but he was his father's child. He seek adventure in everything and every place, and did some of the most unusual things as a boy. It is because of this character that I knew that he and the family didn't hate me, and also it is because of it why I am still alive today."

Mr. Penniston stopped again and took another sip. I could hear the river quietly flowing by and the light wind in the trees. I was also conscious of the small racket being made by the birds overhead as they attacked the fruits in the mango tree. Yet my mind continued its labour, putting pieces in place as regards my family, and in particular Sattou. No wonder he was practically white in colour, I thought. No wonder no one ever spoke of his father. No wonder aunt Shirley was so removed from our family. And no wonder there was this special relationship between him and Mr. Penniston. But Mr. Penniston just admitted that he disliked Sattou when he was a boy. So when did his relationship to him change? What caused that change?

As if reading my mind, Mr. Penniston continued, "Yes, Sattou is a magnificent boy, just like his father, and thanks to that, I am here with you today."

"What do you mean?" I asked.

"Well, it is like this. One evening I was returning home from this very farm and had to cross the river down at the bottom of the village where yo' see they have the bridge. In those days there was no bridge there, and we crossed on a huge tree trunk which was laid from one bank of the river to the next. Now, on that evening it was raining all day, so I could not do much work on the land but stayed in the watch house. I had a good battle ah white rum and with nothing else to do, I sat down and had a few drinks well. So, by evening when I was ready to go home, I was tight like wedge. As I tried to cross on the tree trunk, me foot slip and I tumbled over in the river. I was sure I was dead, 'cause with all the rum I did done drink and the river heavy from all the rain during the day, I couldn't battle it. This had happened to many a man before and we found their bodies three or four days later, out ah sea. So I thought that my hour had come and this was my fate.

"But from nowhere came Sattou, jumped in the river and battling the current, got me to the bank and so save me life. He then realise that I was tight and took me home to me gate. And yo' know to this day he never said a word about this to anyone, not even to yo' grandfather. I know because I have never heard anybody in the village mention this. And no offence meant, but you know nigger people and how them mouth does run like river. So, if he did say something, the whole village would ah know. But even you didn't know, and that shows me that he has never told any member of the family. He is a good, good boy. He is more than Sattou The Great, he is Sattou The Magnificent."

We sat and talked for about an hour more. Mr. Penniston explained to me that he reported to my grandfather on me, not because he disliked me, but because he wanted to see me go the right way. He said he respected my grandfather because he was an educated, decent, kind and forgiving man, and that I must always strive to be like him. He said that this stupid idea about black and white don't mix is a thing of the past and he made a mistake with Sattou and Shirley, and he was going to remedy it.

"So, all this land you see here, is not my land. No Sir. This land belong to my grandson, Sattou The Magnificent. I done make the will and the wife agree with me totally. I don't want you to tell him, he must find out when I dead and gone. So you promise not to say anything?"

"I promise," I said.

"Good boy. This is the least that I could do for a grandson who everybody say is a copy of me in everything."

As he said that, I looked at him closely and was suddenly amazed that I had not seen it before. Mr. Penniston was just a very old version of Sattou. I put my hand to my mouth and fell into deep thought. It struck me that this was the truth that Sattou had spent his life from age seven to now, trying to find. The truth that caused him to travel all over the region trying to get to England or Aruba where he believed it was to be found. It was because of his search for this truth that he almost lost his left hand and indeed his life. And he is still searching, searching for a truth which is just on the other side of the river, just on the bank opposite that on which he grew up. He was searching all over the world for something which was right under his nose, as my mother would say. He just didn't know it. And now I have been given the key to end his search, to reveal to him his own secret. The question was how.

I couldn't help thinking, was Mr. Penniston trying to apologise to my family through me? Did he want me to help patch things up between him and Sattou? Why didn't he approach Sattou himself? What are my grandfather's true views of Mr. Penniston? And why doesn't Mr. Penniston simply apologise to my grandfather?

And the questions continued as I pondered on what I should do. Should I tell Sattou, and if so how? Did my mother know this story and if so, why hasn't she said anything? Why didn't my grandfather say something? Is this why aunt Shirley never comes home from Trinidad to visit? The questions were a million and I didn't know where to turn for answers. But, with all these thoughts running through my head, I realised that there was a pressing need for old man Penniston to unburden his soul to his grandson, and the more I thought of this, the more my own soul became burdened.

"Mr. Penniston," I said, "excuse me for asking. But did you ever try talking to uncle Sattou about this? Did you ever tell him that you are his grandfather?"

"Charlie my boy, the truth is that what I did was so wrong and I am so ashamed that I don't know how to approach the subject with him. I done write his father and tell him that he should come home and we should go to your family together and settle this once and for all. But the truth is I am really ashamed of what I have done, for when all is said and done, Sattou is me blood, and blood thicker than water."

After about another five minutes, I got up to take my leave. I thanked Mr. Penniston and told him that his story was safe with me. He said it didn't matter if I told anyone. The only thing he wanted kept secret was the inheritance, for he wanted it to be a surprise to The Magnificent. As I started to jump the stones to get back on our side of the river he shouted, "Charlie! Charlie!" I turned around and looked in his direction. "Say good evening to the old man for me," I nodded and waited, for I could tell that he wasn't finished. I was right. "Yo' could call me Pen O if yo' wish. I think that is a nice name. I would like for yo' to call me Pen O if yo' don't mind." I nodded, waved and continued my navigation to the other side.

Richard A. Byron-Cox

Lord Orator in the Calypso Tent

Finally, there I was, actually sitting in a Calypso Tent. Waiting. Waiting to experience this feeling that so many others had spoken about with such humour, love, and intoxicating passion. I was bubbling with so much excitement that I felt that my heart would burst open if they didn't start the show soon. I could sense that it wasn't just me who was filled with this air of expectancy. It was the entire theatre. It was as if we were all awaiting something that would give release to our beings, release to our very souls.

Everybody seemed happy just from being in the place. There was a natural gaiety in everything and everyone. It was as if we all knew from here onwards, there could be nothing but relaxation and entertainment to fill, not just the head and heart, but every vein and artery. I can't say for sure why the other people were all in such a mood. As for me, this was the result of a love affair with calypso that began in my childhood. And, being in the Tent was the realisation of a dream I had from since I was little more than an infant. A dream, which until this moment was a cherished hope that I thought, might never come to pass.

My uncles and the books that I had read on the subject, gave varying accounts as to how calypso tents were first formed. They were all interesting, but also very conflicting one with the other. And while I found them, notwithstanding their differences, very intriguing, what really conditioned my love affair with the world of calypsos; what made me feel the rhythms and life of the songs without, in some cases, ever having heard one beat, or note of the music, or one verse or line of the lyrics, were the stories my uncles told of the tents and what took place there. They made it into an unbelievable world of song, music, dance, artistry, theatre, laughter, bacchanal and, above all, joy. Yes, pure and simple joy. And I was about to enter this fascinating world that night for the first time.

The journey to that night and that seat in the House of the Tent began a long time ago. My first recollection puts me at about five years old, and my uncles Sammy and David had come to our house for one of their regular Sunday visits. I remember it as if it were ten minutes ago, for it awoke a cultural element in my soul, which has since then not gone back to sleep.

We were sitting on the front porch of our home, my father, uncles Sammy and David and I, when uncle Sammy started this story. "Dave," he said, "you missed something at Tent last night. This fellow came on stage, saying his name is The Mighty Disappearer. Man, before the music even start up, somebody in the Pit shouted, 'Ah hope you have plenty tricks and good ones too, 'cause ah didn't come to see no magic. But since you is a magic man, show me what you can do. You must be think dis is a circus. Dis is not no circus. Dis is ah Tent!'

"Dave, with that the crowd went wild with laughter. The next thing I hear is the fellow say 'Ouch!' as an old leather boot connected to his forehead. A next voice from the Pit shouted, 'But your disappearing thing is not so mighty at all. Imagine you, ah big time magician, and people lashing you in your face with old shoes. Why you don't disappear before the shoes reach your face?'

"Dave boy, by this time, the whole theatre was roaring, and the MC had to come on stage to try and put some order in the place. He begged the boys in the Pit to 'give the fella a chance, seeing it is his first time.' One man standing in front of the stage, with a dismissive wave of the hand protested, 'What chance? If he want ah chance, make he go buy a bingo.' The crowd joined in, 'Yes, he should buy a bingo.'

"But things calmed down after a while and the band began again. When it was time for the fellow to start singing, he forgot his lines and, Dave, that was the end of him. Somebody in Pit shouted, 'So that is de disappearing thing. All your lyrics disappear? It is time for you too to disappear. When you come next time, you could change your name to Reappear. But for now, your name is Disappear, so please, oblige and live up to your name.' Dave, with that, the Pit started to shout, 'Disappear! Disappear! Disappear!' A minute of that is more than enough for anybody, and the Mighty Disappearer left the stage running from a hail of old shoes and other missiles.

"And guess what? The MC came back and, joining the crowd declared, 'Now I wish all calypsonians would live to their word and name like that fella. He says his name is Disappearer and like this,' he snaps his fingers, 'the fella gone. He good, he real good. If we had a competition tonight, I would have voted him fo' first position. Now lewe move on.'"

By the time uncle Sammy had finished his story, uncle David was holding his right hand over his mouth, laughing and shaking his head from side to side. As for me, I was laughing as if I had lost my mind and wishing I were there in the Tent to see this for myself. Looking back at it now, I suppose I laughed, not because I totally understood the essence of the story. I think it was more because my uncle Sammy had a very uncanny way of relating these things, and also because they were all three, dying of laughter.

When uncle Sammy recovered his composure, uncle David declared, "But Sam, you really wicked you know. You mean the fellow was trying to entertain you and that is the way you all treated him?"

"If he knows he can't sing, why the hell was he on stage? Old people say if you can't stand the heat, stay out of the kitchen. And by the way, whoever hear about a calypso name like Disappearer? Man, the fellow was foolish from the start."

"But, Sam, if it was you, would you want anybody to treat you so?" asked uncle David.

"And that is why I am sticking to sailing. Any singing I doing is when I taking my shower or in the congregation in church," replied uncle Sammy.

"But Sammy, you don't have any heart," said uncle David, still laughing and shaking his head from side to side.

This was my first introduction to the calypso Tent as I recall. I was fascinated and became hooked on these tales from then on. As I got older, I heard more and more stories from my uncles about these tents and all that went on in them. They made it sound like a special world, complete on its own, where everything was done differently from the one I knew. It sounded like a place where people fed their spirits and their hearts and as a consequence, their souls were rested.

These stories gave birth to imaginations a plenty on my part as to what the physical structure of a calypso Tent looked like, and the different sections it had. I was to find out later that in fact, the calypso tents were held in one of the cinemas reserved for this purpose during the carnival season. These cinemas were built in exactly the same style of small theatres in Britain at the time, as these islands were still all colonies of that once great power.

There was a section called The Pit which was closest to, and immediately in front of the stage. It was however significantly lower than the stage, thus forcing those seated there to look up, as they were below those performing. This was one, but not the only reason why this section of the Tent was called such an undignified and belittling name. It had seats which were just hard long benches like the ones we sat on in primary school, only much, much longer and much rougher. It was parted in the middle by a very narrow aisle, and the only limit in terms of patrons Pit knew, was that they stopped taking in people when it was ram cram like a sealed tin of sardines.

The Pit was the place where the poor and bad-behaved went. These were patrons intent on providing additional entertainment to the rest of the theatre by heckling the calypsonians with sharp criticisms, and/or by pelting them with eggs, old shoes and tin cans. More dangerous missiles were used when the situation warranted it, which was usually when the Pit crowd was upset. Many would-have-been calypsonians never got beyond the first verse of their first calypso, owing to the heckling and torpedoes that came from The Pit.

Those were the days when The Pit was the place where everything, anything, anytime by anyone was allowed. It was a place where to sit there you couldn't only be bad, but you had to be brave as well, and be willing to back up your mouth with action. My uncle Sammy told of a Pit episode where a young man's mouth caused him a serious licking.

I remember it was the day Miss Rosetta, our neighbour, was raising the roof of her house to allow better runoff of the rainwater, which was leaking through the roof. My uncles Sammy and Leon had gone with my father to help her that Sunday, following an age-old tradition where neighbours give assistance to each other in situations like those, absolutely free of cost. When the work was finished, they came over to our house to have a drink with my father. Uncle Sammy had gone to Tent the Friday night before and couldn't resist giving my father the full account.

"Fredrick boy, this Tent season is something else. It have good songs, nice music and fun for all who dead. Look Leon there; Barman nearly kill me last night."

My dad, thinking that uncle Sammy had had a quarrel with Barman, looked at him with a measure of surprise. "Sammy, you're crazy, what you want to fight with that brute for?" Barman was the strongest man in that part of town. Besides being naturally built strong with a muscular big-bodied frame, he worked as a small farmer ploughing his land manually with the assistance of a 5P iron hoe. This he did in the boiling heat of the Caribbean, from sun up until sun down. Fighting Barman was like challenging a very strong ox in his prime.

"No Fredrick, don't misunderstand. I didn't have any quarrel with Barman. You think I stupid? It is Barman dealing with the foolishness of a country boy that nearly killed me with laughter."

"Yes," joined in Leon laughing, "I think he must have been from country. No Town man will see Barman liming in a crowd and challenge any member of that crowd."

"So what happened?" asked my father.

"You tell him Leon because sometimes I tell Freddy these things and he thinks it's joke I making. You tell him Leon," commanded uncle Sammy.

"Sam, you know I can't tell things the way you do. You tell him. Go ahead, you tell him."

"All right, all right," agreed uncle Sammy. "Freddy boy, last night we decided that we wanted to try The Pit. Now, knowing how rough it can be down there, we decided that we would go in a group. So we invited Barman, Tyrone, Topaz, Bogzie, Trini and some of the other fellows. You know, the regular crowd that we lime with down by the shop. When we got in, we chose a bench and sat down all together. But Bogzie came late when the bench was already full. As you can expect, he decided that he was not going to sit on a different bench for Pit is a wild place. So we jam up and squeeze up and give him a little space on our bench.

"Little after halfway in the show, this fellow who was sitting at one end of our bench, got up and went outside. Well, we all use the opportunity to make ourselves comfortable. Two twos, the fellow came back in with a bag of popcorn and, finding no place to sit down, demanded his seat. Well, nobody move. He then demanded that Bogzie should get up, for Bogzie was in his seat."

"Not just that," joined in uncle Leon, "you should hear him; 'Gee me me seat! Ah want me seat! Get yo' so and so out ah me seat,' making one big commotion in the place, you would think he is the biggest bad-John in Town."

"That fellow didn't see that you all were with Barman or what?" asked my father.

"This is why I say that he was from the country," answered uncle Sammy. "For it would have to be a mad Town man to see you with Barman and tackle you. And, Freddy, the fellow went further declaring, 'Gee me me seat or we go have trouble here tonight! Big trouble!' Now the moment he said trouble, it became a different ball game altogether. Suddenly I heard Barman's voice booming from the other end of the bench. 'What happening down dey?' 'You shut up!' responded the fellow, 'Who call you?'

"Now Freddy, you know that nobody tells Barman shut up and doesn't expect to pay for it. Barman got up, walked over to the fellow, and without a word burst one slap in the fellow face. The slap spin him round a complete 360 degrees, causing him to drop the popcorn in the process. Before anyone could fathom what was happening, Barman burst another slap in the fellow face and spin him round a complete 360 degrees again. This time, he spin him from the opposite direction. He then took the fellow neck under his right arm, asked Bogzie to move up a bit and sat down quietly with the fellow under his arm kicking and screaming, trying his best to get away.

"Everybody got up, but Barman immediately ordered us to take our seats. So we sat down again. There were three more songs on the cast, and Barman held his captive for those three songs, eating the remainder of fellow's popcorn that didn't spill out of the bag when it fell on the ground."

By this time, my father had the hiccups from laughing and had to beg my uncle Sammy for mercy. "Lord........ Sammy .... Give me.... a break," he said, stopping after each word due to interruptions caused by the hiccups.

I had the hiccups too and couldn't help myself. I thought I would die of laughter. Uncle Leon, seeing my discomfort, became a bit concerned and asked me if I was alright. I assured him I was. But my mother, on hearing uncle Leon's concern, came out and, seeing the state I was in and that of my father, ordered me to go and drink some water, and get a glass for my father as well. Even though I was having the time of my life and didn't want to lose any of the fun, my mother's commands could never be postponed. I dashed off and was back in a flash, hoping that I didn't miss any of the story. I returned to hear uncle Leon urging uncle Sammy to continue his tale.

"But the story is not finished," he said, "Sam, tell him what happened next."

"No Sammy, not yet," pleaded my father, "please remember I have your sister and my children to feed. At least, allow me to drink the water." With that, my father took the glass of water from me and drank the entire thing in one go. His hiccups disappeared. Returning the glass to me, he turned to uncle Sammy and asked, "So what happened next?"

"Well, I doubt anybody in our row heard the first of the last three songs for the noise the fellow was making as he struggled, trying to free himself from Barman's iron grip. Ever so often, the fellow would shout, 'Lemme go! Lemme go!' But Barman sat down eating the fellow popcorn as if he was having a quiet Sunday evening stroll. At one point, he gave Trini the popcorn to hold, clout the fellow hard in the middle of his head with his left hand, asking him, 'What happen, is stupid you stupid? You don't know if you continue to wiggle that you go break yo' own neck?'

"With that the fellow quiet down and we were able to listen to the last two songs and the close of the show. The MC did not forget to thank Barman 'fo' showing those poorly brought up ghetto people how fo' behave themselves in ah Tent of class.'

"With the show over, Barman released the fellow. He made a rush for the closest door which already had a crowd slowly leaving the cinema. He must have thought that Barman was chasing him and so tried to climb on two persons' back to get out. Needless to say, those men held onto the poor young man and started to pelt box and kick like they mad. A war nearly broke out in the place. Barman had to step in and stop the people from bad-beating the fellow, hold his hand and carry him out of the place."

"Tell me…uh…it's a joke," said my father, his voice getting hoarse from the laughter, and his hiccups having returned.

"What joke?" responded uncle Leon, not giving his brother time to answer.

"Fredrick," said uncle Sammy, "you think Tent is just sitting down and listening to a calypso. Oh no Sir, Tent is much more than that. And Pit is the greatest. It is sometimes a boxing or wrestling ring. It is always an overactive debating society. It is the true nerve centre of the calypso Tent and much more."

"Much, much more," nodded Uncle Leon. "It is a whole spectacle with all kind of characters. Believe everything Sam tells you. It is the gospel truth. Tent is all of Shakespeare and more. I hear English people talk of their theatre, but they need to come to a calypso Tent on this island to understand what acting is all about."

"You can say that again," said my father, speaking between his hiccups. "Especially that Pit section. That is a madhouse."

"Yes, Pit is a place of action. There is not a dull moment down there, as the people would say," said Sammy.

"Well, I know for sure that I am not going back down there," said uncle Leon. "Barman or no Barman, I prefer to keep my distance in House. I am not able with those ruffians. And at the end of the day, in

House there is great fun as well, only without the hooliganism, and I am not a hooligan."

House was that area of the cinema where the middle class and the aspirants to that class sat. In House, you had long rows of single seats and space both in the aisle and between the rows. Its first row was a little way behind the last row of The Pit, with a barrier between them. This first row of House was of a higher gradient than Pit, with every row after it gently rising. This gave House a sloping upwards form so that its last row was way under the overhanging Box and Balcony, and was somewhat higher than the level of the stage.

According to my uncles, while House did not have the great sideshows that were put on in The Pit, where everything, anything, anytime by anyone was allowed, it still had wonderful off-stage entertainment. It had many stories of its own, including one they told about a young female lawyer, Jenny Sampson.

It happened that this Jenny Sampson had just come back from London, and, wanting to enjoy her first carnival after about five years in the cold, broke with family tradition of sitting in Balcony or Box. She elected to sit in House to be closer to the little sideshows in House and the action, both on stage and in Pit. To make sure she was in the mood, she had a few beers and, feeling right, she stepped into the Tent.

As things got hot, Jenny Sampson started to enjoy herself with her posse. More beers began to flow and with each additional bottle, Jenny Sampson's temperature rose higher. This first became noticeable when she began shouting at each performer, her approval or disapproval.

She followed that up with standing on her seat in a bid to command as much attention as possible. And she would laugh hilariously at almost every word uttered by the MC, joke or not. All was still under control until the Mighty Stinger came on stage to perform his hit song 'Show them how to do it'.

This was a song about a crazy woman who had come to carnival and decided to show the public how to bacchanal. In the first verse of the song, the woman instructs the revellers to jump up and down. In the second verse, she finds a partner and together they demonstrate to all, the steps of a new dance called 'The drunk and disorderly'. In the third verse, she does everything and anything with everyone and anyone. And in the final verse, she decides to undress, declaring that she wants to have everybody dressed in the costume of nature so that they could win band of the year.

By the time the Mighty Stinger hit the stage, Jenny Sampson clearly had had a beer or two, too many. These convinced her that she not only could, but should demonstrate to the crowd in House all the steps of the song. She decided to play the role of the crazy woman. She began by jumping up and down on her chair, waving the red carnival cap she was wearing. Then she started shouting to everyone instructions as to what to do and how to move. By this time, she was commanding as much attention in House as the Mighty Stinger himself was commanding on stage. He, realising this, advised the crowd that the crazy woman was presently in the Tent and giving a performance right now in House. This brought even more attention to Jenny

Sampson as people now wanted to see who this crazy woman was. Some of the people in Pit turned around and stared at Jenny Sampson. Others started beckoning to her to leave House and join the Mighty Stinger on stage. The whole Pit seemed extremely happy that somebody from the hoity-toity crowd in House really could let go herself and bacchanal in the Tent the way they do.

Not satisfied with giving instructions, Jenny Sampson decided to show the Tent the moves with a partner. At this same time the beers decided it was time to make a final surge. Jenny Sampson held on to a young man sitting in a neighbouring seat, trying to pull him up onto her seat to accompany her in doing the drunk and disorderly. The young man gently resisted. That was enough to knock Jenny Sampson off balance. She fell off the chair flat on her face. As she tried to get up, she fell down twice more and really could not help herself much. The beers were now working overtime and fully in charge of poor Jenny.

Jenny Sampson's friends finally helped her up and, despite her protests, took her straight home. This was an embarrassment to their class, and horror was written all over their faces. Many a man in the Tent that night, including my uncles, were very disappointed that she fell down before the Mighty Stinger got to the final verse of the calypso. They started a great protest when her friends began taking her out of the Tent, "But how all yo' could do that? She still had the last verse to go. Mek she stay and show we how fo' dance that verse."

For the next few years, the Jenny Sampson story became part of Tent folklore. And as things go in the Caribbean, when people tell stories recalling events of this nature, they always add their personal spices to make it hotter and more sensational. So, if anyone were to tell you this story today, Jenny Sampson is simply an unbelievable character. There are those who would swear that she was only removed from the Tent at the end of the fourth verse of the calypso, clad only in her birth suit. And, it is still common nowadays when a young woman goes to a Tent and misbehaves too much in House, to hear people enquire: "Ah who that, Jenny Sampson?"

My uncles also related many of House's other sideshows, including one where a fight broke out between two women. By the end of it, they were both virtually naked, with the men in House and Pit shouting, "Finish de business! Finish de business! You can't leave with unfinished business!"

Even though it did not have the life and naturalness of Pit with its direct involvement in what was happening on the stage, House was not distant or glass-cased from the rest of the Tent as Balcony and Box were. My uncles said that only the "impressionists" went to these two areas. They were physically detached from the Tent in that these were upraised pavilions towering over House, and looking down upon The Pit and the stage with little more than contempt. My uncle Sammy was of the view that, "Generally speaking, the true Tent and calypso lovers did not frequent the Box or Balcony. They were places full of false

English pride and ignorant English prejudice. And English people can't sing calypso."

With each passing carnival and each story my uncles told, I, unlike my father and mother, got more and more interested in the Tents. But there could be no question of my mother allowing her under-aged son to attend a Tent. And even if she did, it was very possible that there was no way I would get in. I was told, that much of what was said and done in the Tents, were not for the ears and eyes of children, in particular, one being brought up in the "fear of the Lord."

Still, when I was fourteen, my uncles pleaded with my mother to send me, if only for the experience. But their sister would have none of it. She insisted that she couldn't knowingly encourage her children to do things displeasing in the sight of the Lord. She was determined that her sons would not turn out like her brothers, if she could help it. Because, for all the efforts of her mother, her four brothers were all hopeless sinners.

On occasions like these, with my mother refusing to budge on her religious principles, my uncles would immediately begin talking about the self-righteousness of some people. This was aimed more at teasing my mother about her iron stance than discrediting her. They would always hold such conversations as if my mother was some incomprehensible being.

"Sammy, I tired telling you to leave Ms. Holier-than-thou," uncle David would say.

"But you can't see the girl running the house like a monastery," uncle Sammy would reply. "I don't know how my brother-in-law could stay married to this nun." He would continue speaking of his sister as if she was a complete stranger and not within earshot.

"You better watch your mouth when you speaking about me in front of my children in my house," my mother would respond, pretending to be more annoyed than she really was.

"I don't know what that woman would have done if my brother-in-law hadn't married to her," uncle Sammy would sometimes say, and then he, uncle David and my father would laugh loudly, further annoying my mother.

"Your brother-in-law and his sons would be like you two and my two other brothers if it wasn't for me. They would be going to Tent, drinking rum and carrying on, and then going to other people's homes and trying to encourage their husbands and children to follow them in this immoral behaviour. And if that is not shameful enough, they would pick specially on their sister's family. You two have no shame!" By this time, all three men would be laughing uncontrollably.

My mother would usually not argue too much with her brothers on these matters. The truth was, she knew that none of them would dare seriously challenge her position regarding this or any other decision which she had taken in the interest of the "proper and God-fearing upbringing of her children." On these matters her word was final!

She came from that age when Caribbean women knew nothing about women's rights; were not concerned with bellowing from the top of the hill how strong they were; and were indeed not as well represented in the professions as they are today. But yet, it was an age that mothered the development of our greatest leaders, and the advancement of the Caribbean in every imaginable way. My mother was no different.

I spent the years between five and seventeen dreaming of going to Tent. But I knew that this would only be over my mother's "dead body", as she put it. She would not hear any arguments that this was part of our culture and such nonsense, as she termed it. No Sir! For her, this was a sin and therefore wrong in the sight of God.

My father never protested against any of these stringent rules. And in all honesty, I think my uncles protested not because they fundamentally disagreed with her, but simply to tease her. She was younger than they and was their only sister. They all had a soft spot somewhere for her, and she and they knew it.

But at seventeen, one year before the maternal decree outlawing my attendance at Tent was to be officially rescinded, fate was kind to me. My long-held dream of going to Tent was realised.

It came to pass that my maternal grandmother got sick and had to have treatment in England. Yes, those were the days when England was still mother country to us in everything, including medicine, and those who could afford it wanted everything from the motherland. Those were the days when demonstrated affinity to the "superior culture" and "refined and educated taste" of the mother country determined your class and social status. Our society was unconsciously consistently rejecting itself.

With Holy Mary gone and only my less than religious father to deal with, I muscled up the courage to approach him on the subject of my going to Tent.

"Daddy, I think uncle Sammy might not be home for Tent this year."

"Why you say that?" he asked.

"Well, his ship is not coming here in the next two months."

"Who told you that?"

"Ron."

"How Ron knows that?"

"His mummy says so."

"Too bad, I hear there are some real good tunes this year. If your uncle was here we would have heard some stories. He would be in the tents first word."

I immediately saw my opportunity and decided to press home the advantage.

"But we could go and see for ourselves. I mean, with you there and thing, I am sure we would be safe."

"Me? No way! Me! Not me! Next thing somebody sees me and come tell your mother when she comes from England. No Sir, not me, for she would say she just turned her back and I am leading her children astray. No Sir, I am not going to no Tent."

My heart sank and I racked my brains for my next sentence, when my father rejoined, "But does Ron go to Tent?"

"Excuse me, what did you say?" I asked.

"Ron, does he go to the Tent?"

"Sure, he went last year with uncle Sammy."

"No. Not so. I mean if he goes on his own, after all, he is what now, twenty or twenty-one?"

"He is nearly twenty-one, and yes, he goes to the Tent on his own."

"I wish it could be more like Sammy with his boys between me and you. But your mother will kill me if she found out that I took you to Tent. Why don't you see if Ron is going and you go with him?"

"You mean it?"

"Yes, I can see you are dying to go to the Tent, and I agree that we should use this opportunity of the absence of your mother for you to do so." I was ecstatic.

And so it was settled. I would go to Tent with my cousin Ron. My conversation with my father was on Thursday evening and the next Tent session was the following day, so my wait wasn't long.

Tent usually began at 8:00 p.m. By 5:30 p.m. I was ready and waiting for Ron, even though we lived in the city about a mile away from the theatre where the Tent was being held. When Ron did not appear at 6:00 p.m., I informed my father that I was going over to uncle

Sammy's to meet him. My father tried to impress upon me that it was quite early. I explained that Ron had told me that there was going to be a big crowd and it was better to be early as we had to get tickets. He reminded me that we were to stay away from The Pit. I gave my word of honour that we would, and was off.

I met Ron liming with Heads, Midnight, Sanks, Socks, Sandy Bay, Country, Bones and Que Pasa. They were Ron's neighbourhood posse, as they all lived in that area which was called Back Road. Those names were not the given names of these boys, but were all aliases or nicknames, something quite normal in those days.

Ron himself was called Priest, a nickname he got because of the fact that he was an altar boy in the Anglican church, the religion of our entire family. I was called Little Jesus for my regular church attendance. I did not know why Sanks and Que Pasa were given those aliases. Midnight was called thus because he was very dark in complexion and was deemed blacker than midnight. Socks, on the other hand, was very light in complexion. But he had had measles and chicken pox as a child, which had left some terrible looking dark marks on his feet and legs, making it appear that he was always wearing a pair of black socks.

Bones' real name was Curtis. He ate a lot and was always prepared to eat anything and everything. Yet he was extremely thin. Sandy Bay and Country were rechristened for the same reason, their origin. They both came from Sandy Bay, a village at the extreme north of the island. When Country arrived in the neighbourhood, his first interaction with the boys was in a game of cricket. He proved himself to be a very good batsman. When asked where he was from he responded, "Me come fram country," and that was it, he was rechristened.

When I arrived, the talk was all about the Tent that night and which calypsonians were expected to give the crowd worth for their money. As I entered the gate, Ron looked up. "Brie, you early man," he said.

"Well, I wasn't sure what time you would leave so I decided to be on time," I replied.

"Fellas, you all know Brie my cousin, right?"

They all acknowledged me in one way or the other. Either with a "Yeer", "How yo' do?", "Yes man" or just a nod of the head. I noticed that nobody called me Little Jesus.

"Anyway, it's good you came now, for I think we would have to leave earlier than planned," said Ron. "Tonight is going to be a hot night with some good songs. Somebody told me that Lord Orator has a good number this year."

"That me hear," said Heads. "Me also hear that they have some new fellas in the Tent that go park up them old men once and fo' all," he continued.

"Somebody say that the Mighty Breeder coming with something strong, and he stand a good chance of making the crown this year," said Sanks.

"But Breeder is not singing in this Tent tonight," interjected Ron. "He is with the Conquerors Tent this year."

"Say way all yo' want, my Road March man this year is Lord Orator," said Midnight. He knew it was difficult for any of the others to argue with him, for unlike them, he used to go to the band rooms where all the calypsonians rehearsed their songs. He therefore had heard most of the songs long before they were released to the public. He had also heard the comments of the musicians and other calypsonians on this or that song. "And the man have stage presence and know how fo' use the stage," he assured.

"Man, I waiting until I get there to make any judgement. It have 'bout fifteen man singing tonight, and a calypsonian is a calypsonian," announced Sanks.

"Sanks you right. Is plenty man singing, so lewe wait," said Que Pasa.

All calypsonians had stage names which all had a handle to them. This was usually either Mighty or Lord. So Breeder was not just Breeder but "The Mighty Breeder," and Orator was "Lord Orator" and so on. According to my uncles, these handles had two explanations. Calypso singing was always a competition and all calypsonians wanted to show they had special prowess as regards writing, singing and performing. They wanted to show that they could not be intimidated or conquered by their opponents. So every singer was mighty or a lord. Secondly, the islands were all part of the so-called British Empire where a lord wasn't too far from the monarchy itself. And in the Caribbean of those years, to be "lord and master" meant to have the ultimate authority. Calypsonians therefore had no problems in making themselves lords, if only on the stage. But this also spoke to a fact which still holds true today. The tremendous influence British colonialism had and still has on these islands.

These stage names of the calypsonians usually had some story behind them. The Mighty Breeder chose his stage name as he had eighteen children with his wife and about sixty with other women. His village felt that he was the greatest breeder they had produced and called him thus. He, being proud of his accomplishments, took his nickname to the stage, simply adding the handle "Mighty."

"Boy, ah looking out fo' de Mighty Builder dis year. That man always ha' something serious and ah think this year is his year," said Sandy Bay, in the most authoritative voice he could.

"Builder is a good calypsonian, but is better he renamed himself the Mighty Buster," said Socks, "if that man could only learn to sing a tune without messing it up, he would have already won the crown a long time ago."

"I agree with Socks," continued Ron, "that man needs to learn to overcome stage fright and the crowd in The Pit."

"What stage fright yo' talking 'bout Priest?" questioned Sandy Bay impatiently. "The man know how fo' handle de stage."

"Yes, he can handle the stage, but his problem is language, just like you Bay, Builder can't talk properly; the man need dictation," said Socks.

"And who is you fo' talk? Pot always want fo' tell kittle he backside black. Yo' behaving as if yo' could talk any better," came the vehement response of Sandy Bay.

"The word is not talk, Bay boy, the word is speak. And I could speak better than you and Builder any day. I was borned in town. Please notice that I correctly add on the 'ed'. And I was bred in town. My whole family from town and you is ah country man."

This last statement by Socks seemed to have offended Country, for he immediately responded. "Socks, you an' Bay ha' thing, way yo' have to call all country people name in dat fo'. Man, keep yo' thing between you and Bay and leave out country people."

"Ok, ok," I said, "the issue is not about country and town. The issue is what really is the best calypso."

"Brie, you better don't get mixed up in the stupidity of Socks and Bay," said Ron jokingly. "These two are too stupid for their own good."

"But I agree with yo' Little J. De better calypso is de important thing," said Sandy Bay, clearly happy that I had come to his rescue. "So who yo' backing this year?" he continued.

"Me, I want to hear what Lord Pretty coming with this year," I said.

"No wonder," said Socks, "you pretty-up, pretty-up. You think is church you going in new jeans and new plaid shirt. Is only a Calypso Tent and nothing more."

"Shut up Socks!" the stern rebuke came from Ron. "My family don't wear jeans and plaid shirt to church. Know your place!"

"Priest boy, what make you so touchy. I was only making a joke with Little J," said Socks apologetically.

"Know your place! That is what I told you!" commanded Ron.

"Alright, alright, I don't know why the people of your family are so untouchable but..." He stopped halfway in the sentence for Ron had sent an "I-dare-you gaze" in his direction, which he had no answer to.

At that moment, there was a sound at the gate and we all looked in that direction to see Ron's mother entering. She was arriving from the hospital where she worked as a nurse.

"Good evening boys."

"Good evening Miss Peters," came the choir response. I followed a second or two later with my, "Good evening aunt Bev."

"Brie, what you doing here and all dressed up?" she demanded. This brought a smile to Socks' face, but it was erased as quickly as it had appeared due to a sharp rebuking glance from Ron.

"He going to the Tent with me tonight," said Ron.

"What you mean he going to the Tent with you?" enquired his mother, her surprise genuine. "You gone crazy young man?"

"No. Uncle Fredrick called me and asked me to take him."

"Don't tell me that Fredrick has suddenly lost his mind to be sending his son to that nest of vice!" said a disbelieving aunt Beverly, her hands now akimbo.

"Yes aunt Beverly, Daddy has allowed me to go with Ron," I confirmed.

"Well, your father sure must have lost his mind. Let's hope Amy don't find out when she comes back, because Brie, you and Fredrick would not hear the end of this. She just turned her back, and Fredrick sending you to Tent. I don't believe it."

"But Ma, is not as if he going alone and is not as if he going to get into trouble," protested Ron.

"Well, for the sake of this family, I hope you are right. And if anything happen to him, I am holding you Ron personally responsible. You hear what I say?"

"All right Ma, all right. You behaving as if I taking Brie to hell. It is only a calypso Tent."

Aunt Beverly stood and stared at Ron for a few of seconds, evidently searching for the proper response. And seeming to find nothing better, she said, "A calypso tent is no place for self-respecting people." With that, she entered the house, denying Ron any chance of a response.

We spent less than fifteen minutes more at Ron's home. With the arrival of his mom, he seemed suddenly impatient to get out of the house and get going to the Tent. I was glad of this, for all the time we spent chatting, I was doing the best I could to hide my impatience and what Caribbean people call my "never-see-come-see" attitude. I was simply tired of this unnecessary delay. My entire circulatory system was pregnant with impatience, for this after all was my first Tent.

Ron got dressed and we left and ambled on to the Tent. On the way, we passed by Howell's rum shop where they bought six bottles of Strong Rum. When I saw that, I immediately regretted my decision to go to Tent. Going to a calypso show was one thing; hanging out with boys who drank Strong Rum was another altogether. My mother was a God-fearing woman who abhorred rum drinking by anyone, not to mention one of her sons. I felt that my mother would be most upset if she were to ever find this out, and that she would unjustly blame my father for something he knew nothing about. I suddenly felt that I had betrayed my parents and my father's trust in particular.

Ron, probably realising what was going through my mind, declared, "As all of you know, Brian does not drink alcohol, so I don't want anybody trying to force him into this. Understand?"

"Ah always say that Christian people should stay out ah calypso business," commented Sandy Bay.

"And I always say that country people should learn how to speak before them open them mouth and make a fool of themself," retorted Socks.

"Fellas," said Ron, "Brie is not a drinking man and that's that. Ok?"

"So what happen to yo' Little J, yo' don't have yo own mouth fo' talk fo' yo' self?" asked Sandy Bay.

"And am I not weary telling you is not talk, that the word is speak," responded Socks.

"Ok, the both of you shut up right now! It is not your business if Brie drinks or not." said Ron with an air of absolute authority and finality. There was an immediate silence and it was not the first time that I envied Ron's authority and power over others. He was a mere three years my senior, yet he commanded the respect of men in their twenties. So much so that he actually ordered them about.

He then proceeded to explain to me on the side. "Listen Brie; don't you worry about the rum. We like to have a little drink to get in the mood for the Tent. Tent Brie, is a place not only of calypso, but real ruction, and a little rum help to lighten your head. You know what I mean?" I nodded to show that I understood, all the while thinking that my mother would have classified Ron and his friends as a bunch of "rough necks", even though they were all about my age or little older, and had never done any crime. But the fact that they were allowed this great freedom by their parents to attend things like carnival shows and tents, and that they drank Strong Rum would have made them all, in her opinion, seasoned graduates of the street, well on their way to becoming vagabonds.

As we walked to the Tent, Sandy Bay tried to resurrect his earlier debate with Socks about the Mighty Builder. "But Priest," he began, "yo' see de problem I have with Socks is that he always know everything, 'bout everybody. Now he saying that Builder is..."

"Bay, I thought I told you to shut your trap," came the curt response of Ron.

I think Ron was capable of ordering his peers about for, unlike me, he was tall and physically very strong. My mother did not consider him particularly bright, but my dad thought that he was a gifted and smart boy who would go a long way in life. With time, my father's opinion proved to be right.

On arriving at the Tent, I was almost full to the brim with excitement. The atmosphere outside the theatre was like that at a grand fair. Everywhere there were people drinking; discussing; getting their money to buy tickets; begging others for a "make up" to purchase their tickets; playing different betting games, some of cards, others with dice, and still others with boards. There were vendors with their trays where you could buy from sweets and corn curls to parched nuts and Strong Rum. There were quarter-steel drums packed with ice for cooling beers, stouts and other alcoholic drinks of any and every description, while their owners tried to convince potential customers to buy.

The women were dressed in all kinds of fashions and styles, and the young men looked relaxed yet energised and excited. Everyone, regardless of how they were dressed or what they were doing, had one thing in common. They were all full of exuberance. One could feel in the air that this was the build-up to something else, something far greater, far more captivating. A climax was waiting in the air to descend.

For me, this was indeed a new world, a world of night life where people ate fresh oranges. In my family, no one ate oranges at night. A world where everyone seemed to be drinking alcohol and every space in the theatre's yard seemed to be occupied with some sort of activity. Ninety percent of my own crowd were by this time quite tipsy. But not Ron. He was as sober as Saint Paul, and as serious as an enraged bull when he gave Sandy Bay the money to buy the tickets. He was also most precise in giving his instructions.

"Bay, if they ask any question, tell them that you are buying tickets for Sammy and David Peters and their friends. If they still not selling you, then call me. Whatever you do, don't go arguing with the cashier or anything like that. We have to show that we are real gentlemen tonight. You understand?" Sandy Bay assured him that he did and left us with the money in hand.

Many years later, Ron explained that he could not and did not indulge in the drinking and carrying on with the boys. He had insisted on the gentlemanly behaviour because my father had called him earlier in the afternoon and let him know what would be the consequence, should my first outing in a Tent become a spectacle. He said that the problem was not really my dad, but his aunt, Holy Mary, Mother of Jesus. We had both laughed then, but looking back now, we realise that my mother was indeed a stern drill sergeant. Everybody had to fall in line when she gave the command.

Sandy Bay did not have any problems in securing the tickets and came running back full of smiles. He handed them over to Ron who distributed them and we entered the theatre.

So, there I was, seated next to Ron, upon his instructions, in the second row in House, that is, counting from Pit backwards. He said this was the best place in the Tent as you got the full blast of everything from the Pit. He wasn't wrong. I observed that there was going to be a very good crowd as House and Pit were practically full and patrons were still pouring in. The musicians were already warmed up, and each was doing his own thing on his respective instrument, waiting for the MC to call the proceedings to order.

As we waited for the show to begin, my restless enquiring eyes kept darting crazily from one place to the other, trying to capture all the activity and excitement happening everywhere. The difference in the behaviour of the people in Pit from all others was very noticeable. They shouted to one another from one side to the other and conducted themselves with absolute freedom, uninhibited by space, time, company or occasion. They were totally at home, behaving as if they knew one another so well, that there was no need for pretence.

In House, you got the impression that people weren't sure whether they wanted to join the "bad behaviour" of The Pit, or maintain their distance. They were certainly less noisy and less rambunctious, and were better dressed and manicured. The young ladies all seemed to have just received barrels from Brooklyn as the latest in back-out, belly-out and miniskirts among other fashions were on display. These people all seemed to be drinking beers and eating popcorn while maintaining some aimless and meaningless chatter. I had the impression that they knew they were being watched and so were putting on a show for the occasion. I somehow felt out of place.

The stage was well lit, while the lights in the rest of the theatre were slightly dimmed. This helped to enhance the central place of the stage. There were young men with baskets of parched nuts, popcorn, sweets and the like, moving up and down the aisle of House encouraging patrons to get their nuts, popcorns and sweets before the show started.

I was so engrossed in the study of these intriguing surroundings that the entrance on stage of the MC completely eluded me. There was a sudden drum roll and a booming voice said, "Welcome to the Tent, ladies and gentlemen. How all yo' feeling tonight? Everybody all right?" The stage immediately grabbed my attention.

The crowd roared the MC a welcome on stage and Ron explained to me that this was Phil Robertson, better known as Spoon Head. He was one of the Caribbean's best stand-up comedians. I had of course heard a lot about him but had never seen him before that moment. As was the custom, Phil Robertson began the show by cracking a few jokes to get the crowd in the mood for the evening.

"Ladies and gentlemen, and River Mouth dey so, in the rough-dry blue shirt," he said, pointing to a man in the first row in Pit. "Gentlemen does listen when other people talking, so give yo' mouth a rest. Yes, as I was saying, ladies and gentlemen, yesterday I hear two fellas arguing about which letter is the most important letter in the English alphabet. Ah third fella jump in the argument and shout out that the first 33 letters is the most important." The crowd broke into laughter. Before the laughter could die down, the MC continued, "All yo' see Piggy not laughing for this joke. That is because he illiterate. He ain't know that the English alphabet only have 26 letters." The audience roared.

Phil Robertson continued for another five minutes or so and had the whole place in an uproar. Our group was laughing so much that we were sometimes out of breath. Even so, I couldn't help wondering what my mother would have said if she knew that I was in the Tent laughing at what she would consider less than clean and proper humour.

Phil Robertson then moved to explaining what the cast was, and warned the bad boys in The Pit to behave themselves. With the crowd charged up and ready for action, we got on our way with an opening number from the Mighty Razor. He got the full attention of the audience with a song entitled "I mashing them up this carnival." He came on stage with a huge hammer and from the moment the music started, he began to jump and prance up and down the stage. He waved the hammer wildly, showing what he would be doing to his opponents in the calypso competition this year. With the people in Pit taking to the song immediately and therefore playing their usual role of supporting cast, he took the Tent almost by storm. Some people got up and danced, enjoying the jumpy beat. Others joined in and sang along with the chorus. All in all, it was an appropriate starting number and I began to look forward to the rest of the show.

Ron explained that there was nothing unusual in the first number being jumpy and catchy. He said that it was the practice of every tent to start with a performance that sets the stage for an interactive show. I never imagined the level of interactivity that I was to witness later.

The show continued and things were going along well enough. Our posse were thoroughly enjoying themselves, with the bottles of Strong Rum being passed up and down the row from one end to the other. Ron's participation in this bottle-passing was to control its frequency, and, to ensure that I was of course, never offered this peace pipe.

After the appearances of six calypsonians, I thought that this was going to be a night of good entertainment, but not one of those specials that my uncles usually talked about. While all the songs were good and got favourable responses, the opening act was still the best up to that point. But everything changed when the MC announced, "Now, ladies and gents, I wish to introduce calypsonian number seven, out of Sandy Bay, the Mighty Roamer."

"Out of where?" came a shout from The Pit. "Sandy Bay? Whoever hear 'bout calypsonian from out dey, you making jokes or what?"

The theatre broke out in laughter.

"No joke," said the MC, "this is de Sparrow from out dey and he doing a number called 'Ah Coming Down'. Them town boys better look out because he says he coming to take de crown."

"Which crown?" was the almost universal response from The Pit.

"Bay, how come you never tell we that you have a man singing this year?" It was Midnight making the enquiry.

"Blackie, me meself don't know dat. Is de first time I hear 'bout he," replied Sandy Bay.

"Man, don't make joke," added Sanks. "You mean you have a fella from your village singing in the Tent and you don't know? Man, you should shame." This exchange didn't last long and we were drawn by activity in the Tent.

"Mr. MC, Spoon Head man, let we forget this Roamer fella and move to serious business. Remember man pay money fo' come in here and we want value fo' we money. Lewe pass this Roamer fella and move on." This demand was being made by a fellow in a white T-shirt, standing and gesticulating in the Pit.

The MC, turning to the man in the white T-shirt, said, "Now, you see you. You too hurry. That is why man like you have no girlfriend. You always in a hurry." The audience roared. With that, Roamer appeared on stage and the MC said, "Well, say something to the crowd."

Clearly tense and somewhat timid, Roamer offered, "Good night and how all yo' do?"

"You better do good or you will soon find out how we do," someone from Pit shouted back.

"Shut up and sing, we don't have time to waste!" somebody else shouted.

With that the band started up and Roamer began:

Ah coming down

Ah coming down

Ah coming down

But the band stopped, for it was clear that Roamer was singing in the wrong key.

"Yo' bus," came the automatic response from Pit, followed by an uproar of laughter from all over the theatre.

"What you country people know 'bout calypso?" demanded another in a broad cowboy hat, standing on the bench so that all could see him. "Boy, come off the stage and rest yo'self."

I immediately realised that this might spell the end of this young man's calypso hopes. But Roamer was not going to give up that easy. He therefore decided to go on.

"All yo' gie me ah chance, is a nice tune and all yo' go like it."

The man in the white T-shirt got up on his bench and shouted back, "We done hear de intro and dat is enough." His statement was followed by universal acclaim from Pit and prompted Ron to say to me, "Boy Brie, look like we are in for some fireworks with this one. Like the real thing about to start now." This was a prophecy.

Being from the country, Roamer was at a serious disadvantage. In those days, calypso singing in Tent was basically a Town thing. People from the country did not usually attend in great numbers for many objective reasons. In the first place, the public transport system was made of big wooden buses which came to Town early in the morning and left latest at 2:30 p.m. Once your bus left you and you had no family or friends in Town, then "crapaud smoke yo' pipe", as my grandmother used to say. There are hundreds of stories of the central police barracks serving as a one-night bed and breakfast for many a country folk. They had to make do with a hard wooden waiting bench as bed, and a cup of water as breakfast the next morning. There were even times when the barracks became a weekend hotel, for if the bus left you on a Saturday, it would only be back on Monday.

Consequently, in those days, carnival and everything to do with it was a town thing. People came from the country only on Carnival Sunday night. They went to the Queen show and stayed for J'ouvert on Monday morning. The young did not return home to the country until Wednesday evening, staying for Mardi Gras until the last band left the streets at 10:00 p.m. Tuesday night. So Roamer was a country boy in a town thing.

And Roamer was a teenager. No boy in his right mind, with no connections to places like Lower City, Largo Hill, La Bassy and the other rough sections of the city, which were the areas that populated The Pit, would say he was singing calypso in Tent. So at age 17, Roamer was but a lamb in the den of The Pit tigers.

But the band came to his rescue, if only for a fleeting moment, as they struck up the music again. Roamer, looking a bit bewildered, began once more.

Ah coming down

Ah coming down

Ah coming down

Carnival Monday

Carnival Tuesday

Again the music stopped and the roar came in unison from Pit.

"Yo' bus again," came the annoyed and protesting voices.

This was followed by a larger uproar of laughter and the Tent suddenly seemed to have added people and greater life. The Pit, in particular, seemed to be buzzing with chatter, all of it loud and lively, and directed to the stage at poor Roamer. The man in the white T-shirt was back on his bench pointing, gesticulating and shouting. But he could not be clearly heard, for a kind of happy and excitement-filled disorder had taken over both The Pit and parts of House. A number of other little pulpits had sprung up in parts of Pit and House, all competing for an audience; all braying about, and to Roamer at the same time. I instinctively knew that he was in deep trouble.

Ron leaned over to me and said that he thought that Roamer is a young calypsonian, and the boys in Pit should give him a chance. As Ron had to shout because of the excitement and chatter all around, Sandy Bay, who was on my immediate left, heard what he said and readily agreed, adding, "That is what I don't like wid Town people! All yo' never want to give ah country man ah chance!"

"Why you don't shut up if you don't have nothing to say?" said Heads, who was on Sandy Bay's left. "He done get two chances and bus two times. Time he come off the stage."

"I agree with Heads," said Bones, "two chances is more than enough. Them country calypsonians too unprofessional; that is why they can't win ah thing."

"Yo' talking 'bout country people can't win. So what 'bout Builder," shot back Sandy Bay, "he did get 4th one time."

"Builder was only born in the country but he live in Town all he life. He is ah Town man," said Sanks.

"But he still born ah country," replied Sandy Bay, determined not to concede his point.

"It's not ah country, Bay boy, is in the country. I already tell you that when you come out to Tent with people of class, talk properly," said Sanks.

"Two of you shut up!" It was Ron. "I want to hear what the MC saying."

"Ladies and gents, please, please let's continue the show," said the MC, trying to regain control before things really got out of hand. "Ladies and gents, let's move on."

"Exactly!" shouted Mr. White T-shirt, standing on his bench and gesticulating like a Baptist reverend in full flight. "Let Roamer go out to roam and let we continue de show."

The theatre erupted into laughter.

"Call on de next calypsonian and lewe move", continued Mr. White T-shirt.

More laughter.

"Most Mouth! Sit down and shut up and let de MC do he work. What happen? Yo' eat cattle tongue before you come here tonight?" a man across from Mr. White T-shirt protested.

"Yes, I eat your cattle tongue," white T-shirt shot back rather aggressively.

By this time, I was almost sure that this was the end of the show. I thought that the MC could never bring the theatre back under control. Ron assured me that there was nothing to worry about, explaining that this was the way generally in the Tent. That the MC was really quite powerful and authoritative, so even a stormy Pit will obey him. He said it had to do with the fact that the MCs were usually people from the same areas as those The Pit crowd came from, or had a good understanding of them and spoke their language. He was right. At that very moment when I thought we were nearing the point of no return, the MC took full control.

"Hey, Piggy, sit down man and lewe go. Black Boy, I weary tell you, you must behave yourself in my Tent. And you Most Mouth," he said, pointing to Mr. White T-shirt, "keep yo' trap shut."

Mr. White T-shirt sat down without another word. It seemed to me that, once the MC called the attention of the theatre to someone, that person would comply with his request for order.

So with things quiet, the MC called back The Mighty Roamer who had disappeared backstage during all the commotion. But before Roamer could say a word, or the band could strike a note, Ghetto Beast went as close to the stage as possible and, looking up directly at the calypsonian, shouted: "Roamer boy, you say you coming down! Well, come down! You can't see dat you can't make it. Man, stop the stupidness and come down!"

The Pit roared its appreciation, with two or three voices shouting, "You say you coming down, come down! Come down!"

Ghetto Beast was a very famous Pit character. He was from a place they called the Slum. This was a rundown neighbourhood in the heart of the city. It was a rough place where non-residents were advised to stay out, and where residents were decidedly tough. His nickname came from having a record of being among the toughest and strongest of his neighbourhood, and from being extremely brutal to his opponents in battles.

"Beast, all yo' need to give de fella a chance," continued the MC. "Roamer is a new man to de business." With that, he gave the signal and the band struck up again and Roamer began for the third time.

Ah coming down

Ah coming down

Ah coming down

Carnival Monday

Carnival Tuesday

And even Ash Wednesday..."

And here, Roamer forgot his lyrics again. Instantaneously, someone in the Pit crowd responded. "You bus again! That is three buses now, more than enough to carry you back ah country. Come off de stage!"

The audience was now falling all over itself with laughter.

"Way you be, ah bomb? Only bussing and bussing and bussing. You want fo' blow up de Tent? Man, come down!" continued the voice without a face.

By this time, some people were standing on their seats, others waving their carnival hats and still others shouting, "Blow man blow!" There was no denying that Roamer, even though he had not got in two good lines of his song, had got the crowd to its feet. This is something every singer hopes to do at least once in his career. But this ovation was more because of, rather than for, Roamer.

I was wondering what would happen next. I didn't have to wait long to find out. Before anyone knew what was taking place, Ghetto Beast jumped up on the stage, grabbed Roamer by the back of the neck, and hauled him down from the stage. The excitement and laughter hit overdrive. People whistled, clapped, laughed, waved their carnival hats, but all around there was nothing but total, absolute joyous insanity. The MC appeared, but it took a good three minutes for him to restore order and quiet. When he finally brought things under control, he asked, "Anybody see the Mighty Roamer? Anybody know where he is?"

"Well, he was trying to come down the whole night and Ghetto Beast help him out!" came a contemptuous response from someone in the Pit.

The theatre roared.

"Well, if he say he coming down, he should come down and stop waste time!" shouted Ghetto Beast. "He lucky I only tek him down and we didn't chase him out de Tent!"

The Tent roared again.

"All right ladies and gents, we now move on with the show. By de way, all yo' hear 'bout the foreign white lady who ate ah hand ah swell belly bonana out Georgetown?"

The crowd shouted, "Noooo!" in unison.

"Well, if you behave yourselves, ah go tell you what happened to she."

The crowd burst out laughing.

"No, no we want it now," someone in Pit protested. "Man Spoony, gee we it now."

"But ah just said that ah only telling all yo' if all yo' behave all yo' selves and all yo' done start to misbehave. All yo' dotish or stupid or both?"

The crowd roared.

"That's better," said the MC. "Now, let we move on and if de good behaviour continue, ah go tell all yo' de joke about the white woman. And by the way; ah see the lady sitting down in House right in front ah me over dey," he said, pointing to a section in House. Half of Pit turned around looking at House, while some people in the section of House to which he pointed, started looking at each other. This happened for about three to four seconds before the whole place broke down in laughter again. There was no white lady in the whole of House.

"So we move on, ladies and gents," said the MC, evidently proud that he had scored one against the entire theatre. "And now I bring to you the Mighty Preacher."

Preacher was number 8 in a cast of fifteen. Looking back at it now; it seemed that he was brought on the stage at precisely that time when the atmosphere most needed him. With his rendition, he brought us back to reason and in effect, stopped the runaway emotions that were threatening to take over the evening during the debacle between Roamer and The Pit.

The Mighty Preacher came on stage dressed in a dark suit, tie and all, carrying in his hand something that looked like a black Bible. He introduced himself and then informed the audience that his song was entitled "The Government is ah waste." I could see from his comportment that he was a seasoned performer, which was confirmed by Ron a second later.

"Bay," he said, "you see stage presence. You see how man should come on stage? Just watch how he will control the crowd. I hope Roamer stick around to see this."

"Priest man; Preacher and them ah veteran in de business. Them man know everything 'bout tent," said Sandy Bay in mild and surrendering objection.

Mighty Preacher gave the signal and the band started the musical introduction, following which he began:

239

Boom boom boom boom by, shoeby

Boom boom boom boom by, shoeby

I don't know what we go do

But this government don't care 'bout me and you

They wasting money everyday

But things getting worse and worse in every way

Look the road in such bad state

Every day I wake up nothing to eat no food on me plate

These politicians don't really care

While the people of this country suffering each and every day

So I tell you to your face

The leaders them have no taste

They mashing up the place

Man this government is a waste

Boom boom boom boom by, shoeby

Boom boom boom boom by, shoeby.

After this chorus, there was a short musical interlude and as the music played, The Pit went wild with shouts of "Blow man! Blow man!" There were people whistling through their tongue and or fingers. Some stood on their benches shouting their appreciation. Ghetto Beast took off his shirt and started to wave it while shouting "Blow man! Blow man!"

I was about to ask Ron what "shoeby" really meant, when the Mighty Preacher began his second verse. There was a hushed reverence as the people drank in every line. It seemed that he, Preacher, wasn't just singing. His was a lecture, a revelation and publication of a terrible truth, complete with the right words, facial expressions, actions and movement on stage. It was clear that he was speaking to the heads and hearts of his audience. His song seemed to embody their message of their need of freedom from want, poverty and social neglect on the part of the authorities. When he hit the chorus the second time, everybody was singing with him. Some people in Pit began to shout "Preacher fo' king dis year! Is Preacher fo' king dis year!"

As the Mighty Preacher sang about the poverty of the ghetto and the negligence of the government, I could see that he was touching the very heartstrings of the majority of the Pit crowd. And even though I was very young, I could sense that he was singing for them. He was their voice of protest against an authority which had power over them, but which didn't care about them. He Preacher was crying the tears of their heart, telling of the pains in their souls, expressing the helplessness they felt, and reflecting the bitterness this all germinated in them. There was a sudden sadness in my soul.

This drastic transformation in the mood of the Tent was like the result of the waving of a fairy's wand. Exactly one performance earlier, the Tent was a threatening riot. Now it was like the most serious gospel meeting, and the Preacher was delivering the Sermon on the Mount. Every patron was suddenly studious. The Tent had changed from a common market place, to an institution of higher learning, and there was a major lecture in governance and political science taking place. It was all simply amazing!

When the Mighty Preacher hit the chorus for the final time after the fourth verse, people were already shouting "Encore! Encore! Encore! Encore!" As the MC made his way back on stage, they began to shout encore even louder, forcing the MC to bring things under control before proceeding.

"Ladies and gentlemen," he said, "now we only halfway through and all yo' already want encore. If we do that, we will never end de show. Believe me, it have plenty excitement to come. Ah matter a fact, ah just come from backstage and ah hear that Lord Orator have something real bad. They say it name 'Them Busy', so lewe move on, 'cause I want fo' hear that. I know you go want fo' hear it too."

The show then went along merrily, with the usual laughter and the crowd expressing approval or otherwise after every performance. Apart from calypsonian No. 9 who slipped and fell, but recovered quickly, and calypsonian No. 11 who burst once and had to start over, with people shouting, "He's another Roamer or what?" and, "What yo' think it is, ah dog show or what?", it looked like all major excitement had passed. But then calypsonian No. 13 arrived with what turned out to be not only a most original performance, but the event of the night.

The MC set the scene by declaring, "Ladies and gents; and Piggy, when I say gents, I am not speaking to you. I weary tell you that gentlemen know how to behave themselves."

The theatre burst out laughing.

"So, as I was saying, ladies and gentlemen, we are winding down and as we get closer to the end, things get sweeter. Now for those of you who have a feel for the English language; but especially those of you who always murdering the Queen's English with your pink adjectives, green adverbs and blue verbs, and wish to improve your situation through tuition, I am pleased to give you, none other than Lord Orator. He will be doing a number called 'Them Busy in La Bassy'. Give him a round of applause."

Even with the favourable applause going on, one could see that the entire theatre was on alert. One could literally feel the wonderings on the mind of the Tent as to what this was about. This was so because Busy was the term used to describe women of questionable lifestyles, with whom most self-respecting men would not associate in public. La Bassy was one of the rougher areas in the city whose inhabitants were very assertive and were always well represented in The Pit. So the question was; what would come next?

"I just love to hear Orator sing," Socks was saying, "the man have dictation."

"It's diction man, not dictation", said Ron. "Socks man, you always talking like somebody who illiterate."

"He more than elitaarate," said Sandy Bay, "but yet he does want to play most eddecated."

"Shut up!" shot back Socks, "you ugly country self."

"But look this Baboon calling people ugly. Fella; yo' need a mirror," said Sandy Bay in a most dismissive manner.

I expected Ron to intervene, but with Lord Orator coming on stage, there was no need for his silence command.

Lord Orator entered the stage dressed in all black with a red piece of cloth tied around his head. There was another red piece of cloth in the left breast pocket of his jacket. He was short in stature, rather slim and seemed to be in his late twenties or early thirties. As a calypsonian with about a decade in the business, and three or four very popular numbers to his name, he was well known in the Tent. He was greeted warmly with applause and a whistle or two. But such niceties would soon be forgotten, once Lord Orator began to sing.

"Good night ladies and gentlemen. The song I am about to do is about a true-life experience. I hope it will not happen to any of you gentlemen here tonight. But whether it happened to you or not, please enjoy." And with that, he gave the signal and the band struck up the music. Lord Orator began:

Bam bam bam bam boui

Bim bam bim bam boui, Shoeby

Love is a painful thing

Love could cause you to commit sin

I know because you see

I fell in love with a Busy

I should have known, that girls from La Bassy

Usually aren't anybody

Cause La Bassy you see

Full of pure Busy

So let me tell you

When you looking for a Busy

Check down La Bassy

You don't need plenty money

Just Check down La Bassy

If you are lost and lonely

Check down La Bassy

You are sure to find company

Check down La Bassy

From the first few bars of the music, one could sense that the song had a sweet beat and catchy tune. But when Lord Orator began his lyrics, it was clear that he had struck a note with the people, and his was going to be one of the more memorable performances of the night. By the middle of the first verse, some patrons in Pit had already gotten out of their seats and were dancing. By the time he got to the end of the first chorus, there were some people already repeating the key line "check down La Bassy" while others simply shouted "Blow man! Blow man!"

Midnight shouted to everyone, "All yo' hear diction. Man dat is diction. Lord Orator is ah Boss when it come to de English language. Tell anybody I tell all yo' so."

"So who doubting yo?" shouted back Country.

"But nobody could doubt me. De man is ah Boss!"

Lord Orator continued:

Women are more than anything, mothers

They are wonderful girls and sisters

But I'm warning everybody

Be careful with those from La Bassy

Don't care how they pretty

They really aren't anybody

I like that place La Bassy

But I'm afraid of them Busy

So believe me when I tell you

To meet them bad girls in the town

Check down La Bassy

Never mind if you smell of rum

Check down La Bassy

If you ugly

Check down La Bassy

Once you have some money

Check down La Bassy

By now more than half the theatre was singing the refrain. Lord Orator did not need to sing the Check down La Bassy line. He simply pointed the microphone to the crowd who shouted it with pleasure. So when he sang, "And if you ugly" he pointed the microphone to them and a loyal choir responded "Check down La Bassy." This was

246

all being done in a most jovial and natural manner, and the stage seemed to have suddenly become one with the rest of the theatre. I was totally fascinated by it all, and my mind was running back to some of the stories I had heard from my uncles.

It might sound impossible, but the truth is that I saw the whole Tent rocking with Lord Orator, anticipating his lyrics and copying his antics on stage. It was as if the whole Tent had become part of the act, whistling, blowing conch shells, demonstrating what he commanded them to, but all just partying. It all seemed one big carnival in full swing, with everybody jumping to the command of the Commander in Chief, Lord Orator himself. And then I saw it.

At first, I didn't realise what it was, for it was just something flying in the direction of Lord Orator. Another second and I saw that it was an old shoe, heading for his chest. He twisted out of the way and it ended on one of the drummer's cymbals with a bang! I was shocked! Although I had heard many stories from my uncles about these happenings, to actually see it, was really a new revelation. But I had to overcome my surprise rather rapidly as this was only the beginning.

On seeing the first shoe, the crowd got more energised and started clapping and shouting, "Blow man! Blow!" And Lord Orator, as if compelled by some strange force, continued singing as if nothing had happened. Then I saw another shoe flying, this time in the direction of Lord Orator's head. He ducked out of the way and continued to sing. This seemed to set the crowd alight and the whole theatre now became fully engaged with this new development on stage, dictated by the missiles coming from The Pit.

The shoes were rapidly followed by the first egg, which smashed into one of the huge speaker boxes on stage. After that, the stage became a virtual firing zone with shots in the form of various objects coming from all directions. Pit was in an uproar. Some people singing, dancing and encouraging Lord Orator on, while others were the marksmen, taking aim and firing away at Lord Orator and the stage. But, regardless of the side they belonged to, the entire Pit was on its feet and the Tent was again transformed.

Beer bottles and beer cans, cigarette packs, more old shoes, eggs and numerous other small articles flew towards the stage at regular intervals. It was obvious that some in Pit came prepared for an occurrence of this nature, and fate was kind to them that night. I could not help but being reminded of a market day where everything seemed to be chaotic. And yet in that chaos, there was an understanding of some sort of order which the shoppers and vendors alike understood.

It also reminded me of Mr. Million and his shop in Town. Mr. Million was a short fat fellow of Portuguese origin, who my mother says was operating his shop in that very same place even before she was born. His name wasn't really Million, and I doubt that anyone really knew his name. But we all knew him as Mr. Million as he had this little shop, which was overcrowded with what seemed to be a million things. However, when you went to buy anything, he would find what you wanted without having to search for it. None of his shelves had labels. One could not discern any kind of order in the way goods were put on them. But yet there must have been some order, at least in the mind of Mr. Million. He always knew where to find anything without searching for it, in what was to the ordinary eyes nothing but a very confusing maze.

Back in the Tent, the missiles continued to fly, but Lord Orator persisted. I saw the piano player duck out of the way of a beer bottle. After that he played a game of see me now, and now you don't, by shielding himself behind the huge speaker box closest to his piano. The drummer pulled one of the cymbals closer to him as his shield after a bottle came flying in the direction of his head. He just managed to raise the cymbal in time for the bottle to crash into it with the resulting Bang! The guitarists, trumpeters and trombonists had an easier time, but were kept like shifting targets, constantly avoiding missiles meant for Lord Orator.

By now, the whole Tent was transformed into a theatre where it seemed no one was simply a spectator. There were those holding their sides from the pain of laughter. There were those shouting "Blow man! Blow!", and there were those waving caps or clapping their hands with glee. Tent interactivity had reached Himalayan proportions.

Ghetto Beast got up on his bench and started to wave the red piece of cloth he had around his head. The one the MC had referred to as Piggy, took off his shirt and started waving it, and more beers and bottles of Strong Rum seemed to appear suddenly all over House and Pit.

Socks said to Ron, "Pass the bottle, this call fo' ah drink."

"Here and pass it down," he said to Socks. Turning to me he said, "Brie boy, this is Tent. I bet you never knew that it could be so good, but this is the real thing. You are lucky, really lucky. The first time you come to Tent and you get to see the real thing. Who would have believed that?" Ron said all of this while laughing, with his hand on his chest as if he was going to have a heart attack.

Midnight, the most musical of us all, was already right in the groove of the sound, singing along during the chorus while affirming, "But dis is de Road March dis year! Dis is de Road March dis year! No body could beat Orator dis year. They would really ha' fo' come good fo' beat him dis year."

With all this commotion going on, in another place and at another time, the performer would have stopped. But not Lord Orator. Through it all, he continued his performance, skipping and hopping out of the way of missiles coming in his direction. He sometimes had to duck, sometimes jump, sometimes skip, and other times twist and turn. But he did it all so naturally that one would have been forgiven for thinking that this was a planned part of the act which Orator organised with The Pit. It was as if he and the crowd in Pit had agreed to put on this show for the rest of the theatre.

"Brie boy, this is Tent! This is the real thing," said Ron.

"Tent without this, is no Tent," Socks joined in.

"Yo' could say dat again," said Sandy Bay. "Dem man in Pit always know how fo' lively up de crowd."

When Orator finally left the stage, there were cheers, laughter, claps, whistles and shouts of "Encore! Encore!" The entire theatre gave him a standing ovation. The MC came on the stage grinning from ear to ear.

"Everybody alright?"

"Yeeheee!" the crowd yelled back in unison.

"So you would like an encore?"

"Yeah! Come wid it! Encore! Encore," they shouted.

"Well, let us clean up this place and finish with the full cast first. Then we go call back Orator to do something."

"Call him now! Call him back now!"

"I done say later. We have to clean up the place first. But I would tell you something. I hear they say that the Prime Minister wants to form an army in this country. Well, I telling all yo' that calypsonians should make up the bulk of that army. In particular calypsonians from this Tent. Way all yo' say?"

"Yeah man!" somebody shouted from The Pit.

"And I think that Orator should be the commander-in-chief. What all yo' think?"

"How you mean man!" somebody behind us in House shouted in agreement.

"I mean, I never see nobody could slip missiles so. Who so brave to take on the whole ah Pit including ah man like Ghetto Beast and come out unscratched. Orator is a boss", reinforced the MC. "I sure the Americans if they hear 'bout Orator go make he ah general in the army. Man, all yo' gee the man another round of applause."

"Encore! Encore!" came the chant, accompanied by great applauding, whistles and laughter.

"When a man like Lord Orator on stage and men like Fishtail in The Pit, we know we have the best around. And look how we Tent happy, so lewe go on. Ladies and gents, please welcome on stage the Mighty Smasher!"

Smasher came on and did a number called "Rolling it out." His was an uneventful act and it was clear that the crowd wanted his performance over and done with as soon as possible. They practically hustled him off the stage, with chants of, "You carrying on too long" and "Time fo' come down." As soon as he was finished, there were renewed shouts of, "Bring on Lord Orator! We want Lord Orator!"

The MC came back, promised the crowd that Orator would be back and called the final act, a calypsonian going by the name of 'The President'. He gave an enjoyable performance with a jumpy number called, 'Carnival on the Moon'. This was a prediction as to how we are going to play carnival on the moon, once the Americans' plans to put man on it was successful. Needless to say, while this song was quite good, the crowd was impatient for him to finish and leave the stage. Everybody awaited the return of the star of the night, Lord Orator.

"Ladies and gents, we had a very good night," began the MC.

"Bring on Orator! We want Orator!"

"Well, I am sorry, but I just went backstage and them tell me that Lord Orator gone home already. So you all will have to come back next week Wednesday night to hear him again. The Tent apologise to everybody."

There was the universal sucking of teeth and a loud "No!" Some people in the Pit started shouting, "Why you all make him leave?" There was no mistaking the genuine feeling of disappointment.

The MC tried to explain.

"Lord Orator sang he song and he can leave when he want. We will have another splendid show next Wednesday night. Tell all your friends to come out and don't forget to make special mention of Lord Orator and La Bassy. This season, this Tent bad like storm, and next week, you could expect Lord Orator to close the show. We will make up for any disappointment we caused tonight. Thank you all and good night. Don't forget, it's next week Wednesday night."

With that the MC took his leave and the show was closed.

We joined the crowd leaving through one of the side doors, with everybody talking at the same time. The subject was of course; Lord Orator and his La Bassy. There were varying views. It was clear however that he was the star of the night, and that everyone would be back the following Wednesday night to get another taste of La Bassy.

As we entered the street and began the walk home, I couldn't help thinking about the stories my uncles had told me in the past. I now understood what uncle Sammy meant when he said, "A calypso tent has two stages, the stage proper and The Pit. The first is for the calypsonian. The other for the all-important supporting cast." I couldn't agree more. Uncle David put it differently. He always said that without The Pit, a calypso tent is only a half-covered tent.

As we got to the point where our paths diverted and Ron had to take me home, we took leave of the others. On the way to my house, we continued to talk of the happenings of the night. I was so taken by it all that I knew it would take me some time to put it all into proper perspective. I however determined there and then that there was no way that I would ever be parting ways with the Tent. It was the greatest and most natural liberation of the human creativity, mind and spirit that I had seen to date. In it all, I saw the many facets that made up my little colonial-island world.

As I opened the gate and entered the front yard, Ron said, "Brie boy, more bacchanal than this tonight is murder. I mean you had a good time, right?" Before I could answer, we heard my mother's voice and stood dead in our tracks. It just couldn't be, after all, she was supposed to still be in London. But sure enough it was.

"Fredrick, I have told you time and again, I don't want any of my children in any calypso tent before they are eighteen years old. I turned my back and Brie is in Tent. How could you allow the child to break my rules like that? If I had come home on the planned date, I would not have known, for this would have been your little secret."

As my mother continued, I turned to look for Ron. He had already stepped back from the gate and was standing a little way looking at me with an expression which said "I sympathise, but I am not going in there!" We both realised that the Tent might be over, but the real bacchanal for my father and me had only now begun. He thoughtfully said, "I spoke too fast. We go see tomorrow if you are still alive." With that, he took his leave while I stood listening as my mother paraded on. Like it or not, I knew that I had to go in and face the music.

As I put my hand on the doorknob, I paused for a second as it struck me that I am going to need some of the antics that Lord Orator had performed. After all, he successfully dealt with all The Pit had thrown at him. But I knew no skipping, ducking or dodging was going to deliver me. Saint Amy was on the rampage. I opened the door and said, "Good night everybody." The silence that followed was deafening.

Richard A. Byron-Cox

Were Mama's Tears

in Vain?

THE DEATH

Boysie was crying and crying. He simply could not stop. In spite of all the consolation everybody around him was trying to give, something in his chest was damaged and the pain was not just real, it was overbearing. It was so real and so overbearing that he thought he would die from it. Although he was very young, he had felt pain before, great pain; like the time he fell over the church wall and ended up on his back on the concrete five feet below. That time he thought he had broken every bone in his body. It took him some time to get up and a few minutes to stay steady on his feet. And he remembered the time when he went to the beach and the needles of the black sea eggs got into the soles of his feet. Mama had to pour boiling hot water on them and dug them out using a sewing needle she had borrowed from Miss Ethylene. Boysie recalled that he had screamed so hard that people heard him in every shack in the tenement yard. Yes, that was pain, terrible pain, but it was only physical pain, nothing more.

But no pain he felt before could compare with that he was feeling today, at this moment. It was as if something essential to his being has fallen out from inside of him. Some irreplaceable part of him has been removed and it was its absence that was causing this indescribable pain. Something told him it might lessen sooner or later, but that it would never ever really go away altogether. Time would prove him to be right.

What he just didn't understand was how God could take Mama at this very young age of his life. What had Mama done that was so wrong? Or what had he done wrong that God would do such a thing to him, take Mama away from him for good. God probably didn't love him as much as Mama had said.

Mama was all he knew, all he ever understood, and the only one who understood him. She was the person who did everything for him. How was he going to survive without her? Nobody loved him apart from Mama. She was the only person he could run to when anything happened, when anything went wrong. She who soothed all the previous pains was now the source of this, his greatest hurt, and there was no one to turn to for help. Yes, these people around were trying to be nice, they were trying to console him. But he needed someone who could speak to his heart, who would actually understand this pain, for they felt it too. Only Mama could do that.

As they shovelled the sand over her coffin, the tears flowed like a river from Boysie. He could not imagine never returning to the one-room galvanise shack and having Mama comb his hair and prepare the cocoa tea which she gave him with a piece of sweat sweet potato or a quarter of doucana, sit and watch him eat, while she drank her cup of pure hot water. He was thin, but Mama was like a rake. In fact, when Boysie first discovered that Mama was dead and called Miss Ruth, the neighbour in the shack next door to ask for help; when she came and confirmed that Mama was indeed dead, she commented that Mama must have died of starvation.

With all the poverty that they lived in, Boysie never knew hunger, and it was only now that he understood why. Mama was determined that he Boysie would not feel any of the pain and suffering she felt. So she fed him with the little she had, while making do with plain hot water on many occasions. He now realised that her frequent fainting was because she bore her hunger, along with that which was meant for him. He could see now why, whenever he asked her why she was not eating, her response was always that she was not hungry. Her love for him denied her the liberty of being hungry, for in situations like those, his contentment could only be had through the sacrifice of hers. Boysie suddenly realised that Mama's death was the price she paid because of love. Yes, love for him. And so the tears just continued to flow.

Boysie would also cry for this, and much more of his mother's suffering on his behalf in later years. He didn't know of it then and therefore only cried because he was burying his mother at the tender age of twelve, and didn't know what awaited him tomorrow. Who was going to be to him the mother of love and compassion that Mama was?

As they sang the funeral hymns and prayed that God accepted Mama into heaven, how Boysie wished that it was he who had died and not Mama. Mama did not deserve to die. He thought that in the least, God should have taken him with Mama, for in that case, they would be together and he would not have to worry about tomorrow. But as it was, he would have to worry not just about tomorrow, but the day after and every day after that too. His was surely going to be a lonely, unhappy and painful road.

As the shadows began to cover the cemetery which was at the end of the church yard, Mr. Woods, the reverend whom Boysie knew better as Teacher Woods and therefore preferred to call him by that name, said the closing prayer. The small group of followers began to disperse. It included aunt Maude, her four boys and Stella, her only daughter. There was Mr. Johnny, the man with the shortened right hand who could work a hoe better than anybody else on the plantation. Mrs. De Fosto, the Portuguese woman whose husband ran the rum shop about two miles down the road from the plantation, was also there. She came because Mama used to clean house sometimes on Sundays for her when she didn't have plantation work to do. And there was Mr. Marshall, the old man who everybody was always saying would die shortly but who always seemed to defy these predictions. His limited mobility, as he had lost one leg to sugar; the mistreatment meted out to him by his children, and the prayers of the estate owners for his death as they saw him as a liability, all seemed incapable of effecting his speedy trip to heaven.

Aunt Maude ordered him and his five cousins to follow her as she led the way out of the small cemetery and to her home. All the way to her house, Boysie's tears kept flowing. He couldn't help thinking that in the same way the shadows had engulfed the cemetery, shutting out all light; and in the same way the dirt was shovelled on his mother's coffin, shutting her out from this world forever, so too today, this day of his mother's passing had shut forever a door of special light in his life. From now on, his was going to be a life with little brightness, if any at all.

As they walked the one mile or so to his aunt's house which was to be his home from now on, Boysie thought about visiting his mother's tin shack just so that he could get the feel and scent of Mama. That he could watch the pictures that adorned the walls of the one-room galvanised-tin-shack place they called home. He wanted for one last time to be alone with her so that she could reassure him that everything was going to be alright.

Theirs was the smallest shack on the whole estate, but Mama treated it with pride and taught Boysie to do the same. Throughout the year, Mama would collect all the old colour magazines from the maid, Miss Ethylene, who worked in the Great House. At Christmas, she would use an old scissors that aunt Maude had given them and cut out all the nice pictures that she found, mix some flour paste which she used to stick the pictures as wallpaper to cover the rusted galvanise sheets that served as the walls of the shack. This made the place look pretty and fresh for the season.

Boysie used to have great fun helping Mama with little things like looking for the best pictures, stirring the flour and water mixture to make the paste, and helping Mama decide which picture fit which spot best. Most of all, he loved when it was all finished and it looked like they had new walls all around, and he could pretend that he knew some of the people in these pictures and so could talk to them and even become friends. He had played such games for as long as he could remember, and every time Christmas came and the paper was changed, there were always new friends with whom to play his game.

But while the inside of the house was renewed every Christmas, every year the outside got uglier and uglier as the rust made it look worse and worse. Boysie did not like how this looked and once suggested to Mama that they should do something about it.

"Mama, why don't we put some pictures on the outside of the house so that it could look pretty like the inside and then all over could be pretty?" he had asked.

"Yes, I wish we could; but if we did, then when the rain comes, it would wash all the pictures away, and we would have wasted our flour for nothing." Mama had replied.

"Well, can't we get some paint and paint it in a pretty colour like one of them houses we see in the pictures?"

"Boysie, what do you mean them houses? What should you say?"

"Those houses, Mama," Boysie dutifully replied.

"Good, remember what I always tell you; always try to speak like an educated person. And yes, one day we will do that when you are big enough to help me with the painting," she had assured him.

He had asked God many times to allow him to grow up fast so that he could be big enough to help Mama with this painting. Now it was too late. Mama was gone forever, and the outside of the house was not beautiful and will now never be.

There were only three real framed pictures in their tin shack. They were all very old and Mama cherished them as if they were made of gold. One was of Jesus Christ. Mama treated it with great reverence. It was hung high on that wall of the shack which faced the door, thus making it the first thing one saw upon entering. In it, Jesus was a white man with long blonde hair and pure blue eyes. He was dressed in a white robe, with outstretched welcoming arms, and there were white doves flying around his head. At the foot of the picture were written the words, 'I am the way, the truth and the life'.

Mama was a Christian woman and took Boysie to church from since he could remember. She explained to Boysie many times how Jesus loves them and always had an angel watching over them, especially over him, for he was a child of God. At first, Boysie found this all a bit hard to understand and so sought answers by questioning his mother.

"But Mama, I never saw Jesus watching me?"

"No, you can't see him", she replied.

"So Mama, have you ever seen Jesus?"

"No, no one can see Jesus."

"So how do you talk to him then?"

"Every time we pray, we talk to him."

"And he hears us?"

"Oh sure, he hears us."

"So, is Jesus dumb Mama?" he asked.

"Boysie, be careful when you speak of Jesus. No, he is not dumb."

"So why he doesn't answer us?" he insisted, "Are you sure he hears us?"

"Of course I am sure. God is everywhere all the time and hears and sees everything."

"You mean Jesus?"

"Yes, I meant Jesus, but God is also there as well."

"So you mean Jesus and God listen to me pray together Mama?"

"Yes, because Jesus and God is one person."

"But how come Mama? Isn't Jesus God's son?"

"Yes, you are right, Jesus is God's son."

"Then how can they be the same person?"

This was one of those times when Boysie's mother was convinced that her child was brilliant many times beyond his age, and would pray to God to be gracious unto her boy, and to make him somebody in this world. In these prayers, she always assured God that she was very satisfied with her lot and did not need anything. But she would be happy "if it so pleases the Lord, that the boy should have a good life."

After thinking for a moment and not knowing how to explain this unusual nature of Jesus and God, she simply told Boysie that he was still too young to understand things of this nature, and he would understand it all later when he was much older.

The shack also had a picture of King George VI. This, Mama considered her very lucky picture. Because of it, she was able to meet and speak to the greatest man on the island and also get a picture of him, the third picture in the shack. Mama truly cherished this last picture for it represented someone powerful whom she had seen and actually spoken to. Above all, thanks to him, she actually owned the tin shack they lived in, that is assuming that Mr. Carson doesn't change his mind.

She considered the picture of the king her lucky picture because she came by it through sheer accident. She was on her way to pick oranges, which was her task for that day, when she saw Ethylene throwing things over the bank they used as the estate's garbage dump. Among those things was this picture of the King which had a badly cracked glass. Mama asked Ethylene for the picture, for she simply couldn't understand how anyone could dump anything with the King on the garbage heap. After all, he was King of the empire. He was our King.

In this picture, the King was sitting on a very nice and high chair called a throne. He wore a golden crown decorated with diamonds, and just sat there with this smile on his face. An intelligent eye could tell he was told to smile, for it was clear that he was doing it solely for the picture and nothing else. At the bottom of the picture was written 'His Majesty King George VI'.

Mama had explained to Boysie that he was the King of the British empire, and, they were all children of the empire, something Boysie must always remember. He therefore must never forget to have manners and respect for the King. "In fact," said Mama, "our King is the King of the world; so Boysie, our King is really special and live in a big house call a palace with plenty servants and everything is gold and silver."

"Is our King house as big as the Great House?" he had asked. The only times Boysie left the estate were when they went to church, and he had never seen a house even half the size of the Carsons' house. He consequently couldn't imagine anything that was as big as, let alone bigger than, the Carsons' house.

"Oh the Carson house is big on our little island, but our King's palace is the biggest house in the British empire which stretch from one end of the world to the other. There is where he and the Royal Family live."

Boysie was silent for a while. A house stretching from one end of the world to the other was beyond his imagination. How does it look? Then he asked.

"Mama, what is the Royal Family?"

"It is the family of the King."

"So why do they call it the Royal Family and not the family of the King?"

"Because the King is his Royal Highness and so his family is royal."

"They have plenty people in the Royal Family?"

"Well, I don't know, but when you look at the size of the palace, you would think is plenty of them," his mother had replied.

"Mama, have you ever seen our King?"

"Only in pictures."

"And you sure he is our King?"

"But of course. He is the king of Mr. Carson and all the other white people on this island, and if he is white people king, what you say about we black people?"

Mr. Carson was the estate owner and came from a family of British origin. They owned one of the huge estates which most people on the island depended on to find jobs, be it ploughing the land and planting the crops, tending them as they grow, or reaping them during harvest. Some, like Miss Ethylene, worked in the big houses as maids and washerwomen. There were others who did jobs like tending the animals and fixing the house and estate fence when they broke down. But whatever they did, most of the people on the island depended exclusively on these estates in one way or the other to make a living.

Mama's tin shack and the land on which it stood both belonged to Mr. Carson. He had promised Mama that she could live there as long as she wanted, and if she could find a piece of land to put the shack, then she could take it and move. Mama would really have loved to have her own piece of land and would many times tell Boysie that when he becomes a grown man, the first thing he must buy is a piece of land, and build a house. She said her father's greatest wish was to have a piece of land, no matter how small so that he could have "knock up something" and move his family out off the Carson estate. But alas, they were too poor for even that. So she was very happy when her sister Maude got married to a man who could take her off of the estate and put her in a house.

Mama cherished the picture of the Colonial Administrator specially. This was her third picture. She had seen him personally and thought that he was a nice man who cared about all the people on the island. She knew this, for he himself had said so when he had visited the estate some years before Boysie was born. She remembered it was around the time when some bad, unreasonable and ignorant nigger people went and staged a riot at the Courthouse in town and one of them got killed.

Mama could not say for sure what happened, but she remembered that Blue, the donkey cart driver, came around that evening. He told everybody that Mr. Carson didn't want them going into Town for there was trouble down there, and he didn't want anybody bringing it on his estate. Mama didn't understand what was meant by this trouble in Town and tried to find out what she could from Blue.

"So Blue, what really happening in Town, is something serious?"

"Me no really know. All me hear is that some stupid nigger people causing trouble in Town and de Colonial Administrator have fo' call out de whole constabulary to deal wid them."

"So what cause it?"

"Well, you know them nigger people ah Town. Them lazy and don't want to wuk hard fo' money. Me hear Mr. Carson telling Mistress Carson dat them start a riot after them went fo' demand from de administrator increase pay fo' labourers from three pence to four pence ah week."

"And then the riot start?" asked Mama.

268

"Well, the Administrator say no; and these ignorant nigger people start to curse and fight, forcing de nice gentleman fo' call out de constabulary to quiet down de place."

"How much people get dead?"

"Me don't know, but if you hear that Sam Browne get dead, don't be surprised."

"What happened to Sam Browne, is he in trouble?" asked Mama, with more than a hint of concern in her voice.

"Well no, nothing ain't happen to him yet. But he should get a bus face or bus head or something."

"Blue, why you saying that, what did Sam Browne do?" asked Mama, starting to show a measure of impatience and worry.

"Me meet him ah go ah Town yesterday saying he going to see what happening down there. And he want black people to put some lash on them lazy white people. And is when me see that me come tell Mr. Carson, and today he tell me to make it clear to all ah you that no body living on his estate is to even think 'bout going to Town. And anybody who go better walk wid them bundle."

Mama couldn't help thinking that this is why she liked Sam Browne as much as she resented Blue. Sam Browne was a man who took decisions he thought were right and didn't care what Mr. Carson or anyone else thought. That is why he had to leave the estate, for he always said that he was a man, and not even Mr. Carson could make him behave like a boy. She hoped that Boysie would be like that one

269

day and confront even Carson in defence of his manhood, in the same way Sam Browne had done.

Although the incident that caused Sam Browne to leave happened quite a while back, Mama remembered it as clearly as if it were yesterday. She was sure that everybody who was there that day had the same vivid memory. It was something that no one ever thought could happen.

It was a Sunday morning and everybody on the estate was being awakened and rounded up by Blue on the orders of Mr. Carson. They had to collect dried coconuts, husk them, bust and dig them out of the shells. They had to then put them in the sun to dry to become copra, which was later put into huge crocus bags and sent to the factory to make soap and coconut oil. They had done this work with the coconut the whole week up until sundown on Saturday evening. However, there were still quite a lot of coconuts to be collected and, fearing the ending of the dry season, Mr. Carson ordered Blue to announce to everyone that they would be working from eight the next morning.

"Everybody, but not me. I not wuking tomorrow. God say six days shall thou labour and the seventh day you shall rest. So I not wuking," said Sam Browne defiantly.

"Sam Browne, you always talking stupidness. Mr. Carson say everybody wuking and everybody have to wuk, including you," replied Blue.

All the other workers stood and just listened. They had grown accustomed to Sam Browne questioning authority, and they knew that

Blue was very circumspect when he had to deal with Sam Browne. They were also accustomed to Sam Browne criticising the Carsons, although never to their faces. But this was the first time that they were hearing him defying an order of Mr. Carson's.

Blue, knowing that power was on his side and realising that this was another of those tests of strength and will between Sam Browne and himself in which he never wins, simply retorted, "Well, you will have to tell Mr. Carson that yo' not wuking tomorrow."

"Well, you go up and bring Carson down and see if me no tell him that I not wuking," came the vehement reply.

This had the group of one hundred and fifty people in shock, for nobody ever refers to Mr. Carson as just "Carson". Even the Carson children, as small as they were, were always referred to as Master and Miss, but never by their first names only.

"Who you calling Carson!" shouted Blue.

"Yo' dotish? You don't know who name Carson?" said Sam Browne, moving towards Blue while speaking.

Blue made a few steps backwards and started to say something. But no one could understand what he wanted to say, as he was stuttering as if he had just swallowed part of his tongue. "Ww.....eee....ll," he began, and the rest was incomprehensible. He then turned around and headed for the Great House. When he was about five or six metres away from the crowd, he turned around to face them and declared; "Remember! Everybody wuking tomorrow,

Sunday or no Sunday, and that include you, Sam Browne boy. You hear what I tell you?"

With that, Blue set off like an express train, heading for the Great House. Sam Browne, for his part, just looked in the direction of Blue and commented, "Moon does run until day catch um", to the great amusement of all the other workers.

Blue did not tell Mr. Carson of Sam Browne's defiance, as he had reported on him once before and got a good beating for it. The story goes that Sam Browne had, on one Friday afternoon, climbed one of the coconut trees on the estate and picked two green coconuts as he had bought a bottle of rum and wanted the coconut water as chaser. On his way to his little tin shack, he met the one person in the world he had begged God not to let see him with these coconuts. Sam Browne sought desperately for an escape route. But alas there was none. He had to meet the situation head on. "Blue, how about you come down to me place and we drink ah rum? I got a whole battle ah Strong rum down there and is me alone and God to deal wid it."

"You get permission from Mr. Carson to pick them coconut?" asked Blue, staring at the coconuts.

"Which coconut?" asked Sam Browne, pretending not to have understood.

"Them same two that you have in yo' hand."

"But who tell you that them is Mr. Carson coconuts? Is he alone have coconut tree round here?" replied Sam Browne.

"Well, don't care way you tell me, I know them is Mr. Carson coconut and ah going up and tell him right now."

"If you call me name, is me and you, you hear me Blue?"

But Blue was not listening. He was already on his way to the Great House.

Mr. Carson, upon hearing the news, rushed down to Sam Browne's shack and caught him red-handed throwing away the coconut shells. "You thief! Ah taking it out ah yo' pay at the end of the fortnight! Nigger people like you, all yo' too ungrateful. I should kick you off the estate right now," began Mr. Carson. "You low down scoundrel! Ah should lock you up and let them jail you, 'cause coconut is session. You no good! No good!"

Mr. Carson was in such a rage that he dispensed with the English language and just rattled off the vernacular, his voice bellowing in the evening quiet. Everybody came out of the other shacks to see Sam Browne being humiliated and treated like a stray dog that was so desperate, he stole even though he knew it was to his detriment. He just stood and stared while Mr. Carson raged on. "Next time you steal anything here, make sure you have yo' bundle packed, 'cause is kick, ah kicking you off this estate! Don't care how I try to help you nigger people, you turn around and thief everything ah have, everything!"

Mr. Carson ranted and raged some more until he finally got tired. He then ordered everybody back into their shacks, warning that the next person he caught stealing anything on the estate, would have to leave and go on the street to live.

Sam Browne's pride was seriously hurt. He was seen as the king of the paupers, and now he had been put in his place. Mr. Carson, with that one action, showed him that he was no lion of the animals on this estate, but was open to the same humiliation as all his fellow paupers. And not only that, but that he Carson, had the power to reduce him to the lowest. So he was now a common thief, and one and only one person was guilty for causing his fall to the very bottom. So now he was determined to get even. But he knew he had to be patient.

About two weeks later, Sam Browne saw Blue leaving the estate to go on the beach which was about a mile away. He knew that this was the chance he was waiting for to teach Blue a lesson once and for all. He hustled out of his shack and took off at top pace for the shortcut he knew Blue always used to get to the beach. He made sure no one saw him as he took off his shirt and entered the bushes to lay-wait Blue. As Blue approached, he remained absolutely still until he was right in front of him. He pounced, grabbing him around the neck with one hand while using the other to wrap his shirt around Blue's head, covering his eyes. He dragged him into the bush and there whipped him savagely.

With every blow he struck, using a coconut broom he had specially selected a week early specifically for this purpose, he asked Blue where was Carson to save him now. He whipped Blue to his satisfaction and then warned him if he said one word to Mr. Carson, he would kill him. Pulling out a huge butcher's knife from his waist, he told Blue that he could kill him now and no one would know.

When Blue saw the knife, for the shirt had long fallen off his face, he lost control of his bowel muscles and a most embarrassing catastrophe ensued. He began to plead with Sam Browne not to kill him, who beholding his pitiful state and sensing the unpleasant smell diffusing in the atmosphere, put back the knife in his waist and left Blue with a final sentence: "You can't say I didn't warn you."

Blue remained in the bushes until nightfall. When he was sure that no one was around, he went down to the beach, bathed, and washed his trousers. He made sure that everyone was in their shack and asleep before he approached the estate and entered his own shack. He was shivering with cold and his skin was ablaze with the burning caused by the salt water in the bruises all over his body. He lay down on his coconut fibre mattress, but this brought little comfort. The terror of how close he came to losing his life simply would not leave his mind. He did not sleep much that night due to being constantly awakened by nightmares of being chased by Sam Browne carrying a cutlass, and demanding his head as a green coconut to chase his rum.

The next morning, his entire body was aching so badly that he couldn't go to work. He managed to peep out of his shack and asked one of the other workers to tell Mr. Carson that he was sick and could not report for duties. He stayed in his shack for the entire week recovering from the beating. When he did finally return to work, he made sure to avoid Sam Browne for a very long time and was always careful how he dealt with him thereafter.

He however always harboured the desire to revenge the beating. His hope was that Sam Browne would make the mistake of crossing Mr. Carson one of these days, resulting in him being kicked off the estate. But although Sam Browne refusing to work on Sunday was a golden opportunity to get even, Blue didn't dare tell as he could risk another confrontation with Sam Browne. And who knows what Sam Browne would do this time. But Blue had little doubt, for Sam Browne had given him a solemn promise.

So Sunday morning came and Blue went rounding up everybody to go to work, but he did not knock at Sam Browne's shack. Everyone else turned out to work and everything was alright, once Mr. Carson did not show up to check on the workers. But at about 11:30 a.m., after returning from Sunday service, Mr. Carson came and took his usual look at how the work was proceeding. He immediately realised that Sam Browne was not there and demanded to know where he was. Everyone looked at Mr. Carson with a stare that said: We don't know. Mr. Carson decided to check down at Sam Browne's shack. As he was about to bang on the half sheet of galvanise that served as the door, Sam Browne opened it and, with his bundle over his left shoulder and cutlass in his right hand, said to Mr. Carson.

"Carson, pay me what you owe me so that me could leave yo' place now!" Mr. Carson jumped back with sudden shock. He was so shocked that he didn't speak. All the blood seemed drained from his face as it became milk-white. It was as if he had come face to face with death. He just stood and stared as if he was seeing a ghost. "Carson, like you no hear me! Me say gee me my fortnight money and let me leave yo' place. Me want me money, Carson!" continued Sam Browne, his voice rising. He stepped out of the shack and towards Mr. Carson who immediately retreated.

"Easy, Mr. Browne, take it e…"

"Carson, you deaf? Gee me my money! I want me money!"

Mr. Carson looked left then right and it was clear he was contemplating an escape. Should he run away, or stay and face what looked like certain death? He wasn't sure what to do. By this time, some of the workers, hearing Sam Browne's powerful voice, came running to see what was going on.

"Carson, you is ah white man and have de law on yo' side. But me have me cutlass in me hand. And as you see, it sharpen back and belly. So gee me my money and let me go, for if me no get my money now, de law go hang me fo' you. Me want my money and me want my money now."

Mr. Carson put a shaking bleached-white hand in his pocket and took out all the coins he found. He passed them over to Sam Browne without bothering to count them. Sam Browne took them without a word, turned, and headed for the road. He never returned to the estate.

By this time, more workers, including Blue, had gathered around looking on as a visibly trembling Mr. Carson stood looking at a departing Sam Browne. A minute or so later, he had recovered enough to bark an order for everyone to return to work. They lingered just enough, all eyes on Mr. Carson, obliging Blue to encourage, "Come on, all yo' hear Mr. Carson; back to wuk, back to wuk."

Blue's fear of Sam Browne multiplied after this incident, and for a while he was all but paranoid. For one, it took a very long time for Blue to venture to the beach, and it was a full two months before he dared leave the grounds of the estate. In the night, he would especially secure the door of his shack, and he sometimes slept under trees in different parts of the estate, just in case Sam Browne came to his shack looking for him. He was dead sure now that Sam Browne would do what he said on the day he was giving the whipping. He prayed that Sam Browne did not suspect him of having had anything to do with Mr. Carson knocking at his shack that Sunday morning.

Three days after his near fatal encounter with Sam Browne, Mr. Carson called Blue to the Great House. He told a story of the new dangers of thieves, robbers and the like going around these days, and the need for estate owners like him to have more protection. "So you see, Blue," he said, "that is why I went and buy me self this new handgun to walk around with on the estate. You know it is just for protection, 'cause one never knows when something could happen. I mean, all the other guns I have here are rifles, and one cannot walk around with a rifle in his pocket. It is just too big and heavy to always carry around. I mean, I know we have cutlasses and thing, but what is a cutlass if you have to come up against a gun, and a powerful handgun like mines? A man would have to be real stupid to know I have my handgun on me and say that he threatening me with a cutlass. Don't you think that he would be begging me fo' shoot him? And guess what? In such a situation like that, I wouldn't even have no case to answer, 'cause it would be self-defence." He then paused a while.

"So, how you like me new handgun?" he finally asked, and, not waiting for Blue to answer, continued, "And guess what? If I shoot you at close range, man, you dead like a nit." Blue physically trembled on hearing this. Mr. Carson, realising he had had the effect he wanted, continued. "I mean, you know I don't mean you, I don't want to shoot you. You is a worker with good behaviour."

Having been reassured, Blue assured Mr. Carson that he liked his new gun alright. He couldn't remember hearing about any new thieves and robbers going around, but if Mr. Carson, a white man, says so, then it must be so. White people know everything and they don't tell lie. He then ran off to tell the other workers about the new gun. "You could imagine!" he impressed upon the others, "Mr. Carson will have his gun wid him wherever he go. He go always have his protection with him. Me tell all yo', dat fella smart, smart, smart. Man, white people, them just too smart."

"So, you mean that if he come down here now he go have de gun?" asked Effie, one of the garden hands.

"But of course, Mr. Carson done tell me that he no leaving it anywhere, he go always have it."

Everybody fell silent and seemed to be in thought. Mama quietly thanked the Lord that Mr. Carson had not bought his new gun a few days earlier. If he had, Sam Browne would certainly be dead today.

"Mr. Carson is right," Blue was saying, "nigger people love to give too much problem. An' anybody who leave de estate and go to town should find them own place and is a good thing that he Sam Browne done left we estate."

"Yes," rejoined Mama, "it is a good thing he did."

But her mind was not at ease. Yes, he had escaped Mr. Carson's handgun but might well go and get himself killed at the riot in town. She later went and found out firsthand that her worry was uncalled for as he was not hurt in any way from his trip into Town. She was happy for that, for him and for herself. He was indeed a brave and strong man, an example that any boy could emulate.

It was about a week after this riot that the Administrator came to visit. The entire estate was ordered to dress in their Sunday best and to assemble in front of the Great House for 10:00 a.m. They formed ten rows of twenty persons each and waited in the bright sunshine for the Administrator to arrive.

Most were barefooted, including Mama who was wearing her one white frock, made from three flour bags and which she only wore on Sundays to church. In fact, there were only three people wearing shoes. Blue had on the old brown leather boots that Mr. Carson had given him with the strict instructions that they were to be worn only on special occasions such as when he was taking Mrs. Carson to town, or if he was going to church on Christmas or New Year's Day. Ethylene and Esmie, the two house maids were also wearing shoes for which Mrs. Carson had no further use.

At the appointed time, the colonial Administrator arrived in his white Vauxhall car. The car drove up the driveway and stopped in front of the Great House, making itself a barrier between the rows of estate workers and the house. It was the first time Mama was seeing a car, although she had heard many stories about them. It made such a strange sound that Mama wondered how the Administrator was not afraid to ride in something like that. She and many others in the rows couldn't take their eyes off the car, it was indeed a wonderful machine.

The Administrator came out and the car was driven off and parked to the side of the house. He was a tall man dressed all in white, including a white hard hat with a shining silver spike at the top. Mr. Carson met him at the bottom of the steps leading up to the veranda. They shook hands and Mr. Carson took him up to meet Mrs. Carson and then presented him to the estate workers. Remaining on the veranda, the Administrator explained that he was happy to be there and that he had brought greetings from the King. He said that the King was very happy with the good behaviour of the people on the island, especially those on this, the Carson estate. He informed them that the King prayed every day to the Lord above that the people will continue to be good and kind, and listen to those in authority over them.

He said the people on Mr. Carson's estate were very lucky as they had roofs over their heads which they paid little for; they had jobs, and they had food to eat. He told them that they must always listen to Mr. Carson, for he was a good man who provided for their well-being, thinking little about himself. He reminded them that it cost Mr. Carson a lot to keep all these people on the estate, and they must not be ungrateful to him for all he was doing in their interest. From his breast pocket he took an envelope which he said was a letter sent by the King to Mr. Carson, thanking him for being so kind to his subjects working on the Carson estate. He finished by saying that he as Administrator, was also very grateful to Mr. Carson for everything he was doing to create employment for the people on his estate.

The Administrator then asked if anyone knew the full title of the King. He said that he had visited many estates on the island and was surprised that the good subjects of the British Empire did not know the full title of their King. That no one has been able to answer this question correctly up to this point was unbelievable. There were two prizes to give to anyone who could correctly answer this question. These prices were sent by the King himself as he was concerned about his subjects whom he really did love.

Blue put up his hand to answer the question and when the Administrator called on him, he said "King George." "Almost but not correct," responded the Administrator. On the encouragement of Mrs. Carson, Ethylene tried, "King George VI?" she enquired. But again the Administrator said that it was not the complete answer.

As she stood there in the sun, Mama's mind ran back to the picture of the King on his nice chair called a throne, and it came to her. Against her own will and wisdom, she raised her hand and the Administrator called on her.

"His Majesty King George VI." She said.

"Splendid! Splendid!" said the Administrator. "Come up here!"

Mama, not knowing what to do, stood her ground for a moment looking at Mr. Carson who was standing behind the administrator for some sign. "Come on up, what you waiting for? Come on up here," insisted the Administrator.

Mama left the row and stepped forward. She mounted the stairs to the veranda where the Administrator was standing. He asked her name, then took the picture of himself from his wife and presented it along with a sixpence piece to her. He stretched out a gloved hand, took her right hand and shook it saying, "Well done, well done." As she descended the steps, he began to clap, "Give her a hand. Give her a hand." And everybody, including Mr. Carson and Mrs. Carson, simply obeyed like loyal servants and began to clap. Mama could not believe that the whole world, including Mr. Carson and the Administrator, were clapping for her. Yes, this third picture was a picture of her triumph, the moment when God specially blessed her.

It was later that same day when it was all over, that Mr. Carson came down to her shack and told her how proud he was of her and that she had done the whole estate very proud. He said that she was free to stay in the shack he had rented her for life. That from that day onwards, he would not be deducting any rent money from her fortnightly wages. He also told her that the shack was now hers and if she wanted to move it off the estate in the future, she was free to do so. Mama, for her part, simply felt that God was truly good. That night, she knelt down and thanked Him from all her heart for being so gracious to her.

Yes, thought Boysie, as he followed his aunt home, their little tin shack had many memories of his mother's life. It was the place where he felt safe. A place he and Mama really loved. Mama was always cleaning everything, not just the shack but the surrounding yard, and always reminding Boysie that cleanliness is next to godliness. She would wash the one set of curtains they had and close the one window and the door and they would stay outside until the curtains were dried and she could hang them up again. Mama didn't like people peeping into her house, even if she was the poorest of the poor.

As they walked, he tried to imagine what living in his aunt's house would be like. He knew that she only took him in because he had nowhere else to go. Mama always said that if anything happened to her, that is where he would have to stay, for he would have no one else. And when all is said and done, aunt Maude was her sister and his aunt. Blood would always be thicker than water. As he thought of these things, he recalled how Mama had first told him that one day he might have to live with aunt Maude.

"You know Boysie, I always wanted that you would have a brother," she said.

"Me, a brother Mama, why?" he asked.

"Because then the two of you could have grown up like me and your aunt Maude."

"Like you and aunt Maude? What do you mean Mama?"

"Well, aunt Maude is my only sister and she and I were always together when we were children."

"I have you Mama, so I don't need anyone else," he assured her.

"Well, I might not always be here."

"What do you mean?" asked a surprised Boysie. "Are you going to leave me?"

"Oh no, Boysie, I would never leave you. Never."

"So then, why did you say that you might not be always here?"

"Boysie, I don't have the lease on my life, and only God knows the future."

"What do you mean? What is the lease of your life? And if you don't have it then who has it?" he questioned, his surprise now being replaced by worry.

"I mean that I don't know how long I am going to live. Only God knows that. Only he can tell how long we all would live. So it might be that I would die before you."

"Oh Mama, please don't die now. Please don't die before me."

"I don't want to die now and I don't want to die before you, but these are things God decides. When he calls us, we have to go Boysie. Please promise me that you would behave yourself very good to aunt Maude when you go to live with her."

"But I am not going to live with aunt Maude. I am staying with you," he had said most adamantly.

"No, not now but one day, and when that day come, you must remember that you must be the best you can be, no matter what happens. No matter what the situation, for she is your aunt and the closest family to you on this earth."

With that Mama began to cry and in between her tears, she kept saying, "You must promise me, you must promise me that you would be good. You must promise..."

"I promise, Mama, I promise, please don't cry anymore," pleaded a now crying Boysie, "You won't have to worry Mama. I promise I would be good."

"And you promise to do as you are told and never question the decisions of your aunt?"

"I promise Mama. Please don't cry anymore."

And Mama was right; God has called her, and now he was all alone and on his way to live with aunt Maude, just like Mama had foretold.

By this time, they were nearing his aunt's home. She told Boysie that they would go to his mother's shack the following day to collect the things that are still there as it was too late to do so now. Boysie did not respond as there was no need to. He knew that it was a decision and he simply had to listen and understand.

THE PREDICAMENT

The first night sleeping in aunt Maude's house was an experience for Boysie. He was given some old clothing with which to make his bed and it was clear that they weren't fresh and clean old clothing. There was the unmistakable smell of stale urine on them. Boysie did not know where to make his bed, and stood with this bundle of old clothes in his hands looking around. Aunt Maude, seeing this, indicated that he should make his bed in the little space on the floor next to the water bucket. Boysie did as he was told. He was given an oversized old shirt of uncle Rick, aunt Maude's husband, to use as pyjamas. As he lay down to sleep, he heard his aunt remark, "Another mouth to feed in this guava crop time."

Boysie fell asleep immediately. Probably it was the result of an activity-filled day, probably it was the tiredness brought on by an emotionally-burdened heart and a broken spirit. Whatever it was, he went to sleep as if dead, a few moments after his head hit the bedding

Mama stood there in her flour bag dress, with the comb stuck in her hair and smiling as she always smiled at him. "Come here Boysie. Sit down, we need to talk. You see, you and I will never part. Like Jesus said, I will never leave you nor forsake you, but will be with you wherever you are, even onto the very end."

"But Mama," he began.

"No buts Boysie. You must follow he who is closest to you and live your life like him. Don't be afraid, for I am watching over you."

"But Mama, you look so nice, so nice. Mama you look just like an angel."

"Yes Boysie, I am your angel, was your angel, and will always be your angel. I will always be watching over you."

"Always?"

"Yes, always, but don't forget to ask Sam Browne, he will know. He is a good man and he is also very kind, never mind he drinks rum now and again."

"But you said that rum drinking is not good and..."

"Yes, rum drinking is not good. But remember who Sam Browne is, and rum drinking is his only fault. I see that you are going to need him now more than ever, but have faith, for God is good and you will always be safe."

"But Mama, ask Sam Browne what? What must I ask him? Mama, Mama..."

"Wake up Boysie, wake up."

Boysie awoke to find aunt Maude standing over him. At first she looked like Mama and he almost said Mama, but stopped himself just in time. As he became fully awake, he looked around him hoping to see Mama. Then it came to him, he was only dreaming. What he just experienced wasn't real in anyway, and the tears welled up in his eyes. But he refused to be overcome by his emotions. He got up and took up the bedding but didn't know where to put them. Aunt Maude, seeing his dilemma, asked.

"Did you pee your bed?"

"No aunt Maude, I don't pee my bed. Mama taught me not to drink a lot before I go to sleep and therefore I would…"

"Ok, ok, I understand," said aunt Maude. "All the same, you need to put them bedding outside to catch some sun. So take them and put them on the rock stones in the backyard. Now remember that it is cloudy today and the rain might fall. So you have to look out for rain and move your bedding before rain wet them or you will have nothing to sleep on tonight," she warned.

After putting his bedding outside, Boysie got a tin cup of water and the root of a nut grass as he could find no coconut shell fibre which was always plentiful on the estate. He scrubbed his teeth vigorously with the nut grass root then finished the process by using his index finger, and rinsing with the water. As he stood in the yard thinking what he should do next, aunt Maude called, "Boysie, why you standing up in the yard? Come and get your tea."

Boysie went and found a medium-sized tin cup of bush-water tea but no sweat sweet potato or bam-bam, and he didn't understand it. He remembered that his mother had said that unlike her, his aunt had married well and therefore could afford a lot of the things she couldn't. So why was there no sweat sweet potato or bam-bam?

Aunt Maude didn't live on the estate in one of its shacks like his mother did. She had her own good board house that her husband had built. It wasn't big, but in the eyes of Boysie, it was better than anything that he and Mama ever had. Aunt Maude had a wooden kitchen outside in the yard; she also had a coal pot, some tin pots, and even three water buckets in the kitchen.

All of this struck Boysie for he and Mama had nothing like it. Mama used to cook outside in the open air on a three-stone fireside, using the dry wood she gathered as fuel. There were many times that due to rain, Mama couldn't put a pot on the fire. On these occasions, she would give Boysie some sugar water while pleading with God to stop the rain, so she could cook and give her one child something hot. Mama had told him that aunt Maude had things far better and this is why she wanted him to get an education so he could leave the shack and with it, the dependence on Mr. Carson and his estate to make a living.

Later that day, Boysie went with aunt Maude to the shack to collect the remaining things that she considered might be useful. As they got closer, Boysie just couldn't stop the tears that had welled up in him. He tried to cry silently but couldn't help it. As the sounds began coming out muffled by his hand cupped over his mouth, there came a voice behind them, "Maude." They turned around to see Mr. Carson.

"Oh, good morning Mr. Carson," said aunt Maude in her best Queen's English.

"How is Boysie holding up?" he asked. "Poor fella, he must feel real lost and heart-broken. But at least he has you."

"Yes, you are right Mr. Carson. It is sad that his mother had to die now. But what can we do? I have five of me own and in this hard guava crop it ain't easy. But I will do me best with him. By the way, we came to get the things from the house. We can't take all one time so I hope you don't mind we making a few trips."

"No, I don't mind; this house is now for Boysie as I did give it to his mother. The Administrator himself asked me to give it to her. And I can't take it back now, for I will be going back on me word to the Administrator. I also promise his mother that he could have it when she dead."

Aunt Maude was taken aback by this news and Mr. Carson, noting this, continued. "His mother care about she one child and would have given she life for him. Before she dead, she specifically called me and ask me about this house and I give she me word and will keep it. After all, it is the least I could do. He is now motherless and fatherless, and only God knows what will happen to him in this world."

It was true that Boysie did not know who his father was. His mother had promised to tell him all about his father, but died not having done so. Boysie wasn't sure that he had a father at all, but never really felt the need for one as Mama fulfilled both roles.

"So you mean that we can move this house for Boysie and put it somewhere else?" asked aunt Maude.

"Well, I told his mother that I know you have no land. So the house should not be moved for now until Boysie gets a little older and can be independent. You don't have to worry, I give the Administrator and Boysie mother me word. This house will always be waiting for him."

Aunt Maude knew better than to argue with the de facto mayor of the village. She simply said, "Of course, of course. I am sure he mother would want it no other way." With that Mr. Carson took his leave.

Under the direction of his aunt, Boysie gathered his things and aunt Maude took a few of Mama's things she said were needed. They stepped out of the shack and she pushed in the door and spun the piece of wood nailed on to the doorpost which acted as a stopper, effectively keeping the door shut.

As they walked back to aunt Maude's house, Boysie thought of what Mr. Carson had said and he realised once again that he was right. His Mama was the best Mama in the world, and he was very special to her. He instinctively knew that he will never be that special to anyone again in life. Never ever.

Even if life at aunt Maude's was new to him, he had to settle down rather rapidly. School was on holidays and he was given his daily chores to do. These included filling the large water barrels and the various water buckets by fetching water from the river; tending the goats and sheep; feeding the chickens, and sweeping the yard every morning. These were things he never did when he lived with Mama. But he remembered what Mama had said, "Anything aunt Maude tell you do, you do it without murmur."

Boysie noted that anytime there was need for one of the children to do something around the house, whether it was roasting a breadfruit, running to the shop to buy some sugar, washing the tin cups and plates, or watering the vegetables in the kitchen garden, he was the one called to do it ten out of ten times.

Sometimes at the end of the day, he was so tired after these chores that he would fall asleep like the dead. He was often very hungry during the day, for he found that the tin cup of bush tea with the infrequent piece of sweat sweet potato, Madungo bakes or bam-bam were not enough to keep his hunger at bay. After getting this bush tea at 8:00 in the morning, by 11:00 he was so famished that he sometimes thought he would faint and fall down. He however soon found a way of dealing with this. He would dig out and eat the raw sweet potatoes he found in the fields already harvested, or by picking and eating the green peas when his aunt Maude and other members of the family were not in sight.

Life was much harder than he ever thought it could be, even though Mama had told him he mustn't expect anything easy, especially when she would not be there to look out for him. He remembered how she had explained this to him just a few months before her death.

It was a very rainy day and one-legged Mr. Marshall had fallen down as he tried to enter his shack, due to the land in front of it being waterlogged and swampy from the heavy rains. He tried to raise himself up but couldn't, and had to crawl on all fours to get inside. Mama went with Boysie and tried to help him up, but she was too weak to raise such a heavy man, and so was heartbroken that she couldn't help. When they went back inside drenched to the bone, she was overcome with sympathy and empathy for Mr. Marshall.

"Boysie," she had said, "life can sometimes be very cruel, especially when people lack basic love and feelings for others. You might meet people like that sometime in life, but you must forgive them, and you yourself must never become like that. Always remember that Jesus says that we must love one another."

"Mama, I know I will never meet anyone like that."

"Don't say that Boysie, for one never knows."

"But Mama, you are not like that, are you?"

"No, I am not like that and I can never be like that."

"You see, I will never meet anyone like that for I will always live with you."

"Boysie, I am tired telling you that anything can happen to me, and then you will be on your own."

"But Mama, you said that if anything should happen to you, I will be living with aunt Maude."

"Yes, that is true. You will be living with your aunt Maude."

"And is she like that?"

"No Boysie." Said his mother softly and hesitantly, "No, your aunt is not like that. And remember, please never forget that aunt Maude is my sister and would never see you die. But still, everybody have their rough seas to cross. Whatever happens, whatever other people might be, once it is something bad or wrong, you must never become that.

You hear me, you must never become that. And always remember it is not always easy to forgive, but it is always the right thing to do."

As the summer progressed, Boysie became accustomed to his routine and never did he complain. He realised that even though his aunt was much better off than his mother, life was still very hard for her and her family. And even with this hardship, she had done him and his mother a tremendous favour by taking him in.

He visited his mother's shack as often as he could and would have loved to do so more often, but his chores at home didn't allow much time for that. Apart from that, aunt Maude had forbidden him to go to the shack too often as she felt that Mr. Carson would not like this very much. At least this is what she told Boysie.

Day-dreaming about Mama and remembering how she cared for him became a regular activity with Boysie. He would remember the conversations they had and the very stern instructions his mother would give. He remembered the times she would insist that he did things she thought were right but which he didn't want to do. These included his going off to school the first time and taking his lessons seriously once he was in school.

Mama also appeared often in his dreams. On these occasions, she was always sad and took him on her lap the way she used to do up until he was about 10 years old. She would give him instructions, always reminding him never to be afraid, that she will always be with him, and that everything is going to be alright.

Those dreams always seem very real to Boysie. He would quite often awake in the middle of the night, only to find it was nothing more than a dream, and end up wishing that he hadn't woken up. It was in one of those dreams that Mama told him a second time about Sam Browne, and the need for Boysie to listen and follow him. On this occasion, Mama once again appeared in her one and only white frock, and was explaining to Boysie how to cook rice and peas. As she stood over the three-stone fireside, Sam Browne appeared and said hello to them and so started a conversation between him and Mama.

"So what you trying to teach Boysie now? You know that he is ah boy and should be taught things that fellas do, not so?" said Sam Browne.

"Yes Samuel, I know you are right and that is why I am sending him to you so that you can teach him a thing or two."

"Me, you sending me away, why, why, why do you want to send me away?" demanded Boysie.

"No, I am not sending you away; I am sending you to Samuel."

"But why? Why are you sending me to him?"

"Please Boysie, follow Sam Browne, follow Sam Browne. Let him hold your hand now and we will meet later. I can't carry you all the way, so let him help us and you and I, we will meet later."

"Come now Boysie," said Sam Browne, "you is a big boy now and you need to learn to be independent."

"Thank you Samuel," said Mama. "I know you will take good care of him. Never mind what I said before, I know that you understand your responsibility now."

"But you know I can't do this alone, and Boysie would never believe me. He know me only as…"

"Samuel, you will not be alone, for I will never leave you nor Boysie. I just ask that you do your part now. If you do, Boysie would make us both very proud."

Sam Browne took his hand and, as they walked away, he admonished Boysie that he needs to grow up and not always depend on his mother. As they walked, Boysie would glance back now and again, and as if by magic, his mother stood in the same spot and ever so slowly vanished.

He awoke to find Mr. George shaking him and saying, "Boysie, wake up. Wake up Boysie. You dreaming about yo' Mama again. You have to stop thinking about yo' mother so much. She done dead and you can't bring she back." Boysie awoke and looked around him as he didn't understand anything for the first few seconds. But his environs soon reminded him of where he was as his dream gave way to reality. Yes, Mr. George was right, Mama is dead and he must find some way of accepting that.

One day after he had been living with aunt Maude for just over two weeks, she called him into the kitchen. "Boysie, you will be thirteen this September, isn't it?"

"Yes aunt Maude, on the 19th."

"I know that, and I think is time you learn a trade. Boys don't go to school up to standard five, and it is better that you have something useful to do. With the help of the Lord, I find you a good job."

Boysie's heart almost stopped at that very moment. His breathing became irregular. No, not this, this just couldn't be, his mind immediately began to rebel. Mama had always said that education was his future, that he was one day going to be a doctor or a lawyer, somebody important and respected. He was supposed to swell Mama's nose by showing that he was indeed very bright. Yes, brighter than any black person in the village, and just as bright as any white person, if not brighter. His success in education was to be the recompense for Mama's struggles and pains. As she put it, his education was to be proof of her talents, that she was poor but not stupid. That she didn't get anywhere not because she was dunce, but because she never had a chance due to one thing and one thing only, poverty.

As his aunt spoke, Boysie's educational journey up to this point flashed through his mind rapidly. From the beginning to what now seemed to be the end, all stood out vividly. He remembered the first Monday when he went to school and his mother's determination that he must go.

"Boysie," she said as she bathed him, "I don't want you to come like me, working in people's fields for nothing. I want you to have a better life."

"Mama, I don't want a better life; I want to live with you."

"You will still live with me, only that our life would be better."

298

"How better?"

"Remember you said you want to buy me a big, big, big house?"

"Yes, bigger than that of Mr. Carson," said Boysie, stretching his arms as far as they could extend.

"Well, my boy, if you really going to buy such a big house, then you are going to need a lot of money and without good learning, you can't get money, so you need to go to school."

"But why can't I stay home and you teach me?"

"I would like to do that but I don't know enough."

The truth was that, as regards literacy, Mama could only read, add and subtract. With writing, she could accomplish little more than a friendly letter. As far back as one could trace, she and Maude were the first two members of their family to ever attend school. This happened because a Methodist minister had advised her mother that she should send them to school to learn to read so that they might be able to read the Bible at least. He would later comment that Mama had a very good head and could go very far indeed. This was not to be.

At school she did learn comparatively rapidly. But it was all cut short with the death of her own mother and the resulting need for her to go to work on the estate, to feed herself and her younger sister Maude. Mama had never forgotten that. She had heard many people say poverty is no crime, but she wasn't sure. From her experience, it always had a very heavy and terrible sentence for its victims. In her case, it had imprisoned her in a multitude of ways, and threatened to do the same to her son. She was determined to prevent this from happening to him if she could.

She had come to realise the value of an education, if only in the most cruel of ways. She was the only worker on the entire estate who could read and/or write. The most all the others were capable of, was the simplest of addition and subtraction, nothing more. And this they all knew because they needed it to be able to count the pennies they were paid by Mr. Carson for their labour on his land. If they needed to write something, even their names, they came to her. It was the same if they needed something read.

And she will always remember the time when the colonial Administrator came and asked the question about the King's title. Even though Ethylene had seen the picture of the king every day of her life, she simply could not read the words His Majesty written at its base, and so could not answer the Administrator's question correctly.

So on that first morning after bathing him and giving him his cup of bush water and a piece of sweat sweet potato, she had dressed him in the light-blue shirt and khaki pants, which was the school uniform. He put on the pair of gunslingers she had bought for him to wear to school, and she reminded him that he should take care of them. She took him to the school and watched as they said prayers for assembly that first morning. As they prayed, Boysie had opened his eyes to see if Mama was still standing there. He saw the tears flowing down her cheeks as she wiped her face with the back of her palms. He was doing the same.

These first few days of his schooling were very hard for both Boysie and Mama as he felt absolutely lost without her around. He was in a situation where he knew no one, as he was the only child in the school from the Carson estate. Everyone and everything was new to him. It broke Mama's heart to know that she had to force her Boysie to go through something which she knew must be hard for him. But yet it had to be done.

Within a few weeks however, they both were very satisfied, even happy that she had made such a decision. Boysie returned home every day with new stories of what he had learned in school. Mama was more than happy and excited that he was learning so quickly. The teacher was so impressed with Boysie's ability and performance that he confided in Mama his belief that Boysie was something special and he was going to become a doctor or a lawyer, certainly somebody important. This was much, much more than Mama could ever hope for. A teacher yes, a policeman or a messenger in an office was Mama's high hopes. But a lawyer or a doctor! Not in her wildest dreams. She always knew that he was a very bright boy, but here now was the proof. The teacher himself had confirmed it. And from that day on, she was determined to do everything in her power to make sure that Boysie became somebody.

Over the six years of his attending school, Boysie had just gotten better and better. He was so good that the teacher had indicated to Mama that he knew for sure that Boysie would pass the Standard Six exams with flying colours when his turn came to sit them. She knew that that would mean the beginning of great things to come. As he spoke, Mama had looked away, for tears had begun to well up in her eyes. She did not want the teacher to see how touched she was by the academic performance of her Boysie.

That evening, Mama made some cornmeal porridge with the little bit of cow's milk that Maude had given her. After they ate Mama told Boysie that he must never forget to thank the Lord for all he had, regardless of the situation he was in. She told him that today they had plenty, for they had cornmeal porridge with milk in it, but who knows what tomorrow brings. But whatever it brings, he must always remember to thank the Lord.

And that night, try as she might, Mama could not fall asleep. After a while, she got down from the wooden bed, got on her knees and started to pray. In her prayer, she told God that she didn't get Boysie the right way in his sight, but that she knew that He understood and had forgiven her. She said that she alone was guilty of this sin and not Boysie and, while she knew that the sins of the parents follow the children, she was asking God that he would spare her Boysie this. She thanked God for having given him such a good head, and pleaded with God to make him into somebody successful. She said she would not be able to help Boysie in achieving any of this and was leaving it in God's hand; she was surrendering her one and only child to him, like Samuel's mother did. She told God that, even though she would love to see Boysie become a doctor or a lawyer, she would still be very satisfied if God had other plans, for she was prepared for His will and not hers to be done.

When she got up off her knees, Mama felt reassured that even though she would not live to see what her son would become, he was definitely going to be a success. She felt that she, through that prayer, had received a promise from God that he was going to bless Boysie.

Boysie knew all of these prayers and tears of his mother; and believed he had an obligation to succeed in his educational pursuit, if only for her. He remembered her always reminding him that his education was the most important thing in his life and that it was something to be cherished to the utmost. She had explained to him that it was the only thing he can achieve in this life which, once acquired, he would die with, for nothing and no one could ever take it away.

"Boysie, you know," she had said, "this house belongs to Mr. Carson and he can throw us out whenever he wants, and we will have to live on the streets for we will have no place to go."

"Mama, you mean that Mr. Carson can tell us to leave and we have to leave?" he asked incredulously.

"Yes, he can, for he owns this house. But not just this house; all the other houses on the estate; and as a matter of fact the whole estate."

"But this is our house, you yourself said so. So how can he come and throw us out?" protested Boysie.

"He can because he only lent it to us, but it is his house."

"That is unfair; he already has a big house and the whole estate. Why should he have our house as well?"

"It might be unfair, but that's the way it is, and there is nothing we can do about it."

"Well Mama, we need to get our own house and move out."

"Well, that is easier said than done, Boysie."

"But how can he take something that belongs to us?"

"Boysie, it doesn't belong to us and, even when things belong to us, people can simply take them and do what they want. And sometimes it is not even someone, but something can take what we have and we can do nothing about it."

"What do you mean?" asked a slightly confused Boysie.

"Well, we can for example build a house and as soon as we finish building it, a hurricane or great storm blows it down. Or we can buy a goat or a sheep and then it falls sick and dead, and what can we do?"

"Then we can lose everything we have Mama, everything."

"No, not everything, for whenever you have education, it is yours until you are dead, and no one and nothing can take it from you. It is in your head until you are dead."

"What do you mean Mama?"

"Well you see; I can read and write and spell and wherever I am, on this estate or another, I would still be able to do that, and nothing and no one can take that from me. They can take this house, my job, even my life, but my little bit of education no one can take. I would die with it."

"And that is why you want me to have a good education?"

"Yes Boysie, but that is not the only reason why."

"Then why else?"

"Because you have good brains, and one day you are going to be a great man in this country."

"You mean like Mr. Carson?"

"No, not like Mr. Carson, you need to think higher, much higher."

"Mama, you mean that I should become the colonial Administrator!" exploded Boysie.

"Well, I don't know if you could become the colonial Administrator, for he is a white man. But you sure are going to be someone more important than Mr. Carson."

So that was Mama's dream for him, to have such an education that he would be more important than Mr. Carson. But here now was aunt Maude telling him that his road to that success had ended, even though it had not even begun. It was simply not possible.

"Boysie," his aunt's voice called him back to the present. "What is wrong, you feel sick?"

"No aunt Maude," managed a bewildered Boysie.

"Then what is the problem? What cause this sudden change in you?"

How was Boysie to explain to her that he was destined to be a lawyer or a doctor, somebody great in this society? How was he, a twelve-year-old boy, to explain to her, a grown woman, that his future was not in learning a trade but in books? No, he did not know what to say, he did not know how to begin to explain.

"Well… well, Mama said," he began but was not able to finish as aunt Maude interrupted.

"Yo' Mama is dead, and now you live here with me, and so time to forget what yo' Mama said and do as I tell you."

"But Mama said that I…"

"Forget yo' Mama, I tell you!" shouted aunt Maude, losing her patience.

Boysie stood in silence. This was the first time in his life he was faced with a situation where he needed to say something and didn't know how to say it. He could sense his chest beginning to heave up and down and as he looked at the floor, he was conscious of the louder breathing of aunt Maude.

"Yo' life now depend on me," continued aunt Maude. "And you would be better off making a few cents which would help you later in life than going school and wasting yo' time."

Boysie still felt like telling her that his teacher had forecasted that he would pass the standard six exams and become a very educated person later in life. But he knew that this would just bring more recrimination, and therefore decided to let his aunt have the last word.

"I talk with Mr. Carson yesterday about giving you a hold on at the estate. He said he has no space for anybody right now as things slow, but because of me, he willing to give you a hold on in the stable to help Blue take care of the horses. This is ah good opportunity for ah boy yo' age, so hold on to it with both hands and make good use of it."

All that Boysie could think was that Mama had said that school was the most important thing in his life, and that whatever he did, he should never forget that. He just knew that his aunt wasn't right, that she was making a terrible mistake. How he wished Mama could be there to make this clear to aunt Maude. But alas, he had to face this on his own. There was no Mama.

"Mr. Carson say that yo' start Monday coming and he expect you there early," continued aunt Maude. "He say it is not much work but at least you will learn to tend horses and become useful to yourself and society."

Boysie now had a serious battle taking place in his head. He was caught between two instructions of his mother and didn't know what to do. She had said whatever he did he must attend school. But she had also said that he must always obey aunt Maude. What was he to do now, when carrying out one meant disobeying the other.

After aunt Maude was finished with him, Boysie went around to the back of the house and sat in the breadfruit tree thinking what to do. He then remembered that Mama always prayed whenever she had a problem and always made him do the same. How to pray was something Mama began teaching Boysie since he was a very small child. So it was something he knew how to do, and was accustomed to doing. And this was what he now did.

On Monday morning aunt Maude woke Boysie at 5:30 a.m. He fetched water from the river and filled up the barrels, took out the animals, had his cup of bush water tea and a large piece of sweat sweet potato and headed off to meet Mr. Carson and Blue. He liked horses, but just knew that caring for them was not what his mother wanted for him. No, she had big and great dreams.

He also knew that his mother would have resented him working under Blue. While she never said anything bad about him, at least not in his presence, he had the distinct feeling she had a serious dislike for him. She never praised him, but instead was always saying how different he was from Sam Browne whom she saw as being strong and capable, and wasn't afraid of anyone, including Mr. Carson.

As he walked Boysie could see the stables in his mind's eye. He saw everything on the estate, for he knew where everything was on that property. Like his mother before him, he had grown up there. He had never worked before and knew not what to expect, but aunt Maude had told him that he must do all that Blue required of him. Indeed he was to call Blue, "Mr. Blue," and always answer Mr. Carson "Yes Sir". As these thoughts and pictures of the estate filled his mind, he remembered how his mother had always hoped that Mr. Carson would never have over him the power, he had over her. He remembered that she had said that what she admired most about Sam Browne was his independence of Mr. Carson and the estate.

"Boysie," she had said, "you see Sam Browne, he might not be better off than anybody here; but he sure ain't worse, 'cause he is his own man. And mark my words, you see those bamboo brooms he selling, one day he is going to have the money to buy his own piece of land and build himself a good board house. You watch and see if I am not right. When God say something is for you, no man can take it away. You watch and see."

Boysie was so taken up with all of these memories and thoughts that he didn't see Sam Browne coming out of the small pathway on his right. He also didn't hear when Sam Browne called to him the first time. As he walked on contemplating what was to be his fate in life under the power of Mr. Carson, and being a victim of the poverty and ignorance of the life of an estate worker, he heard the voice.

"Boysie!"

He was startled by the sudden break in the quietness which caused a consequential break in his thoughts. He turned around to see Sam Browne pulling his wooden cart and instantly thought: where was Sam Browne going this early morning with his cart? Certainly not to sell brooms, for there was none on the cart and anyway, it was much too early to go waking up people to try and sell them anything.

Since leaving the estate years earlier, Sam Browne had built himself this wooden cart which he used on weekends to transport his brooms from house to house and village to village seeking customers. This was hard and demanding work. The wheels of the cart were made of wood, which were covered with rubber, cut from discarded tyres. The only things metal on this cart were the bearings which were placed into the middle of the wooden wheels to allow their smooth spinning while preventing their corrosion. Pulling and pushing this cart up the many hills of this rugged island demanded muscles of steel.

"Boysie, what happen? You don't know me?" asked the approaching Sam Browne. "Is me, Sam Browne Boysie." Boysie had been so startled that he had not answered Sam Browne's first or second call. "Where you going this early morning?" enquired Sam Browne, "I no see you since yo' mother dead. How they treating you?" Sam Browne seemed to want to know everything all at once. Boysie did not know where to begin to answer.

"Good morning Sam Browne, I didn't see you there."

"Where you going this early morning?" repeated Sam Browne.

"I am starting work today on the estate by Mr. Carson."

"What! Which wuk? Who send you to wuk on de estate and fo' what?"

"Aunt Maude said she talk with Mr. Carson and he agreed to take me on to help Blue tend the horses."

"Wid Blue tending horse!" said Sam Browne indignantly, "Why she sending you to wuk on that estate under a fool?"

"She says I am going to leave school now and therefore I need to learn a trade and she got this hold on for me from Mr. Carson."

"What does she mean you going to leave school soon? She don't know that you is the brightest boy in the school and you going for the exams to go higher in education? What is this at all with this woman? She gone crazy?"

"I don't know," said Boysie. "And I know Mama wish me to become somebody important and respected and get off from Mr. Carson estate just like you did. And, and, aunt Maude is now sending me back to the estate to work with Blue. How am I going to please Mama now?" asked Boysie, his spirit clearly broken. Not being able to contain himself anymore, he broke down in tears, becoming a complete picture of resignation and hopelessness. His spirit simply needed this release.

Sam Browne became silent for a while as his anger at Maude gave way to compassion for Boysie. The memories rushed to his mind and he thought how justified was Boysie's mother's fears for the future of her child, once she had departed this world. She had told him that Boysie would be orphaned when she was gone. She had insisted that this would not merely be because of her physical absence, but because there would be no one to connect with him through the heart. Sam Browne was seeing that now. It made him sad, terribly ashamed and genuinely heart-broken that he was still alive, and yet Boysie was so alone in spirit, so lost in grief, and so abandoned by love. He knew he had to do something. At least that he owed Boysie.

"Ok Boysie," he said as gently as he could. "I know how you feel, but crying never helped nobody; we have to do something about this. I don't know what, but we have to do something. I have to do something." After thinking for a few seconds, Sam Browne continued as if speaking to himself. "How could she do this? You is she sister only child and everybody say you have a good head. Everybody say you the brightest boy in this village. How could she do that?" And as if suddenly boiling over, he declared, "Not over me dead body you going to wuk under Blue on Carson estate! Never happen! Never happen!"

The anger seemed to return to Sam Browne with a great rush. Boysie, not knowing much about him, apart from what his mother had said, didn't know how he should respond. He looked at Sam Browne speechlessly, and then the dream he had of his mother telling him to follow Sam Browne returned to him. He decided not to tell this to him. Sam Browne continued, "You is not going to any wuk, you coming wid me. I slaved for nothing for Carson. Yo' mother slaved for nothing for Carson, but you not going to do that. Not over my dead body. No, not even if I have to go to Calvary and back. No, you not doing it!"

"Sam Browne," Boysie said, "I have to go because…"

"No, you don't have to," said Sam Browne, not allowing Boysie to finish. "Why is you who have to and not any of her own children when the whole world know not one of them is half as bright as you?" he asked rhetorically.

But Boysie insisted. "You see, Mama made me promise her before she died that I would never disobey aunt Maude, never ever."

That stopped Sam Browne dead in his tracks. He didn't know what to do. This was a period in Caribbean civilisation when one's word was a bond, and when obeying one's parents was a sacred duty, in particular the commands of your mother. More so if it was a promise made to her on her death-bed. And even though Sam Browne was the village's champion rum drinker, he knew one must never break these basic norms of the code of social behaviour. Disobeying your parents was tantamount to breaking God's commandment. He was also pretty sure that Boysie's mother was somewhere up there looking down on them, and she would expect him to tell Boysie that he has to obey his aunt.

"You right Boysie," he said after a few moments of silence. "Yes; you have to obey yo' mother, but I am not going to leave it so. I have to do something about this. By God, I have to do something about it."

They continued to converse and Boysie recovered his composure. He found it very interesting that Sam Browne wanted to know everything about his life at aunt Maude's. Were they feeding him enough? And where was he sleeping? How the other children related to him? And how was George, aunt Maude's husband, treating him?

Boysie answered as favourably as he could, not wanting to make Sam Browne angrier than he already seemed to be. More importantly, he wanted to carry out his mother's wishes of always being grateful to aunt Maude for everything that she did, and never saying anything bad about anyone.

But even though Boysie had done his best to paint a rosy picture of his life at aunt Maude's, Sam Browne couldn't help feeling that something was wrong. At least Boysie was being denied that which he and his mother cherished most. That which he, Sam Browne had hoped would prove that there is something good in him after all. He knew there was more to him than just drinking rum. Boysie's mother had seen it and he was sure that Boysie would be the proof of it.

But now it might never happen. All of Boysie's brains would rot just like his mother's had, without ever being used. The world would never know how truly intelligent Boysie is. And this was all his fault. He was to be blamed for this, for had he done the right and Christian thing and stood up and be responsible, this would never have happened. He then and there vowed to change it. He reminded himself that Boysie's mother used to always say to him that it was never too late to change from doing wrong to doing what is right. And it was indeed not too late for him to redeem himself. His decision was taken. He would do what is right.

As Boysie took his leave to continue his path to the Carson estate, Sam Browne reassured him that he would be attending school the coming school term. He Sam Browne is going to make sure that this happened. As Boysie proceeded on his journey, he glanced back to see an energised Sam Browne, pushing his cart back up the small path from whence he had come. He pushed it vigorously as if he couldn't wait to get back home.

When he arrived at the estate, Blue took him around to the horse stables and ordered him to get them clean. As he worked removing the horse dung, Blue would return time and again to order him to do this or that area once again. Boysie complied without a word. He spent the entire day cleaning the stables, guided by the periodic instructions of Blue. During the lunch hour, he did not have anything to eat but told no one. Instead he went and stayed in his mother's old tin shack. The memories came rushing back.

As he lay down in the little shack, he remembered the many discussions he had with Mama and he realised that she was really preparing him for life after her death. Little did he know that this would be so soon.

He recalled her one day telling him that life is never easy. He would have to struggle for what he wanted and even in the best moments of life, there are rainy days. This conversation was occasioned after Mr. Carson's small distillery where he made rum on the estate caught afire and the whole thing was virtually destroyed. This made Mr. Carson cross with everyone on the estate for weeks. He blamed all the workers for the mishap, claiming it was because he had to be following them around to ensure that they didn't laze about, that he didn't have time to attend to the proper running of the distillery.

But to Mama, this was simply one of Mr. Carson's rainy days. This was one of those where it was more than just rain, and more like a storm which always comes from time to time. But she knew that no storm endures forever, for they are all followed by a calm.

"Life Boysie," she had said, "very often brings us things we wouldn't like to have, but if we have faith, we can and will come through alright. You must never be afraid when life brings you such challenges, for you will always beat them."

"But how do you know that?" asked Boysie.

"Because I know life without challenge just does not exist."

"No, I am not talking about the challenge. How do you know that I will always beat these challenges?"

"Because I know that you will have the strength to succeed."

"Mama, you yourself always say that I am a small weak boy."

"Boysie," said Mama, getting very serious indeed, "remember this as long as you live. Strength is not always muscles or force; it is most times the will and determination to succeed. Do you understand me?"

"Yes Mama."

"Are you sure?"

"Yes Mama."

"Boysie, I want you to say it after me. Strength is not always muscles or physical force; it is most times the will and determination to succeed."

Yes, all those episodes were Mama's way of preparing him for life after her passing. Now the moment of testing had come, just as Mama had predicted. But even with all her preparation, he wasn't really sure how he was to respond to the challenge. Life, as his Mama had said, really wasn't simple at all.

By the time the day had ended, Boysie was so tired that he simply went to the river, had a bath and hoped that he could get something to eat and go to sleep. He wasn't that lucky. When he got home, aunt Maude ordered him to full the water barrels and so he had to go to the river with his bucket a few times. Then he had to go and get the sheep and goats. When he was finished, he didn't even bother to try and get something to eat. He simply got his bedding, made his bed, and went to sleep.

His mother visited him that night, and with her was Sam Browne. They promised him that all would be well. He simply had to have faith in God, for He sees and knows all things, and He cares about His children, and he Boysie was a child of God. It all seemed so real that the next morning when Boysie, on his way to work, met Sam Browne waiting for him on the road, he almost felt that his mother would also appear.

"Boysie good morning, how was the wuk yesterday?"

"Good morning Sam Browne, it wasn't bad."

"What did they tell you to do?"

"Well, Blue asked me to clean the horse stables."

"As if I didn't know," said a reflective Sam Browne. "But don't worry, I promise you things will change and sooner rather than later. Yo' mother never had much faith in me. Not that I blame her. But I promise you that all will be alright and sooner rather than later."

"Why do you say that Mama had no faith in you? This is not true at all. Mama even came in my sleep and told me that I should listen to you and follow you."

"She really did that?" asked a surprised but obviously pleased Sam Browne.

"Yes, she did, and last night I saw both of you in my sleep telling me that everything would be alright, for you are watching over me."

Boysie watched as Sam Browne turned away for a moment or two and, even though his back was turned, Boysie saw that Sam Browne had taken his hand and was wiping his face. As he turned back to Boysie, he was looking at the ground, with his right hand over his face. He stood like this for a few moments and then he looked up and spoke, and Boysie was sure that he could see water in his eyes.

"Yo' mother is right," he said softly. "And I again want to let you know that if it is the last thing that I do, I going make sure that you get a good education, even if it cause me me life."

Boysie suddenly understood the dream in which his mother had ordered him to follow Sam Browne. He saw now that Sam Browne really had his interest at heart and he quietly said to him, "Thank you. I know my mother would only tell me to follow you because you are a good man. She always said you are a good man. After a small pause he added, "And she is right."

Now Boysie actually saw the tears run down Sam Browne's face and he became ashamed. He looked at the ground, for he simply could not look at Sam Browne. It was the first time he was seeing a grown man cry. Sam Browne was also unable to look at Boysie but looked away while taking his shirt collar to dry his eyes.

A few moments of silence passed, and then Boysie told Sam Browne that he had to leave as he must get to work on time. Sam Browne did not speak but nodded his understanding. As Boysie left, he was afraid to look back and kept his head straight. When he was gone about 30 yards, Sam Browne shouted, "Boysie!" and as Boysie turned to face him, he simply said, "God is love and we must trust him to see us through." Boysie nodded his agreement and continued his way. His heart was, for some strange reason, feeling much lighter.

Boysie worked from Monday to Thursday cleaning the stables, brushing down, feeding and watering the horses and cutting elephant grass for them. It was laborious work not made any easier by an ever demanding Blue, clearly enjoying his role as boss. It was always "Boysie, wash that part down again." Or, "Boysie, you need to cut more grass for the horses, that's not enough." There was always something that Blue was not satisfied with, or wanted Boysie to do again and again. These orders did little to help Boysie feel comfortable with his performance on the job. So even though the work was not always strenuous, the atmosphere was always unpleasant for Boysie, as Blue, in a determined effort to show authority, was a constant humbug and a nuisance.

As Boysie was going through his chores on the estate, Sam Browne sat at home wondering what he could do to change Boysie's plight. On Wednesday morning it came to him. He got up and set out on the four mile journey to the nearby village of Petty Palm to see Teacher Woods. All along the way, he planned and planned how he was going to talk to him. He wondered if he should try and speak the best English he could so that Teacher Woods would not think him totally dumb and stupid. After all, Teacher Woods was a Headteacher and a reverend, a very educated white man. Or should he speak as he usually does, for

Teacher Woods had an idea of his literacy level anyway, and he therefore couldn't fool him.

He got to his destination without deciding what to do, how to approach Teacher Woods, how he should speak with him. But all his worry was in vain. He was to be disappointed, for when the door opened, Mrs. Woods came out and, without waiting to hear what Sam Browne had to say, explained that her husband had gone into town and would only be back on the Saturday around midday. Sam Browne's heart sank. Till Saturday, but what was Boysie to do all this time?

As he set off on his way back home, he realised that the absence of Teacher Woods was in a way to his advantage. He now had the time to actually plan what he wanted to say to him. He wasn't sure how Teacher Woods could help, but if he couldn't, then no one else could. He wondered whom he could go to and ask some advice on how to approach Teacher Woods. But he knew the answer to that already, and he didn't have the power of Christ to call her from beyond the grave.

On Thursday morning, Mr. Carson had Blue gather all the workers in the yard in front of the Great House. He told them that everyone was expected to work until late for the remainder of the week and into next week, as they would begin to grind the cassava to make farine, bam-bam and starch. Boysie knew that this meant that he would have to tell his aunt that he would be getting home later than usual. He remembered that when his mother was alive and they were making farine, she sometimes got back to their shack when he was already fast asleep.

The making of farine was a very long and laborious process and all the estate workers were involved in it. They had to dig the cassava out of the ground, grind it, and then bake it. During all this back-breaking work, everybody was kept busy, as the whole exercise was fully labour-intensive and everyone was expected to work to full capacity until the last bit of cassava was turned into farine and cassava starch.

After Mr. Carson had made his announcement, they all marched onto the fields to start the digging of the cassava out of the ground. As the others marched off, Boysie decided that he had to seek Blue's permission to go and tell his aunt of the new development at work, which would mean him returning home later than usual.

"Mr. Blue," he said.

"What happen now? You ain't hear Mr. Carson done give the orders?"

"Yes Mr. Blue, but I want you to allow me to go and tell my aunt Maude that I will be working late and so I might reach home late tonight."

Blue realised that what Boysie said made sense. After all, he was still a child and he needed to tell his guardian of this new situation as regards his working hours. He took Boysie and they approached Mr. Carson.

"Mr. Carson Sah, you see Boysie here live with he aunt since he mother dead. An' now that he have to wuk late from today, he need to go home to tell he aunt that he not coming home early from today until we done wid de cossada and farine."

"Yes, you right Blue. Let him go and tell his aunt, 'cause she go start to wonder when it start to get late and he ain't come home." As Boysie turned to leave, Mr. Carson stopped him; "But by the way, you have your mother house here. It would be better if you tell her that you will stay there when you done wuk than go home and wake them up if they done sleeping."

When Boysie got home, aunt Maude was shocked to see him. She immediately assumed that he had done something wrong and Mr. Carson had become annoyed and fired him.

"Boysie, what you doing here?" she began. "Why you not at wuk? I told you, that you must behave yo' self 'cause it so hard to get wuk these days."

"Mr. Carson send me home..." began Boysie. But an impatient aunt Maude interrupted him.

"I can see that Boysie, I not blind. The question is what you did to make the man fire you. He was so kind to give you the little hold on, after I plead with him and through goodness to me he take you on. Now look what you gone and do, embarrass me. So what you do there to upset the good man?"

"I didn't do anything," Boysie meekly replied.

"So Mr. Carson is ah crazy man to just send you home just so? He is ah crazy man, eh Boysie?"

"No aunt Maude."

"Exactly not, so why did he send you home?"

"He sent me to tell you that I would have to work late from tonight until next week, as we have to make farine starting today."

Aunt Maude was silent for a few moments, not knowing what to say. She finally recovered herself and demanded, "So why you never said so in the first place, boy? Why is it you want to give me ah heart attack thinking that the man fire you? Lawd, look on me cross and trial. Boysie, you couldn't say that all the time?"

"He said I should sleep in my mother house from tonight as I would finish work late and he doesn't want me to wake you up after you have gone to sleep."

This caught aunt Maude a bit off guard and she thought a few moments before answering. "Of course that make sense. This farine-making business could sometimes go on all night long."

"Well, that was what I came to tell you and I must go back to work for they are waiting on me."

With that Boysie left and returned to the estate and joined the others chopping cassava plants and digging them out of the ground. They worked until dusk and then, when there was no more light in the field to continue the digging, they turned to the grinding. By the time they were finished for the night, Boysie was so tired that he was glad he didn't have to walk home to aunt Maude's. He went straight to his mother's shack and immediately went to sleep.

The next morning, Boysie got up and was so hungry that his head began to hurt. He hadn't had a bath the night before and so went down to the river and bathed in the cold clear water. His next desire was to get something to eat, but this turned out to be rather difficult. Even though there were many fruit trees on the estate, he didn't dare pick any without the expressed permission of Mr. Carson, as that was tantamount to stealing. He therefore headed off to the field to work with an empty stomach.

In the morning session, he joined the gang cutting the cassava plant and digging the tubers out of the ground. They worked until midday. During this time, he from time to time visited the water bucket drinking small calabashes of water in the hope that it would ease his hunger. At lunchtime while the others headed off to eat, he went to his mother's shack and lay down on the wooden bed. He used the time to look through some of the old magazines. His stomach was now in open protest.

They returned to the field at 1:00 p.m., with the sun blazing down mercilessly on their heads. Most of the men and all of the women were wearing broad-brimmed straw hats as a form of protection. Boysie did not have one. After ten minutes of work, he went to the drinking bucket to get some water. Ten minutes later he was back again, and this prompted a reaction from Blue. "You ain't weary go to de bucket fo' water; you here to wuk, not to drink water."

"Yes Mr. Blue," was Boysie's only response. He decided however that he would not go back to the bucket for the rest of the day, for he preferred to avoid further rebuke from Blue. The afternoon sun was relentless in its torture and as he worked, Boysie felt its intensity more and more. He remembered feeling weak and then as if he was going to fall. Then everything around him just went black.

When he came to his senses, he was lying on the ground in the shade of a breadfruit tree, with his head in Miss Ethylene's lap. Realising that he had regained consciousness, she began reassuring him that he only fainted and everything was going to be all right. She kept asking him how he felt and if anything was hurting him. He assured her that this was not the case and that he was alright. Then she realised what was the problem. "Boysie," she said, "did you get anything to eat this morning?"

"No Miss Ethylene."

"Did you eat anything last night or yesterday?"

"No Miss Ethylene. I didn't have anything to eat."

Ethylene sighed, rested her right cheek in her right hand and began to shake her head from side to side. "When yo' mother dead and gone, dog better than you," she said. "This boy has been working for two days in boiling hot sun without ah thing to eat. Blue, God go punish people like you. For God sake, he is nothing but a child, and not one ah you saw it fit to even give him a piece ah food. That is why he was drinking water so. It was nothing than the poor pickney was hungry. Blue, I blame you, 'cause he wuking directly under you, and you know he mother dead. At least you could look out a little bit for him. But, mark me words, Blue, God go punish you. And if I dead, ants go bring news, but me words no go drop on the ground. God go punish you."

"But, but, but, Ethylene, the boy never even say to me that he hungry, that he want something to eat," said Blue, trying in vain to defend himself. "Ask him if he ever tell me that he hungry. Boysie, you tell me you hungry, eh Boysie? Did you ever tell me you want something fo' eat?"

"He not suppose to tell you," said Ethylene, not waiting for Boysie to respond. "You is a grown man and commonsense should tell you that. After all, he has no mother. Oh God, how she must be crying in she grave. She one pickney have to suffer even though he wuking with people who he know since he born. God go punish you Blue, remember me words."

With that, Ethylene made Boysie sit up. She got up and marched off to the kitchen of the Great House. When she came back, she carried a buttered penny bread and an old enamel cup of lime swank and gave it Boysie saying, "Take this, Boysie, your mother was a good woman, and I can't watch you suffer."

At first Boysie just looked at her and did nothing. It's not that he hadn't seen kindness before, for his Mama was nothing if she wasn't kind. But this was all new to him. He had never eaten a penny bread before. The truth be told, bread was a luxury he very rarely saw, much more ate, let alone with butter. And he had never drunk anything from an enamel cup before, although he had seen them. And to think this was all meant for him!

"Go ahead Boysie, eat the bread." Said Ethylene, "Only God knows how you ain't done drop down dead from hunger. To think that you starving here when everybody, every one of them know your mother and that she was good to all of them. When they want letter write and them pickney name spell, they went to she. But she dead now and not one of them is willing to give ah helping hand to you. But mark my words, God doesn't sleep, no Sah, God doesn't sleep. All them who make you suffer will pay for it one day."

"But Ethylene, I tell you that Boysie never tell me he hungry, he never tell me, I swear to God, he never tell me he hungry," repeated a now ashamed and embarrassed Blue.

"Blue, you should shame to call God name, but I done with you long time. I leave people like you in the hands of the Almighty. He go' deal wid you, in he own time, not me."

The others just stood there listening. Nobody dared challenge Ethylene. Not only because what she said was true, but also because of the fact that she worked in the Great House and was closer to the Carsons than any of them, including Blue. They knew that she was trusted by Mrs. Carson who was the real boss of the estate when push came to shove.

When Boysie was finished eating, Ethylene took the cup and told him that from now on, every morning before he started work, he was to come to the door at the back of the kitchen for his morning tea. She said she wished she could do much more, but she had six children to feed without a soul in the world to help her. Boysie thanked her profusely.

Boysie felt better after eating, and worked all through the evening. At about 6:30, Ethylene came and informed him that she went down to his mother's house and left something down there for him. Boysie continued to work until 10:00 p.m. He helped to keep the fire under the huge iron copper ablaze and gathered and dumped the cassava peel. When he got to the shack after work, he found a small tin cake pan on the little wooden bench that his Mama used as a table. It was full of rice and peas and chicken neck and foot. He clasped his hands, placed them under his chin and gave God thanks just as his mother had taught him from as far back as he could remember. He asked God to bless the food and to "specially bless Miss Ethylene and all her children." Then he sat down on the door step in front of the house in the splendid light of the moon, just as he and Mama used to do, and had the rice and peas and chicken foot and neck. It was the best dinner he had in a very long time; and certainly the best he had had since his Mama passed away. "May God always bless Miss Ethylene," he said, as he finished the last spoonful. And he meant it with all his heart.

As Mr. Woods' horse was about to enter the small path leading to his house, he realised the person sitting on the big stone about a hundred feet ahead was Sam Browne. The bamboo broom vendor from the neighbouring village and a fellow who everybody said was a notorious rum drinker. Mr. Woods had always wanted to talk to Sam Browne about coming to church; and so decided that he would stop and chat with him a bit. But before he could get as close as he would have liked, Sam Browne got up from the stone and waving said,

"Teacher Woods, I know you just from town, but I want to talk to you right now."

Although a little taken aback, Reverend Woods tried not to show his surprise, and calmly responded, "Good day Sam. Like you had a good sales day today; you are finished quite early."

"I sorry to forget me manners. Good morning Teacher Woods. No, I didn't sell any broom today."

"Oh, how come, you didn't make any recently? I was planning to get three from you this week."

"No, I mean yes, I have broom and I done left three by yo' Madam already; but I have a problem and…"

"Oh, she didn't pay you yet?"

"No, no, Teacher Woods, is not about the money. It is a big, big problem I have and if you can't help, then I don't know who can help me. But you see, I pray to the Lard and he sent me to you and that is why I come here."

Mr. Woods was a white Englishman and, apart from his role as Headteacher of the village school, he was the reverend of the village Methodist church. He knew everyone in the village and knew that Sam Browne was a drinker who did not attend church. He seriously doubted whether Sam knew anything about praying.

"I know you just come from all the way in Town and you very tired, but I beseech you to just give me a little bit ah yo' time, for this is very important and it can't wait. Please just a little bit ah yo' time is all I ask. It is not really for me but for somebody who really need help."

Mr. Woods was very intrigued by all this for many reasons. In the first place, he had been the Headteacher and village reverend for more than 10 years and he couldn't remember ever speaking to Sam Browne. Secondly, it was known that Sam was a very independent-minded man who even Mr. Carson, the most powerful man in the village, was very careful with. And thirdly, he was a man who stuck to himself, drinking his rum, selling his brooms, and rarely mixing with anyone. But now, here he was saying he wanted to help someone. Mr. Woods got down from his horse and simply said, "Please tell me Sam Browne, what is the problem?"

Sam Browne took a deep breath, told Mr. Woods to please excuse his broken English and related his problem. When he was finished with his story, Mr. Woods assured him that he would do all he could to help. He remounted his horse and took his leave, but then turned around and thanked Sam Browne for helping him with his sermon for the next day. A surprised Sam Browne requested of him to explain how did he help with the sermon when it had not even been preached yet. "Never mind that. The important thing is that you did help and in a mighty way indeed. Go home now and continue to pray for God's mercy and grace." With that Mr. Woods patted his horse and rode the remaining 800 yards home, knowing that he had the perfect sermon for that Sunday.

As Sam Browne walked home, he couldn't help thinking that it all turned out to be much easier than he had ever imagined. Then he was suddenly overcome with the fear that Teacher Woods was not going to help him after all. He knew that one could never trust a white man, and then to ask a white man to go against his own colour is even worse. When he remembered that Carson was the richest man, not only in the village but on that side of the island, his fears increased. "Maybe," he thought, "this Teacher Woods only say he would help to get rid of me as quickly as possible."

But then again he thought, the man is not just a teacher, he is also a Christian and a reverend. As a God-fearing person he is not supposed to lie. And, he didn't ask for anything for himself. No, he would never do that. He asked on behalf of the boy and not for his sake, but for the mother's sake who had become a full Methodist and Christian, because the same Teacher Woods had encouraged her to do so in the interest of the same boy's education. He wondered whether Teacher Woods had any suspicions of the reason for his actions. But now he really didn't care. He needed to help the boy; it was the least he could do and not just for the boy's, but for his mother's sake as well.

THE HOPE

That Sunday morning, Reverend Woods waited at the church door to welcome all his parishioners as was his custom. As he shook Mr. Carson's hand to welcome him, he said, "Joey, I think I want to take you up on the glass of wine you promised me. Are you going out this afternoon?" Joey Carson assured his reverend that he had no plans, and in fact he and Mrs. Carson were thinking of having the reverend over after service for lunch. Reverend Woods accepted.

Reverend Woods remembered that when he was first told that he would be stationed on this island, he was rather apprehensive. Now he felt like a modern day Jonah and was very contented with his work thus far. He saw that God really needed a servant in this vineyard to help these miserable, poor, illiterate and ignorant black people. When he saw their absolutely desperate state, he often wondered what sin they could have committed so that their lot in life should be what it was. He himself found them very naive but friendly, gentle, kind and obedient people who were easily satisfied with so little, indeed next to nothing. This was one reason why he always felt obliged to help them in whatever way he could, and why he agreed to assist the drunkard Sam Browne. For even he, notwithstanding all the alcohol-induced bad behaviour, was of a kindred soul, as he clearly demonstrated yesterday in the most selfless of ways.

So yes, after service, he would join the Carsons for lunch, and would spend the afternoon explaining to Joey the plight of Boysie. If a non-Christian drunk could have compassion for the helpless, how much more should he the Lord's servant do? After all, he was called to be his brother's keeper.

***

It was Monday morning and as Boysie stood in the front veranda of the Great House waiting for Mr. Carson to come out, his mind and his heart were very troubled indeed. What could have caused Mr. Carson to summon him to the Great House? It was known that he never called anyone to the Great House unless he was terribly dissatisfied with them, and wanted to read them off his premises. Boysie silently prayed to God that Mr. Carson would not fire him. It's not that he cared very much for the work. No, it was more about the wrath of aunt Maude he was certain to be subjected to later. But what could he have done? Was it that Mr. Carson found out about the food that Miss Ethylene was giving him and was upset about it? Or could it be that Blue was dissatisfied with his work and so told Mr. Carson to fire him? Whatever it was, he knew that only God could help him now, so he continued praying.

"Boysie," a voice said suddenly, and Boysie jumped back to the present. It was Mr. Carson. Boysie was so deep in his prayers and with his back turned to the door and looking out on the fields, that he didn't hear Mr. Carson step out of the house and onto the veranda.

"Good morning Sir, I come because Mr. Blue said that you..."

"I know." said Mr. Carson, "I want you to read this," he continued, handing Boysie a copy of The Nation, the island's only newspaper published once a week. Boysie was taken aback. He looked at Mr. Carson with enquiring eyes. "What you waiting for? Take the paper and read! What happen, you afraid I going to bite you?"

"No, no sir," responded Boysie. "I was…"

"Well then, take the paper and read it."

Just then, Mrs. Carson came out and saw Boysie. "This is the child Reverend was talking about yesterday?" she asked.

"That is he self."

"So you are Boysie?" she said enquiringly.

"Yes please Mistress Carson. I am Boysie."

"Well, why are you standing? Sit down and read the paper for us. Your mother was a good reader and a young lady with potential, and it is not surprising that you have some abilities." The tone and attitude of Mrs. Carson made Boysie feel a bit more comfortable. He remembered his mother saying that she was a lovely lady who was concerned about all the workers on the estate.

"Use that chair there," said Mrs. Carson, pointing to one of the whisk deck chairs in the veranda. Boysie looked at Mr. Carson and waited. Mr. Carson hesitated for a second or two and then gave the smallest of nods and Boysie sat as instructed. "Come on Boysie, read," urged Mrs. Carson, "there is nothing to be afraid of."

Boysie began tentatively at first, for he was expecting anything else but this, and he really didn't understand why they wanted him to read a newspaper to them. But with the encouragement of Mrs. Carson, he soon found his courage and was reading fluently. He was doing so well that Mrs. Carson could not hide her surprise and satisfaction.

"No wonder the Reverend said that you are more than just a very bright boy," she said when Boysie had reached the end of the article. "Where did you learn to read so well? I think I agree with Reverend, you will indeed go very far."

"At school Mistress Carson," replied a more at ease Boysie.

"Give me a moment Joey," she said as she left them and entered the house. Moments later, she returned with a King James Version of the Bible. "Boysie I want you to find Psalm 119 and read it for me." Boysie did as he was told, and before he could have read three verses, Mr. Carson got up and left, telling his wife that he would return in a moment. Boysie read the Psalm to its end. "Child, the Lord has blessed you specially. Do you pray?" asked an ecstatic Mrs. Carson.

"Yes Mistress Carson, my Mama taught me how to pray."

"Well, you must thank the Lord for your wonderful gift every time you pray, for He has really blessed you specially."

"Yes Mistress Carson."

By this time, Mr. Carson had returned and he brought with him an exercise book and a pencil. He pencilled down about ten different exercises in arithmetic and ordered Boysie to solve them. This Boysie did with seemingly great ease, forcing Mr. Carson to nod his head in appreciation.

"Boysie, who is the Prime Minister of Britain?" asked Mr. Carson.

"You mean Great Britain Sir?"

"Yes Boysie," answered Mrs. Carson, looking at her husband with eyes that said: You better be careful now.

"Sir Winston Churchill Sir."

"And who is the greatest playwright of all time?"

"William Shakespeare Sir."

"And the greatest novelist?"

"Charles Dickens Sir."

The Carsons continued to drill Boysie for another fifteen minutes, but whatever the challenge, he was equal to the task. Mr. Carson finally relented. "And to think that I thought that Reverend Woods might have overstated his ability," he commented.

"He obviously didn't," responded Mrs. Carson. "And Joey, now thinking of it, I think his message Sunday about being our brother's keeper was intended for you, and only you."

"So you have only now reached that conclusion?" said Mr. Carson. After waiting for a response and getting none he continued, "Oh yes, I forgot, you had gone in to lie down when he raised the subject with me yesterday afternoon after lunch. From the moment he opened his mouth and began to tell me about this business with Boysie and his mother, my mind went straight back to his sermon in the morning. He was simply preparing his path to tackle me later in the afternoon."

All of this conversation the Carsons conducted as if Boysie wasn't there. He of course did not understand what it was really all about, but he sensed that it concerned him and had something to do with Teacher Woods. One thing he felt sure about, was that he wasn't called because Blue had reported on him having done something wrong. Knowing that he wasn't there to be given his marching orders, he felt relieved. He didn't have to explain anything to aunt Maude. While he wasn't sure that what was presently going on between Mr. Carson and his wife had much to do with him and his work, he still had no choice but to sit there, listen and wait for their next command.

"So what are you going to do with him Joey?" asked Mrs. Carson.

"To be honest, I don't know. I simply did not expect him to be so intelligent and bright."

After thinking a few moments, he said, "Boysie."

"Yes Sir."

"You know how to tally?"

"Yes sir, I learnt it in school."

"You know weights and measures?"

"Yes sir, I was taught how to use them at school."

"Can you write a letter, and do you know how to use a pen?"

"Yes Sir, Teacher Woods taught me those things," Boysie replied.

"Joey, the Reverend was right, that boy will be a good help to you. I think you should remove him from the field and let him do the stocktaking and reckoning for you."

"All right, all right," said Mr. Carson. He sat for a while contemplating. He then ordered Boysie to follow him. He took him to the estate storeroom, where, he detailed all of the new duties he expected Boysie to sooner or later take over as his office and clerical assistant. These included keeping the storeroom records, tabulating all bills and making up the pay sheet for all the workers on the estate. He told Boysie that he would teach him as they went along so he had nothing to worry about.

Boysie mastered all of these tasks in an extremely short time. In fact, it was such a short time that Mr. Carson was completely amazed. It took him less than a week to realise that Boysie did indeed have a very bright mind which, if properly trained, there was no telling how far he could reach. He also realised that it was in his power to assist Boysie in the realisation of this great potential, but knew that, as his grandfather and father had said, "Once nigger people reach somewhere, they become arrogant and up-started. They don't want to acknowledge white man as boss anymore." What was he to do?

With all these thoughts going through his head, Mr. Carson was forced to face the truth that he might well hold in his hands the key to this orphaned child's future. He honestly wished that he could just brush these thoughts aside. But he couldn't, for he constantly heard the sermon of Reverend Woods on that Sunday morning instructing, "You must be your brother's keeper.

***

Boysie had started his new job four weeks before the new school term began. He felt very special and lucky, indeed blessed to be given such a position on the estate. In his new job, he had a chance to read all the newspapers and even the books that Mr. Carson had. Mrs. Carson had told him he was free to borrow any of the books she had in the house. All the other workers looked up to him, especially after the end of the first week when he held the sheet which they made their X on before receiving their pay from Mr. Carson. Blue went around telling everyone that it was he who had advised Mr. Carson that he should give Boysie that job, as he saw how talented Boysie was and knew he would reach far. He said he always knew that Boysie could do good "brains wuk", and thank God Mr. Carson trusted him enough to believe his word and promote Boysie so high.

Of all the people on the estate, Boysie knew that the one who was most happy for him was Miss Ethylene. She continued to provide him with his morning tea, but now she did so openly, as it was being done with the blessings of Mrs. Carson. For Ethylene, this was proof of what she had always believed and declared: that Boysie's mother was a very intelligent, nice, good, decent woman. So although she was gone, God would not leave her son undone.

But not even this "big job" could get Boysie to forget his mission. So while all the field workers rejoiced in his success, his mind was on school and passing the final exams. His further education was ringing like a church bell in his head and he could hear his Mama reminding him "Nobody can take your education from you. Nothing can take your education from you. You will take it to your grave, for once you have it, it will remain yours to the end."

In keeping with his new job, Mr. Carson told Boysie to bring his best clothes so that they may determine what is suitable for him to wear to work. He said that Boysie was now no field labourer and therefore had to dress properly. So on Wednesday evening, Boysie went to his aunt Maude's house to collect his Sunday Best. As he was returning to the estate, he met Sam Browne in the middle of the road waiting for him. He had seen Boysie coming from Maude's house and took his pot of green-peas soup off the fireside and went to wait for when Boysie came out.

"Evening Boysie. How you do me boy?"

"Good evening Sam Browne. Everything is alright. I just went over to aunt Maude's to get these things and I am going back to the estate."

Sam Browne couldn't help feeling that this boy really doesn't belong on an estate. No, he belonged somewhere in the church, as an altar boy and later as a reverend. He could just sense that Boysie had something more to do in life than just dig potato banks and clean horses' stables. He was simply too intelligent for that. Just listening to Boysie speak made Sam Browne marvel, for "the boy talk English like one Englishman." He didn't know how he was going to help to make this come through, but he was going to make sure that one day Boysie would be free from that estate. Free from the burden of profitless labour for the Carsons.

"Them is yo' clothes?" Sam Browne asked.

"Yes, these are my clothes."

"So why you carrying them back to the estate?" he wanted to know.

"Well, because I have to work late sometimes. Mr. Carson and aunt Maude have agreed that I should live in my mother's house for the time being, and I need these clothes for my work, as Mrs. Carson says, I must look better in the office. So I went to get them."

"The office!" exclaimed Sam Browne. "What you mean by the office? You mean that you wuking in Carson office!"

"Well," said Boysie rather hesitantly, "I work as Mr. Carson office clerk and assistant. So I have to be in the office and storeroom, checking things and writing things for Mr. Carson, so I don't work in the field anymore."

"Tell me that again," said a disbelieving Sam Browne. "You say that you writing things for Carson and that you in charge of the storeroom? When me wuk for Carson, the only time me see the storeroom, was when he make me carry something heavy in or out of that place; and you is now in charge. Is that so?"

"Well, I never ask him; it was Blue who told him that I could do this work and…"

"That lying son of ah … ah," said Sam Browne, stopping himself just in time. "Next time I see him, I will remind him what happen to him the last time he talk too much. And this time, all he is chatting is lie. But this is not really time to worry about Blue. We should give God thanks. We should really give him thanks, and I must thank Teacher Woods, 'cause he is a man to his word. And when you go back to school in September, you must also thank him. Did you see him on the estate?"

"You mean Teacher Woods?"

"Yes Teacher Woods, did he come to the estate?"

"I don't know if he came to the estate, for I did not see him."

But Boysie wasn't at the moment thinking of Teacher Woods' visit to the estate. He was thinking of what Sam Browne had said about his returning to school. Sam Browne spoke of it as if it was something finalised, a done deal. As if there is an assurance that he would be indeed returning to school, and he wanted to ask Sam Browne about it. But Sam Browne was continuing about Teacher Woods. "I am sure it was through him that God has answered me prayers."

After his discussion with Teacher Woods, Sam Browne had felt the need to go down to De Fosto's rum shop and buy a quart of rum. But he remembered the words of the Reverend that he should pray. And that is what he has done since that Saturday afternoon to now, ignoring his urges to have a drink. "God is a good God, and I hope you are praying as your mother always insisted, and thanking God for all these blessings," he said to Boysie.

Boysie assured him that he was praying. Sam Browne then enquired of him if Mr. Carson had said anything about his return to school next term. When Boysie answered in the negative, Sam Browne seemed taken aback, and Boysie saw him go into a moment of unquiet thought. Then slowly nodding his head as if he had understood it all, he said, "There is nothing to worry about. Yo' mother is watching over you. Everything go be alright."

Boysie reminded Sam Browne that he had to get back to the estate, took his leave and started off. As he was about to turn the corner which would have put Sam Browne completely out of sight, he looked back and saw Sam Browne standing in the same spot, his chin resting on his right fist. Boysie could see that he was far removed from the present. He was a man in the reality of a different world, a world of his thoughts and contemplation.

***

With each passing day Mr. Carson passed more and more clerical duties to Boysie. He had proven that he could efficiently accomplish any task, once the procedure was explained to him. While Mr. Carson was impressed with Boysie's work, he was very circumspect with his praise. His wife though, openly showed appreciation for Boysie's efforts and was truly impressed with his passion for reading. While they were paying the field labourers at the end of the first fortnight since Boysie took up his new position, Mr. Carson told him that they need to talk about his future. When they were finished with the payment, he took Boysie to the office and sat him down.

"Boysie," he began, "Reverend Woods, your teacher, say that you is a very bright boy, and he is absolutely right. For the fortnight you work here, you did ah good job and I please wid you. Reverend Woods want you to go back to school next term. He say that if you lucky, you go pass the school exams and further yo' education. That is not ah bad thing, and I know how much you like read. The problem is that wid the death of yo' mother, you have nobody to support you in school.

You can't count on yo' aunt, for you know she is the one who send you to work here in the first place. She can't afford to feed you and keep you in school.

"I notice how bright and how willing you is," continued Joey Carson, "and also that you is ah hard worker. Mrs. Carson also think that you is ah good boy. We trust you and she agree that you should stay here and work wid we instead of going back to school. Here you go' have the opportunity of a good life, round people you know and who know you."

Mr. Carson stopped, and Boysie wasn't sure if a response was required of him, and if so, what that response should be. It had all been so unexpected that he was caught in a moment of incomplete understanding. He sat without saying anything, for he simply didn't know what he should say. Mr. Carson, realising that this was all so unanticipated by Boysie that he was completely surprised, continued.

"Boysie, me and Mrs. Carson decide to ask you to work permanently for we. I know that one day, with your brains and me training you, you will know how to run everything. Me and she could then relax and leave you to run the whole estate. Needless for me to tell you that when that day come, you go be the only black man running ah estate on this island. Probably in the whole ah the West Indies. Of course, it go take some time; after all, you is still only ah boy. But there is no doubt in me mind that in a few years, you will know everything and you would make a good manager of me estate.

"I saw your aunt Maude, and she say that she is glad that I give you such a job because she now don't even have to worry about feeding you. So this is the best thing for you and she and me. Boysie, you see, it is the best thing for everybody. And I know your mother would ah been proud and happy if she was alive to see that you get such ah big job, manager of the estate where she born. You see Boysie, you could go back to school, but nobody sure that you go pass the exam, not even Reverend Woods himself. And he should know; after all, he is the Headteacher and he is a very bright man. He must know who go pass and who go fail. I mean he didn't say that you go fail, but then he not sure you go pass. And what go happen then if you fail? You go lose such a good opportunity to one day become manager of this whole estate, and the only black man in all ah the West Indies to become manager of ah estate.

"But even if you pass the exam, then you have to think how you going to continue yo' education. You know they doesn't give black people scholarship. So way you go do, eh, way you go do? That is the question you have to ask yo' self. If you stay here, one day you go become the manager and be the boss of everybody here, with ah good salary and everything. So this is ah good opportunity for a boy like you to make yo' self somebody in this world. Here you will have a bright future for I know yo' mother from she is a little girl. I know you before you even born. So you come like family to me, 'cause we family go way back together.

"Boysie, your great grandmother wuk for me grandfather. Your grandmother wuk for me father. Your mother come and wuk for me, and now you come and wuk for me. So we is all one family and you must continue the family tradition."

Boysie was listening to all of this and wondering what he had done to make Mr. Carson empty his soul to him like that. Was Mr. Carson drunk? Mama had always warned him about drinking rum. She had said that that was Sam Browne's weakness; he drank too much rum. And when people drink rum, their tongue becomes loose; they talk and talk, but it was always all foolishness. So was Mr. Carson drunk? And was this the reason why he was talking the way he was?

Boysie knew that his grandparents had worked on the estate, and all of that. But, according to his mother, this was because they had no alternative. The truth was, his mother had said, that as far as she could remember, her family had always been tied to this estate. It embodied their survival in the past. It was all the history her family ever knew. And it was essential to her very existence at present, for it was the only employment she ever had.

He, Boysie couldn't understand a fundamental contradiction in his mother as regards this issue. She was always telling him how good the Carsons had been to her family. All the nice things they had done like allowing her family to live in the galvanised shack that they lived in. How Mr. Carson ended up giving it to her upon the request of the colonial Administrator. And how, thanks to the Carsons, the estate was not only their source of income, but their home for they lived on it.

But yet, her one true wish was to leave that estate like her sister had done. Indeed, the main reason why she wanted Boysie to have an education was so that he could get a good job and become independent of the estate. Leave it and the Carsons behind and find his own road in life. She was unable to do it through marriage as her sister did, but her son would not use marriage. No, he was going to use brains and education.

Boysie also remembered that the only person from the estate his mother seemed to not only genuinely respect, but also appreciate was Sam Browne. He was the only one brave enough to stand up to Mr. Carson, demand his money and leave the estate. And she had a hidden but deep resentment for Blue, the worker who was closest to Mr. Carson, the one who was seen by everyone as Mr. Carson's spy. He remembered that he would hear his mother praying at nights, asking the Lord to make her son independent so that he could stand on his own two feet and don't depend on anyone for a living.

So yes, Mr. Carson was right. There has been a history of family connection between the two families. But Boysie knew it was one his mother wanted to break. If not completely and comprehensively, at least she wanted to bring an end to her dependence on the estate for a living and lodging.

"We could see you helping Hamlet in the future with this estate," Mr. Carson was saying. "Even though he is five years older than you, you and he grow up here on this estate just like yo' mother and yo' aunt and me. And believe it or not, it was the same way wid yo' grandfather and me father. Wid yo' brains and yo' love for hard work, Hamlet will do wonders here with yo' help."

Boysie knew Hamlet well. He had gone to school six years before Boysie, but was in a grade, one year behind him. Something many on the estate always seemed ready to comment upon, once Mr. Carson wasn't in earshot. Many were the whispers on the estate that Hamlet was "dunce like bat"; but Boysie wasn't sure of this. Hamlet was a student at Mrs. Yoke's, a private school in Town, where only white and very high-coloured children went. It was said that the money their parents paid for a term for one child was many times more than any estate worker made in a whole year. At least, Boysie knew that that was the rumour on the estate.

"And Hamlet is definitely going to need you when he come back. Me and Mrs. Carson might be dead and gone and you would be the one with the full knowledge about everything on this estate. So two ah you go make ah good team, ah very good team, me dear Boysie.

"So this has been the place of your family for as far back as they could remember. This is your place too. And you know, I done decide that, once you get a little bigger, I moving you out ah your mother little place and ah putting you in one of them big board house behind the Great House so you go be more comfortable. As you grow each year, we go increase your salary. What I telling you is that you have a future here and that future already start, so you don't have to worry about passing no school exams. You hear what I telling you Boysie? 'Cause I don't see what sense it make you going back to school and wasting your time when you done know all them things you know. Believe me, as little as you be, you done have more than half the education ah man like me have."

Mr. Carson rattled on some more, and then had to stop as he realised it was getting late. Boysie left the estate and headed home to aunt Maude with a very heavy heart. After his conversation with Mr. Carson, he would normally be very happy. For, imagine him being the manager of that huge estate one day, and everybody, including Blue, taking orders from him. As Mr. Carson himself said, he would be his right-hand man, and later when Hamlet comes back, he would be Hamlet's right-hand man as well. But wait; where was Hamlet going? Was he going to stay a long time in Town? Anyway, that was another question. Now he was supposed to be happy. But instead, his heart was heavy. Heavy because Mr. Carson had made it quite clear that he had to choose between school and the job. It was also clear that there could be no question of him finishing school and then returning to the job. Opportunity knocks only once. It was now or never.

But Mama had always made it clear that education was to take precedence over all. She had told him that in all his getting, get education, for it was the only way out for the poor like him. She had said in no uncertain terms that a better life depended on whether he had a good education. It depended on being independent, and not upon waiting on handouts from anyone.

When he got home, he found himself in a deeper predicament. As soon as he entered the yard, aunt Maude met him and was all smiles and joy. This was not totally surprising to Boysie for, during his discussion with Mr. Carson, he had advised that he Carson had already given Boysie's wages for the fortnight to his aunt.

"Boysie, you now coming? We here waiting on you to congratulate you. Boy, you make me family proud, and yo' mother would ah been so proud and happy if she was alive to see this. I sure she up there looking down and smiling. You is a bless child and whoever yo' father be and wherever he is, like yo' mother, you prove you don't need a helping hand from him to get on in life. God really bless you Boysie, and you must pray hard and thank him. Imagine you start wuking only three weeks ago and Mr. Carson paying you more than everybody else on that estate." On hearing this, Boysie looked at his aunt incredulously, and she, realising his disbelief, continued, "Oh yes, he tell me so he self. And Boysie, when you pray, remember to pray for Mr. Carson so that the Lord bless him. And don't forget all them who help you along the way. Mr. Carson done tell me that he going to make you manager one day. Me own little nephew Boysie, to be the manager of that whole estate one day. Gawd does really wuk wonders."

Boysie saw that he was in really deep trouble. There was no doubt that his aunt felt that school was not a place for him anymore. And through her efforts, he had a job which, in such a short time, had placed him squarely on the road to success in life. This is the dream of every poor black person, not just on the Carson estate, but on the island as a whole. And thanks to her, for him it was not a dream anymore, but a living existing reality. How could he say no? How could he turn his back on the efforts of his aunt, the goodness of Mr. Carson and the pride of the estate people who would all glory in his achievement? For them, he was a symbol of one of their own proving himself brilliant enough to do office work for a white man.

But still, Mama's voice would not leave him alone. It kept reminding him that education was the key, and it matters more than anything else. It was the only thing that he would truly own which could not be taken away from him. But more than anything, it was what would make her proud, because it would make him independent and respected; somebody in the society. He knew however that despite her ambition for him, there was one all-important factor. Mama was dead, and all the others were alive, and now they, not Mama, held the key to his fate.

***

The weekend passed, and Boysie reported for work the Monday morning, with his heart heavier than it was on the previous Friday. He had prayed about his situation several times over the Saturday and Sunday, asking God for a sign as to what he should do. But none came. He knew not what to do, for while he felt sure that his mother would have said that he should return to school, doing that under these circumstances would be impossible. It would mean incurring the wrath of aunt Maude, losing his job, having no place to live, disappointing all the estate workers, and having no one to support him. Yes, he was really in a predicament where it was impossible to choose without serious consequences.

He also knew that there was no use appealing to anyone. Once it had been decided by aunt Maude, then it was decided. In her eyes, she had done him a grand favour by placing him in such circumstances. Yes, through her, he, her motherless nephew, had found favour with the Carsons. Now he had a better chance than most of being removed from the abject poverty, illiteracy and perpetual hopelessness which the rest of the estate wallowed in. Yes, it was still within the boundaries of the estate and the confines of dependence on the Carsons. But progress beyond these was not the rule; it was rather the rare exception. Most on the estate accepted that a change in their status would only come when they went to the great beyond, to rest in peace with their Lord and Saviour. No wonder that "Freedom over me" was their favourite hymn.

Yet, even with this knowledge of the real, he knew his heart would always yearn for the dream. That dream that Mama had placed there from the first day he remembered himself. And now, he could see no way of moving from the real to that dream, for he was trapped in the real. Yet, he knew the dream would not stop calling until he converted it into the real.

Everyone on the estate couldn't help but notice Boysie's reserved and melancholy state. And as always, it was Ethylene who showed the most concern. She enquired of Boysie whether he was feeling well, thinking that he had a health problem, or that he missed his Mama. He consistently reassured her that he was fine. Most people on the estate attributed his state to his mourning the loss of his mother, and concluded that with time, he would come to himself. But Boysie kept his burden secret in his soul while twisting and turning it around and around in his head, the way one would do with a difficult algebra problem, in the vain hope his brain would find a solution for him. But regardless of his mental juggling, his brain supplied the one logical answer it could. He had no choice but to resign himself to his fate.

***

It was now the middle of the last week before school was to begin. Boysie felt it was useless hoping any more. That Wednesday morning, he went down to the river to have his early morning bath before heading off to work. As he was on his way to the estate, he heard his name and looked around to see none other but Sam Browne.

"Good mawning, and how things going Boysie?" he asked.

"Good morning Sam Browne; everything is alright."

"I so glad to hear that. Is Carson treating you right in the new job?"

"Yes, he and Mrs. Carson are very nice to me, and the job is very good."

"Yes, this job is very good; but when you finish yo' education, you will be much better off, for that is what education does do. It does give you a good job and make you respectable. And that is why I went and buy these fo' you," he said, handing Boysie the package he had in his hand.

"What is this?" asked an unsuspecting Boysie.

"That is yo' school clothes for next term, all brand new. I even buy a new boots for you, so you don't have to walk barefoot simply because yo' mother dead."

Boysie's face lit up, but only for the briefest of moments as he remembered that as regards school, his days with that were over. He politely told Sam Browne that he couldn't take it.

"What you mean you can't take it? Maude has told you not to take anything from me?" demanded Boysie.

"No, no, no," Boysie hurriedly answered, realising that Sam Browne could completely misunderstand the situation.

"So she already buy you new school clothes, or Carson buy them?"

"No, they haven't bought me any new school clothes."

"So then, why you don't want these? Don't tell me that you done have so much pride like yo' mother and don't want to take anything from me, even when you need it? I don't..."

"No, no, it is nothing like that," said Boysie, interrupting Sam Browne's rising annoyance and arresting his thoughts of Boysie's rejection of him through rejection of his kindness. "I will not be going back to school next term, and so I don't need new school clothes."

Sam Browne was dumb for a moment or two, the time it took for the information to properly register. He was expecting anything else, but not this. Oh no, not this. Not after all the promises he made to Boysie's mother in his prayers. Not after Teacher Woods had promised to help. Not after he had promised himself to invest all he had in

Boysie's education, and was sure that the rewards were going to be great. No, anything else; but not this!

"What you mean that you not going back to school?" questioned a clearly confused Sam Browne.

Again, Boysie wasn't sure how he should explain this to Sam Browne. He didn't want him to blame aunt Maude or Mr. Carson, which he felt sure would be the case. He therefore, choosing his words very carefully, proceeded to explain the situation in the best way he could, being mindful of not laying blame on anyone, in particular his aunt Maude. He was observing Sam Browne's reaction as he spoke. Sam Browne, for his part, had put his face in his hands and began silently lamenting the passing of Boysie's mother, shaking his head from side to side. He saw most clearly now that she had correctly foreseen everything that would happen to her son, once she was gone. This melancholy state of Sam Browne so affected Boysie that he pitied him. So much so that anyone observing could have easily believed that it was Sam Browne who was facing the unfortunate circumstance and not Boysie.

When Boysie had finished his story, Sam Browne seemed to be so deep in thought that Boysie was convinced that his mind had left his body. Standing in front of him was an uninhabited shell of flesh and bones, void of any spirit, soul and consciousness. He waited a few moments and then announced that he must leave as he must get to work on time. Sam Browne came back from his mental travels, and the change was most evident to Boysie.

"Boysie." he said, "You want to continue yo' education?"

"As I just explained, I…"

"I know what you just say. I not talking about that. I asking you ah question. You want to go back to school, and if you go back you will study yo' book?"

"Yes, I want to return to school, but I…"

"All right," said Sam Browne, not allowing Boysie to go on. "If is the last thing I do in life, you going back to school. Nobody not telling me what I could do. Not even you mother could tell me what to do, much more anybody else. Leave them to me."

After making it clear to Boysie that he might have to leave the job to continue his education and that, all in all, he would have to make up his mind to see some hard times, he assured him that, "Come what may, you going back to school, and no Maude nor Carson is going to stop it!"

All that day on the job, it wasn't just Boysie's heart that was heavy, now his mind was also anxious. He did not know what Sam Browne was going to do, but there was no doubting his resolve. He had left Boysie that morning like a man on a mission, and it did not escape Boysie that the last time Sam Browne had promised to do something on his behalf, it resulted in Mr. Carson giving him the big job. He didn't know what this was going to lead to, and he waited expectantly all day for something to happen. But nothing did. He therefore thought that he would meet Sam Browne on his way home. But here too, he was to be disappointed. He went to sleep that night more confused and uncertain than ever.

Thursday went by very much like Wednesday did, and Boysie began wondering if Sam Browne had failed in his efforts. After all, who was Sam Browne anyway? He was a friend of his mother, who tried to help him, and that's all there was to it. If only there was a way to let aunt Maude see that his education was what meant most to him and Mama. Probably if he had gone immediately to Sam Browne and told him when he found out about the plan to make him into Mr. Carson's permanent office clerk and not send him back to school, it might have given him time to do something. But now, with only the weekend left before the reopening of school, it was certainly too late. Boysie was so taken with these thoughts that the sudden shout of "Whoa!" startled him a little, and he awoke from his world of dim hope. He looked through the office window to see Teacher Woods dismounting his horse and giving the reins to Blue, as Miss Ethylene stepped out of the Great House to greet him and usher him in.

After about an hour, Teacher Woods came out of the Great House, accompanied by Mr. Carson. They exchanged a few words and Boysie could see that Mr. Carson seemed to be agreeing to something. Teacher Woods took his leave of Mr. Carson, collected the reins of his horse from Blue, and was on his way. Boysie returned to his work.

Ten minutes following the departure of Teacher Woods, Mr. Carson came into the office and sat down. He ordered Boysie to do the same and proceeded to explain the situation. "Boysie," he said,

"Reverend Woods has just come to see me about you, and has asked that I allow you to go back to school this term. I know you have just one more year before you finish school, but yo' mother dead and yo' aunt Maude can't afford to send you to school. So I give you this very good job because I understand the situation. But Reverend Woods want you to go back to school, which, as you and I know, is useless to yo' future, especially since you have this new job. But I promise him that I will ask you what you want to do with yo' future. So, as a good Methodist, I asking you now: you want to go to school or to continue in you nice job with me and everybody on the estate?"

Boysie did not expect this, for he knew that the offer made to him a little over a week ago was not an offer but an order. A command that he was informed about and with which he was expected to comply, no questions asked. What was he to do now? What was he to say? He was truly at a loss. Going back to school is what Mama would want him to do, but this was not an option. In the first place, where would he live? Aunt Maude had made it abundantly clear that she couldn't support him in school. He couldn't very well go against her and expect to live in her house. How would he eat? No, it was simply not possible. He simply had to accept his fate.

But yet, he couldn't bring himself to tell Mr. Carson that he did not want to go back to school, for that simply was not the truth. His mother had always taught him to "Speak the truth Boysie, and speak it ever, cause it what it will." So he just sat there staring at Mr. Carson without saying anything, caught between the reality and the dream, between his possession and his ambition.

Mr. Carson, not getting the response he expected, was more than surprised. He therefore decided to press home his argument. "Come now Boysie. Don't tell me ah bright boy like you don't have the good sense to see that you stand a better chance staying here with you own on the estate. Yo' grandparents born on this estate and yo' mother born here and you born here. It is easy for Reverend Woods to talk about school. He is an Englishman and his bread done butter. Your mother work hard to see you get this far, and I know if she was here now, she go tell you take this job."

Mr. Carson continued speaking, but Boysie did not hear anymore, as he was suddenly transported back to his mother and her words, "We have lived on this estate all our lives, not knowing anything else. My sister did the right thing to marry a man who took her off this place. Boysie, I am not saying this place is bad. No, not at all. Look how good Mr. Carson is; he gave me this house 'cause the colonial Administrator asked him to do it. No, he is not bad and the estate workers are all good people. But this estate is not your place, and education is what is going to take you off this estate and make you find your place."

"Excuse me, Mr. Carson Sah, but Mistress Carson say that you need to come now." It was the housemaid Ethylene and her unannounced entry that brought Boysie back to the present. "Blue done already prepare the buggy, and Mrs. Carson is dress and waiting Sah."

"Alright Ethylene, tell she I coming right now," said Mr. Carson, upon which Ethylene responded, "Yes Sah," turned around and left the office. Mr. Carson returned his gaze to Boysie. "Boysie, you have no mother, no father, nobody who care for you but me and yo' aunt Maude. I know you would like to get as much education as possible, and that is not ah bad thing. But you must be realistic. Think about how much everybody on this estate care for you, ok?" And with that Mr. Carson left, and Boysie was left alone to fight with confusing thoughts which he knew would never become clear unless he had the intervention of someone else. She always had the answer, no matter how difficult the question. But the reality was that she was no more.

Two hours later, Boysie left the estate and began his journey home. He walked aimlessly without seeing or hearing anything. Oh how he wished that Mama was around. She always knew everything. She always told him what to do and how to do it. As he walked he kept thinking of all those things that his mother told him, how she would remind him that his heart would always tell him what is right, so he must always follow his heart.

As he turned the first corner, putting the estate out of sight, he saw in the grey of the evening, a figure standing about five hundred yards away. His pace quickened. As he got a little closer, he realised that the person walking in his direction was the one he hoped it would be. Still about a hundred yards away, Sam Browne shouted, "Boysie, it's me, and we have to talk now." There were little breaks in his speech, and

Boysie could tell that he was a bit out of breath. As they came upon each other, it was clear that Sam Browne was upset and annoyed.

"You is going to yo' aunt now, right?"

"Yes, I finish working and I am going home now."

"Well, when you get there, I want you to take what you have there and come back here and meet me right now. Your aunt don't have yo' interest at heart. No, not at all, at all, at all. She want to make you into another Carson slave, but that go happen only over me dead body. She just too wicked, just too wicked." Not comprehending any of this Boysie stood speechless. Unaware of his listener's incomprehension, Sam Browne continued, "I think she yo' aunt would try to understand the situation and try to help you. But no, all she could see is the few cents that Carson paying you, and telling me stupidness that you have good future on the estate. Which kind of future, I want to know," said Sam Browne, his tone betraying much more than anger, something close to rage.

Finally recognising Boysie's incomprehension and the need to explain himself fully, Sam Browne made a conscious effort to control his emotions. He then related to Boysie the reason for his evident disquiet and heightened blood circulation.

It transpired that he had gone to see aunt Maude to try and convince her that she should allow Boysie to return to school to finish his primary education. She flatly refused. He then tried to induce her by offering to give her a small monthly sum to do so. She again refused, saying that the sum was too small. Sam Browne then hiked the amount, but to no avail. All else failing, he was forced to threaten her with exposing her opposition to Boysie's education to Teacher Woods. He further warned her that if she didn't allow Boysie to go back to school, he would ask God to curse her and her children. She then relented, saying that if Sam Browne wanted Boysie to go to school, he could take him. So Boysie now had a choice to leave aunt Maude and live with Sam Browne and continue his education, or stay with his aunt and forget all about further education.

While for Sam Browne this was finally the solution, for Boysie it only meant more problems. He was simply terrified of the consequences of what Sam Browne had done, and really couldn't fathom how he was going to repair the damage. He remembered that his mother made him promise never to annoy his aunt and always to obey her. How was he to face her now? And after she had done so much to get him the job with Mr. Carson, how was he to take the side of Sam Browne? That he knew would be ingratitude of the worst kind. What was Sam Browne thinking to have gone and done something so mindless?

Sam Browne, seeming to read Boysie's thoughts, began to reassure him that it was all for the best. He reminded Boysie that his mother cherished education more than anything else. He argued that if she were there, she certainly would not have done it the same way; that is by threatening his aunt. Nevertheless, she would have done the same thing. She would not have let anything or anyone come between Boysie and his getting an education. With that latter part, Boysie had to agree;

but still it was going against aunt Maude, and that was not his mother's instructions.

As they walked to aunt Maude's house, Sam Browne kept up his argument. He assured Boysie that this was all good for his future, and he should not think that his mother would be angry with him, for he was doing the right thing. Boysie just listened not knowing what to say. Sam Browne explained further that he had gone to see Teacher Woods and had asked for his help, and Teacher Woods had promised to help by speaking to Carson. He said he believed in Teacher Woods, for he was a man of God; but he wasn't sure if he had the time to speak with Carson as yet. Boysie then confirmed that he had seen Teacher Woods visiting Mr. Carson, and that sometime after Teacher Woods' visit, Mr. Carson had talked to him about not going back to school. This revelation Sam Browne took as proof that he was right and that God was on Boysie's side, and had sent him, Sam Browne to help him. But Boysie was still troubled, still worried about disappointing his mother by disobeying his aunt.

Then Sam Browne reminded him that his mother had told him to follow Sam Browne. And suddenly Boysie saw it. He realised that even if he disagreed with his actions, somewhere, somehow Sam Browne was right, and there was no turning back now. He had to do as Sam Browne said, for in the dream with his mother, those echoing words came rushing back and he could hear her voice in his head saying, "Follow Sam Browne, Boysie, follow Sam Browne. Let him hold your hand now, and we will meet later. I can't carry you all the way, so let him help us, and you and I, we will meet later."

As they approached aunt Maude's house, Boysie could see the flambeau burning through the kitchen window. He stopped, turned to Sam Browne and said, "It's alright, you don't have to come any further, just wait here and I will get my bundle and come." He said it with such assuredness that Sam Browne instantly knew that in that walk of about one mile since they started on the journey to his aunt's house, Boysie had changed and would never be the same again. He couldn't see his face or eyes, for it was already too dark for that. But he knew he didn't need to. He had heard such resolution in that young voice, that it reminded him of someone who spoke in the same decisive manner. He knew that now that the decision had been taken, he didn't need to say anything, and he didn't need to follow Boysie any further.

He stood and watched as Boysie entered the yard and proceeded to the kitchen, knowing that for once in his life, he Sam Browne had helped good to prevail. And he felt real proud of himself, for he knew that Boysie's mother was looking down with that worried look she always carried. But at this moment, she was thanking him for ensuring that her dream for Boysie would come through.

As Boysie approached the kitchen, his aunt Maude stepped out and he was abruptly face to face with her. Boysie opened his mouth to say good evening, but before he could do so, his aunt began. "Boysie," she said, "that Sam Browne was here and talking 'bout you going to live with him. I hope he didn't come meet you on the road and tell you any stupidness. Your mother left you in my care, and I don't know what business of his it is. Did he meet you on the road and tell you any foolishness?"

"Yes aunt Maude, he met me and told me of his plan."

"What plan? That old drunkard! You don't bother with he and he foolishness. He is ah drunkard with no respectability! He is no family of yours and will not care if you grow up ah drunkard with no respectability just like him. I have with the help of the Lard, get you that good job wid Mr. Carson where you will have ah future. Mr. Carson he self done tell me so. If Sam Browne ever come talk to you about living with him, you make sure you tell him to go with his cross and leave you alone in Jesus name."

"But he wants me to go back to school," said Boysie, in a tone slightly uncertain yet firm and challenging.

"What you mean that he want you to go to school?" inquired his aunt, her tone surprised by, but immediately rebuffing the challenge.

"Yes, he wants me to go to school," said Boysie in a more matter-of-fact manner as if daring his aunt to deny this truth. A few moments passed before there was a response.

"And what can the school do for you? What is going to come of the school? You have ah good job wid Mr. Carson and will have ah good future on the estate." This last statement set off a train of thoughts in Boysie's head, and he felt more determined and surer than ever that he was to leave his aunt and join Sam Browne. "You cannot leave me your aunt and your good job with the estate to go and live with that drunkard."

"But he wants me to go to school." Boysie quietly but defiantly insisted.

"And what can this school do for you that the estate and Mr. Carson can't do for you?", a clearly annoyed aunt Maude demanded, in a voice reflecting her increasing impatience and dissatisfaction with how the conversation was going.

"Well, Mama wanted me to go to school and get an education. She wanted me to leave that estate and be independent and respectable someday."

"What is all this foolishness about education and respectable and leaving the estate!" responded aunt Maude, now shouting, her dissatisfaction in Boysie's behaviour boiling over. "You are ungrateful to me and Mr. Carson, after all that we do for you! Your mother dead and left you and I take you in and find ah good wuk for you! And now you telling me about school and leaving the estate. Lard have mercy, you ungrateful, ungrateful, ungrateful!" shouted aunt Maude as she broke down in tears, unable to contain herself further.

Boysie, seeing her tears, couldn't help but be moved and stood looking at the ground pondering on what he should do next. He felt sick inside and knew that he had done his aunt great harm. But what troubled him even more was the greater pain that he had caused his mother. He knew what he was doing was wrong, but his heart told him that he had to continue along this path and his mother always said he should follow his heart. Without knowing exactly why, he broke down in tears and found himself saying, "I am sorry aunt Maude, I am sorry."

"Boysie, this is your home now," said a slightly recovering aunt Maude. "If you leave us and the estate and go with Sam Browne what will happen to you? Who would look after you? You are my only sister only child, and I don't want to see you suffer the way she did."

"You are right," said Boysie, "that is exactly what Mama said, that she didn't want me to suffer the way she did, and therefore she wants me to get an education and leave the estate. She said the best thing she ever did in her life was to get the little education she had, and the best thing that you and Sam Browne ever did, was to leave the estate, and she would have done that if she had a chance."

With that aunt Maude began to cry even more. She said she knew she should have done more to help her sister, especially after Boysie was born; but she couldn't as she had her own cross to bear. She told Boysie that life was not always easy and she really wanted the best for him, for his mother was her only sister and God saw it fit to take her but leave him, and she wanted to make sure she did what was right by Boysie. She said she knew that life was not easy on the estate, and that his mother always wanted something better and she can't blame him for being the same. She continued expressing sorrow at the pain and suffering her sister went through and said that she knew that life was changing, that the new generation such as Boysie wanted a better life.

Boysie listened to it all, sometimes silently crying, other times lost in the thoughts and the memory of his mother and all she had taught him. And he was really and absolutely sure now that he had to take his bundle and go. So at the end of it all, he simply said, "Aunt Maude, I know that Mama would want me to have an education, a good education. And I know that Mama always wanted me to do like you and leave the estate. The only chance for me to do that is to go and live with Sam Browne, so I will go and get my bundle."

***

Boysie moved in with Sam Browne in the little wattle and daub. He was very apprehensive at first, for Sam Browne was a known drunkard and not a respectable person in the village. But he was however to be pleasantly surprised, as Sam Browne was orderly in every way and in everything. He made sure that Boysie did everything right in the very same way Mama demanded. In some cases, he was even stricter than she was. He made sure that his clothes were always clean for school, that there was always enough to eat, and he even introduced Boysie to molasses to sweeten his tea and milk. These were things that Mama simply couldn't afford. He sometimes allowed Boysie to help him in chipping the bamboo to make the brooms, but only after he had done his homework from school, which was always the first thing he had to do on arriving home each day.

Another thing that surprised Boysie was that Sam Browne insisted on his going to church every Sunday, where Teacher Woods was Reverend Woods. At these services, he would see Mr. Carson and his wife and aunt Maude and his cousins. At first, they avoided him, but gradually they began to speak to him. He sometimes met Miss Ethylene who was always nice to him and was always concerned about his welfare. One Sunday, she told Boysie that she was now even more convinced that he had a great future ahead of him. After a few weeks, Reverend Woods began giving him lessons to become an altar boy in the church.

The whole village was amazed at how clean he always was and how concerned Sam Browne was about him. But what shocked everyone most, including Boysie, was the fact that Sam Browne stopped drinking rum completely. He who was the most notorious rum drinker in the entire village had just suddenly stopped, and had no interest in it anymore. Unlike the public, Boysie was also privy to the fact that he had gotten a Bible and would read it daily. Many would be the time when he would come to Boysie, asking how a word was pronounced or what was its meaning, especially words in the Old Testament. His care for Boysie, preparation and sale of his bamboo brooms, and his reading of the Bible now became the centre of Sam Browne's life.

But they both knew that while all of that had the positive endorsement of the village, its ultimate judgement of Sam Browne's ability to look after Boysie would come later. They knew that there was a specific hour of reckoning and that hour wasn't too far off. Sam Browne was determined not to fail, and so did everything in his power to ensure that Boysie would "turn out right", as he put it. He went and spoke to Teacher Woods on many occasions, just to find out about Boysie's progress. He insisted that Boysie be given additional homework, and he went looking for old magazines and ensured that

Boysie read them all to him. He made Boysie read at least one chapter of the Bible every night before he went to sleep. On Sundays, Boysie had to go to church and then read the lessons to Sam Browne when he got home. And he made sure that Boysie understood that in everything, his lessons came first.

At nights, he would get on his knees and plead to the Lord to have mercy on him and don't punish him as much as he deserves. He would tell the Lord that he knew he deserved to be punished, but the boy and his mother should be spared as they never did anything wrong. And even if the mother fell by the wayside, it was his fault and not hers, and she had suffered enough for it. Many a night Boysie would hear Sam Browne and try to understand the full meaning of his prayers, but never really did. He however determined that Sam Browne, like Mama, wanted the best for him, and made up his mind not to disappoint him.

Then the Sunday before the exams came. When Boysie awoke, he realised that Sam Browne had already gone to the river and had a bath and was preparing the cocoa tea with the celement bush. It was the sweet scent of the bush in the boiling cocoa that woke him. Sam Browne ordered him to go to the river and take a bath. When he returned, he found Sam Browne fully dressed in suit and tie, his hair nicely combed. He was wearing a pair of black leather shoes. After Boysie had had his breakfast of hot chocolate and sweat sweet potato, he donned his own new suit and tie which Sam Browne had already set out on the bed for him.

As they left the house and headed for the church, Boysie couldn't resist asking Sam Browne about all these strange things he was doing. Sam Browne didn't go to church ever, but here he was dressed in jacket and tie headed for church. He had stopped drinking rum and was committed to being respectable in the eyes of the village. He had changed, but what has caused the change? Why was he so different from the Sam Browne everybody knew in the past?

"Boysie," he said, "I know that everybody think I am worthless and no good, and me can't blame them, because I was worthless and no good. But you see, if I did follow your mother, I would have been better, much better. She said you is better than me and I didn't believe she at first, but now I see for me self and I want to make you somebody, educated and respectable. I am going to church today 'cause I want to beg the Lawd to help you with your exam tomorrow, 'cause, 'cause I want you to become somebody respectable so that your mother will smile as she look down upon you. And you know, I don't want to fail you, 'cause you left your aunt and come with me. And, and, I don't want to make you shame 'cause they will say how stupid you was to leave your job and go live with a drunkard. You see, you trusted me, believed me, and respected me enough to come with me, even when I deserved none of that. Now I want to have your respect, but I must deserve it." Sam Browne stopped speaking and looked away. As they walked in silence, Boysie noticed that Sam Browne took his jacket sleeve and wiped his eyes.

It is here that Boysie realised that there wasn't just a change, but that a radical transformation was taking place in the life of Sam Browne. He suddenly saw that even his language had changed significantly. He was speaking more and more standard English each day. He would now say good morning or good afternoon to everyone he passed on the way, and didn't speak of Mr. Carson, Blue and aunt Maude in the bitter tones of the past. Yes, there was a radical transformation taking place.

As they approached the church, Sam Browne turned to Boysie and said, "My mother died when I was your age, and I never know me father 'cause I was not born when he died from accident. I is…" and he suddenly stopped and began breathing heavily, while Boysie waited for him to continue. After about forty five seconds had passed, Sam Browne continued. "I want you to pass this exam more than anything in the world. I rather dead than you fail. Your mother and now you are the only people who ever believe in me and trust me." With that, he fell silent and simply looked away. While Boysie didn't know why, he saw that Sam Browne was overcome with emotions, and so determined that maintaining his silence was best at that time.

But he was moved by all this and made up his mind that, come what may, he couldn't fail tomorrow. In the past, he studied hard because of Mama, but now he wanted to pass because of Sam Browne. He was sure that Sam Browne wanted him to succeed as much as Mama had wanted. And he was prepared to do everything to ensure this. He simply couldn't disappoint him now. No, he must succeed, for he couldn't let all Sam Browne's labours go in vain. As they reached the church door, Teacher Woods stretched out his hand, taking Sam Browne's firmly, and simply said, "Welcome Sam, it is really good to see you. I have a special seat for you and Boysie. Turning to Mrs. Woods, he smiled and requested, "Please show Mr. Browne and Boysie to their seats."

***

The next day the exam was simple enough, but Boysie had his problems. At first he found it very difficult to settle down as he thought that he had forgotten everything. He began to sweat and fidget so much that even the invigilator noticed how uncomfortable he was. But then he remembered that his mother had said, "Boysie, in whatever you do, let God go before you; for he who trusts in God has nothing to fear. With God all things are possible, and as David said, I have never seen the righteous forsaken." So he settled down and, once he had done so, he began working on every question in the most thorough and meticulous of ways. This resulted in him taking more time than all the others to complete the exams. He left the hall feeling sure that he had made it, but the results would only come three months later. He already knew that these would be three months of unease for him. When he came out from the examination hall, he met Sam Browne waiting for him in the exact position that he had left him more than three hours earlier. Upon seeing Boysie, he simply smiled and said, "That's me boy; I know you done pass."

The truth was that Sam Browne was very nervous about this exam and how Boysie would perform. But after Boysie had entered the exam hall, along came Teacher Woods who, on seeing the troubled look of worry and fear on Sam Browne's face, reassured him that there was no need to worry. He said if Boysie couldn't pass this exam, then no one could, not even he the teacher. This was great reassurance to Sam Browne, for Teacher Woods should know. After all, he was Boysie's teacher. Apart from that, he was a white man, and white people are not stupid, "say what you like." Yes, it might be that he deliberately lied to put Sam Browne at peace. But then again, he was a Christian and not just any Christian, but a reverend in the Methodist Church. He simply couldn't sin his soul by lying like that. And in all that he had promised so far, he had delivered. He left Sam Browne at peace and full of confidence.

The three months waiting for the results seemed to take an eternity to pass, and every day was counted and marked by Boysie and Sam Browne. In those three months, Mr. Carson went to aunt Maude and Reverend Woods asking them to convince Sam Browne to send Boysie to the estate to help him as a clerk in the office. This information was relayed to Sam Browne; but after thinking carefully about it, he decided that Boysie was not going to return to that estate under any circumstance. He had left it once and for all. He Sam Browne had had his experience with that white man on that estate. Outside of being taken there in a coffin, he would only return there if he knew that in so doing, he could help bring some dignity to those perishing ignorant souls that laboured there in vain day in day out. No, Boysie will not be returning to a life of absolute subservience. Never!

Sam Browne used those three months to learn a lot about the Bible. He had determined that it was to be used as the reading text for his lessons with Boysie. Their little wattle and daub house became full of old newspapers and magazines that he collected from Teacher Woods and the police station, and he took great pride in seeing Boysie read them. Through all this reading, he was learning many new things and was discovering a new world. He learnt of how a Spanish man named Columbus had discovered the island and how the British fought the Spanish, beat them up, and took away the island from them. And so the island became British and that is why the Queen of England is now his Queen.

In this way, with him cutting bamboo to make brooms for sale, his going to church every Sunday and reading his Bible, and his explaining to Boysie different aspects of his life as a boy on the estate, the three months came and went. However, the results never came, and Sam Browne began to worry. At first, he thought that they had come and Boysie had failed, and so as not to disappoint them, Teacher Woods had hidden this fact. But each Sunday they went to church, Teacher Woods would assure him that the results would come sooner or later and there was nothing to worry about.

And then they came.

It was a Friday morning. Sam Browne was just about to leave with his bundle of bamboo brooms to make his usual weekly rounds when

Talbert, the servant boy of Teacher Woods came galloping on his tall entire donkey, "Mr. Browne, Mr. Browne, good morning." Sam Browne looked up and, upon seeing Talbert, immediately knew that the results had arrived. "Mr. Browne," continued Talbert, not attempting to dismount his donkey, "Reverend Woods tell me fo' tell you fo' come now an' bring Boysie. He say you go know what it is about. Me can't stay as me have fo' go back fo' go ah market with Miss Woods."

"Yes," replied Sam Browne, and his heart began this massive pounding in his chest. He put his right hand on his left breast as if trying to slow the rate. This was the day he was waiting for, and now that it had arrived, he was suddenly anxious to the point of frightfulness. His thoughts seemed to be all over the place. What was he to do? "Yes Talbert, tell him we coming now, tell him we coming now. Boysie, Boysie, look out here." As Boysie opened the door of the house, he saw Sam Browne running towards him. "Boysie, Teacher Woods send to call we. Put on something presentable; we have to go now, he waiting on we."

It took them 50 minutes to foot the journey to Mr. Wood's residence. It was a bright morning, with the sun radiant. By the time they got there, the perspiration was literally flowing from every pore on their skins. On that entire journey which, under normal circumstances would have taken Sam Browne two hours, his mind was in a state of excitement. What did the result show? Did Boysie pass? And suppose he did pass, what were they going to do? And if he didn't pass, what were they going to do? The questions were a thousand and, try as Sam Browne might, he couldn't remain calm.

From a distance of more than a hundred yards off, Sam Browne and Boysie could see Teacher Woods in his garden sitting talking to Mrs. Woods. As they got closer, Mrs. Woods got up and went inside. By the time they got to the gate, she was leaving with Talbert. They bowed to her and proceeded to a beckoning Teacher Woods.

"Good morning Sam Browne, Good morning Boysie. I am glad to see you," said Mr. Woods.

"Good morning Teacher Woods," they answered in one voice.

Mr. Woods, seeing that they were sweating and seemed a little out of breath, inquired if they wanted some water to drink. They both responded in the negative. Mr. Woods understood. The quenching of thirst could wait. Of course, everything else could. Without another word, he took a brown envelope out of the breast pocket of his white shirt and handed it to Sam Browne.

The latter, not understanding, looked at him enquiringly, and Teacher Woods realised that he needed to explain. "Sam Browne," he said, "this is Boysie's results from the exam. I did not open them, for I felt that you his…" Teacher Woods hesitated a little, "Well, you as his guardian should have the honour, the right to open it."

"You mean you don't know if he pass or if he fail?" enquired Sam Browne, his tone and manner betraying genuine surprise, terrible anxiety, but yet great hope.

"No, I don't know, for I didn't open it," replied Teacher Woods. "I think it is only right that you as... well his guardian should see it first." Sam Browne, nodding his head in agreement, took the rectangular shaped brown envelope and looked at it from both sides. On the front it said "To Mr. M. Woods, Headteacher, Moune Village Primary School." On the back was written "The Colonial Office of Education." As Sam Browne tried to tear the envelope open, his hand began to shake vigorously, so vigorously that he couldn't accomplish the task and had to return the envelope to Teacher Woods who tore it open and passed it back.

Sam Browne, with still trembling hands, took out the white paper and looked at it for a while, obviously reading carefully. After about a minute and a half, he looked up to the heavens and the tears began to roll down his face.

Acknowledgements

While the stories in this book were written by me, the book as such might never have been written, much more seen the light of day, were it not for the encouragement and, in some cases, the practical assistance of many friends. Indeed, the belief that these stories should be written and offered to the reading public as a book never originated with me. It came from some of these friends who stumbled upon them and convinced me that I should share them with the public at large.

When you grew up in a world where everyone is a doubting Thomas as regards your abilities, these encouragements are not merely kind words. They are a statement of faith, thanks to which I began this journey and because of which you, the reader, are holding this book in your hand at this moment. If you didn't enjoy it, there is only one guilty party, yours truly; for these stories are all my doing, and I unreservedly apologise. If however, as I hope, it did bring you some joy, then you will appreciate even more the role of those being acknowledged herein. They were not only the lights, cameras, stage and all those other very important elements which created and set the scene. Most importantly, they all shouted, "Action!" Thanks to all this, I wrote and published this book.

Many, many people deserve to be thanked for the realisation of this effort, and I wish to thank again all those who had a direct influence on its writing and publication of the first edition to fruition. In this regard my special thanks go out to Pamela 'Miss Charles' Charles who taught me the beauty of language and literature, and to all the teachers both formal and informal who laid the foundation of my love for stories, and later literature.

A very, very special thank you is here extended to Her Excellency, Mrs Andrea Bowman for writing the preface to this, the second edition, and for offering guidance as regards its editing.

Richard A. Byron-Cox

April 2025

Konigswinter

Germany

Brief Historical Notes

Generally speaking, universal adult suffrage did not come to the English-speaking Caribbean until after the Second World War. Before that time, franchise was limited in one way or the other, and all the countries were not granted this franchise at the same time. For example, Jamaica was granted universal adult suffrage in 1944, Trinidad in 1946, while St. Vincent and the Grenadines achieved this in 1951.

With the introduction by Europeans of plantation economy in the Caribbean on a universal scale from the 17th century onwards, Africans were brought in large numbers and enslaved on the sugar, tobacco and cotton plantations. These people were considered animals, merely part of the estate stock until their liberation on 1st August 1838.

The Spiritual Baptists religion is one of the oldest religious faiths practised in the Caribbean. It has its own practices, rites and doctrines, some of which have African origins. It was the only religion during colonialism which was led by black people. This and its African roots were among the fundamental reasons why the colonial authorities sought to and did make it illegal in many territories, including Trinidad and Tobago and St. Vincent and the Grenadines. However, with the coming of universal adult suffrage and internal self-rule, the laws were changed, thereby allowing freedom to practise this faith. Indeed in the

Republic of Trinidad and Tobago, and in St. Vincent and the Grenadines, this faith now has its own national holiday.

Even after a long colonial history, most Caribbean countries, especially those of the Windward and Leeward islands, had no real developed deep-water harbour. Big ships were therefore anchored out at sea and all goods and passengers were taken to and from land by smaller boats called lighters.

During the colonial period, the English-speaking Caribbean used the British or imperial system of weights and measures.

After the end of the Second World War, many people went to the Dutch islands of Aruba and Curacao to work in the oil refineries. Pay and working conditions were better there, while unemployment was a serious problem in the English-speaking Caribbean.

In 1955, the powerful Hurricane Janet hit Grenada, resulting in serious damage to the island.

The use of tractors is a fairly recent thing in some Caribbean countries. As they were predominantly agricultural societies, the garden hoe was an extremely popular and necessary tool. It still remains the main tool for many a small farmer.

The English-speaking Caribbean, like many other colonies, was heavily influenced by the so-called mother countries. These societies therefore tried in various ways to copy the lifestyle of the mother country, as was aptly described in V.S. Naipaul's "The Mimic men."

Many of these islands still give out the Member of the British Empire (MBE) and other such useless relics although there is no

British Empire. And many states still retain the Queen as head of state, even though they claim to be independent.

At the beginning of the 60s, US President J. F. Kennedy promised that the USA would put a man on the moon before the decade was out. This news, for some unknown reason, got sections of the Caribbean very excited.

The 1930s was a very turbulent time in the Caribbean. Due mainly to economic hardship, there were many disturbances, including serious riots. These were experienced in St. Kitts, Trinidad, St. Lucia and British Guyana (Now the Republic of Guyana), among others, including St. Vincent and the Grenadines.

At this time in Caribbean development, many had not even seen a suitcase, much less owned one. It was therefore very common for them to wrap their belongings in a sheet or large piece of cloth when they had to move on. This was called a bundle.

Throughout colonialism, the Caribbean territories were basically agricultural economies producing crops for the Mother country. As the demands changed, so did the crops. Coconuts were produced in many islands on a commercial scale, including in Dominica and St. Vincent. It was primarily used for making edible oils and soaps.

Set in the Caribbean between 1900 and 1960, this book of stories is an exciting, engaging, suspense-filled and revealing biography of its fictional characters. The reader empathizes with their pains, sorrows, ignorance and suffering, but ultimately joins them in celebrating the sunshine of triumph.

The Dead Man Living with Us:

Tony is almost strangled to death in his sleep and wakes up to the sound of invisible footsteps leaving his room. He is worried that there is something sinister about his home. His fears multiply when his mother makes a startling revelation.

When Japheth met Lucifer:

Japheth terrorised his village to the point where he is recognised as its champion bully. He shows no mercy for anyone, as he thought he would never need it from anyone. But that was until the night he met Lucifer.

Sattou's pain and Mr. Penniston's burden:

Sattou spent thirty years of his life searching the world for a family truth. He never suspected that it was in that man living on the opposite bank of the river, whose life he saved when aged seventeen. Charles, his cousin, finds that truth, but is it too dangerous to be revealed to Sattou?

Lord Orator and the Calypso Tent:

Lord Orator is hurt by love and seeks revenge on the culprit, a La Bassy woman. He must however get past the anger and missiles from the La Bassy patrons in the Calypso Tent. Who will win this contest of wills?

Were Mama's Tears in Vain?

As the shadows lengthened in the cemetery, 12-year-old Boysie sees no prospect other than returning to the estate to a life of ignorance, subservience and poverty. He is tormented that all his hopes and dreams will be locked forever in that grave. Or will fate be kinder to him and offer the redemption that Mama so pleaded for?

Richard A. Byron-Cox was born and grew up in the Caribbean. He was educated in the Caribbean, Europe and Latin America and is trained in the fields of law, international relations, diplomacy, and international law in which he holds a PhD. He is also multilingual.

 Dr. Byron-Cox worked as an advisor in the Ministry of Foreign Affairs in St. Vincent and the Grenadines before becoming an international civil servant with the United Nations Organisation, which he served for more than twenty five years. Apart from Were Mama's Tears in Vain?, he has also written to critical acclaim, "The Sory of Paulene Bramble: Book One: Springs Blossoms and Young Thorns."

www.ingramcontent.com/pod-product-compliance
Lightning Source LLC
Chambersburg PA
CBHW051256120626
46547CB00015B/1973